# Ethics at the End of Life

Ralph Baergen
*Idaho State University*

**WADSWORTH**

**THOMSON LEARNING** ™

Australia • Canada • Mexico • Singapore • Spain • United Kingdom • United States

Philosophy Editor: Peter Adams
Assistant Editor: Kara Kindstrom
Editorial Assistant: Mark Andrews
Marketing Manager: Dave Garrison
Print Buyer: Robert King
Permissions Editor: Bob Kauser

Production Service: G&S Typesetters, Inc.
Copy Editor: Barbara Norton
Cover Designer: Yvo Riezebos
Compositor: G&S Typesetters, Inc.
Printer: Webcom, Ltd.

Library of Congress
Cataloging-in-Publication Data

Baergen, Ralph.
    Ethics at the end of life / Ralph Baergen.
        p.   cm.
    Includes bibliographical references and index.
    ISBN 0-534-55845-3
    1. Terminally ill—Care—Moral and ethical
aspects.   4. Medical ethics.   I. Title

R726.8 .B33 2000
174′.24—dc21                    00-043760

**WADSWORTH**
**10 Davis Drive**
**Belmont, CA 94002-3098**
**USA**
**www.wadsworth.com**
1-800-423-0563 (Thomson Learning
Academic Resource Center)

**For more information about our products,
contact us:**
Thomson Learning Academic Resource Center
**1-800-423-0563**
http://www.wadsworth.com

**International Headquarters**
Thomson Learning
International Division
290 Harbor Drive, 2nd Floor
Stamford, CT 06902-7477
USA

**UK/Europe/Middle East/South Africa**
Thomson Learning
Berkshire House
168–173 High Holborn
London WC1V 7AA
United Kingdom

**Asia**
Thomson Learning
60 Albert Street #15-01
Albert Complex
Singapore 189969

**Canada**
Nelson/Thomson Learning
1120 Birchmount Road
Scarborough, Ontario M1K 5G4
Canada

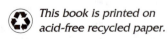

# Contents

# Section 4: *Futility and Fighting Death*

# Section 5: *Resuscitating the Dying Patient*

# Section 6: *Assisted Suicide*

# Section 7: *Euthanasia*

# Preface

*Ethics at the End of Life* is a collection of important essays on medical ethics dealing with the moral issues that arise as people approach death, and is intended as a textbook for courses in medical ethics. The majority of cases addressed by hospital ethics committees involve patients who are approaching death; therefore, the end-of-life focus of this book also makes it of great practical value for the medical professionals, patients, and families who are concerned about these issues. Furthermore, addressing only end-of-life issues is a good way of making manageable the vast literature and scope of medical ethics, and does so in such a way that implications can be drawn out for many topics that are not addressed explicitly. Thus, although there is no section on rationing medical resources, the section on medical futility has much to say about allocation decisions. And although there is no section on abortion, the discussion of treating seriously ill newborns takes up the hard questions of moral personhood, of balancing the child's interests against those of the family, and so forth. Such breadth makes this text appropriate for a full-scale course on medical ethics.

This book has a number of valuable features, some of which are rare among medical ethics texts. For instance, a glossary of philosophical and medical terms is included, so that readers who are new to these matters will find the selections much more accessible. Also, there is a full index for the book—an uncommon but welcome feature in an anthology.

This collection includes both the seminal articles that have shaped the current debates, and new works likely to determine where these discussions go from here. These selections are well balanced, providing a broad view of each debate. Each section of the book covers a different topic and begins with an introductory essay that makes clear the central issues, defines the relevant terms, and gives the primary lines of argument. Some articles have shortcomings that should be pointed, or play a role in the current debate that needs to be identified. The introductory essays do both, as well as filling in any gaps left by the selections.

There is also an annotated bibliography for each topic, directing students to other important work in these areas. Along with the introductory essay, this feature will give students an excellent picture of the literature on each topic. Instructors will welcome the inclusion of discussion questions in each section, many of which take the form of case studies. Also of considerable value is the overview of ethical theories and principles that begins the book.

I am grateful for the aid of my editor, Peter Adams, his assistant, Mark Andrews, and Kaila Wyllys. I also wish to acknowledge those who reviewed this book and offered many valuable suggestions: Robert Baker, Union College; Mary Ann Cutter, University of Colorado at Colorado Springs; Kathleen Dixon, Bowling Green State University; David Fletcher, Wheaton College; and Robert Audi, University of Nebraska.

# Section 1

## *Ethics at the End of Life*

## Troubling Questions

The family sitting across the table in the hospital conference room was clearly very upset. The patient's father was tense and quiet, his wife close to tears. The patient's sister was nervously chewing at fingernails that had already begun to bleed. The patient himself was not present. He was in a bed in a nursing home across the city, minimally conscious, minimally functional, apparently unaware of the television spouting game shows and soap operas in the corner. Until recently, his food had been given to him orally, but a few weeks ago he had begun refusing to eat. The physician had then begun tube feedings—over the family's objections. We were all here at the ethics committee consultation because the family and the patient's physician were deadlocked about what sort of care he ought to be receiving. The family was pleading with us to have the tube removed and nutrition and hydration stopped so that he could die in peace, but the doctor staunchly insisted that he had an obligation to continue full treatment.

The parents told of how their son had tried to commit suicide nearly a decade earlier, of the brain damage that had resulted, and of the bleak years since, stuck in a nursing home with no hope of ever leading what they called "a meaningful life." No one, they argued, would want that sort of life; he would be better off dead, free of the indignities of his present existence. After all, they said, had he not tried to kill himself years ago? Did not his refusal to eat indicate that he still wanted to die? Would not stopping his nutrition and hydration just be helping him to do what he had been unable to do for himself? Did that not fit with what we had called respecting patient autonomy? Did he not have a right to die with dignity?

1

The nursing staff who cared for this man told us a different story. They described a patient who seemed to recognize them when they entered his room, who seemed to enjoy having his back rubbed, who seemed to pay attention to the television. True, things had been different for the past few weeks. The patient seemed depressed and withdrawn, and no biological cause had been found for this. The nursing staff certainly did not agree with the family's claim that the patient's life held only suffering or that death would be a welcome release for him. If only his depression could be treated, the quality of his life would justify keeping him alive. Unfortunately, attempts to deal with his depression had so far been unsuccessful. The nurses also pointed out that the family rarely visited the patient and suggested that the family was not a reliable source of information about what sort of treatment this patient would want.

The attending physician was impatient with this speculation about the patient's wishes or the quality of his life. Although these factors might play a role, we knew far too little about them to give them a significant place in making the decision at hand. What we knew for sure was that the patient was alive and had no life-threatening condition. The doctor reminded us that it was his responsibility to keep his patients alive unless they were "overmastered by disease," as Hippocrates had put it.[1] Well, this patient was not overmastered by anything just yet, so treatment had better continue despite the entreaties of the family.

This case illustrates many of the factors that make medical ethics important and difficult. Notice first the many uncertainties in this case. It is not clear what this patient's life is like; we do not know how much he is suffering nor whether he finds his life acceptable. Also, something has changed for this patient in the past few weeks, bringing on this apparent depression, but what that is or whether anything can be done to reverse it is not clear.

A second factor is that although it is evident that a decision has to be made about this patient's treatment, it is not plain which rules or principles should guide us. We feel an obligation to act in ways that are morally appropriate, not just medically sound. But we are pulled in different directions. Should we focus on doing what the patient would have wanted, or on doing what will minimize his suffering, or on traditional guidelines, such as a physician's obligation to keep patients alive? When these come into conflict with one another, which considerations should be given priority? Are we just guessing, or is there some reliable and defensible way of settling these questions?

Third, there is a question of decision-making authority to be settled. Is the physician in charge of the patient's care? Or does the patient's family speak for him? And what if the people who know the patient best are the nurses who have cared for him over the years? They are neither physicians nor family members, but they may be able to tell us more than these others about what his life is like, what he would want, and what would be to his benefit. What, if anything, is their role in making decisions about the patient's care?

Fourth, there is a legal dimension to be considered. Is it against the law to stop feeding a patient and let him starve to death? Is it legal for the physician to insert a

---

1. Hippocrates, "The Science of Medicine," in *Hippocratic Writings,* ed. G. E. R. Lloyd (New York: Pelican Classics, 1978), 139–47, esp. section 8 (143 f).

feeding tube or make other changes in the patient's care when the family objects to this? Apart from questions about what the relevant laws say and how they should be interpreted, there are moral issues here, too. How should we respond when our moral obligations conflict with our legal ones?

To all of this we might add the religious beliefs of those involved. These frequently bear upon how we understand our moral obligations, our central values, and the meaning of life and death. But what should we do when people's religious beliefs lead them into decisions that others involved in the patient's care regard as medically unwise or morally unacceptable? Suppose, for instance, that a patient with a life-threatening but treatable condition decides to forgo the recommended treatment and travel to one of his religion's holy places to seek healing through prayer and animal sacrifice. Does the religious nature of this decision make it morally impermissible to interfere with it? What if this patient had decided instead to seek healing through celebrity-recommended diets or aromatherapy? Is there a moral ground for responding differently to these different reasons for rejecting a medically indicated treatment?

Rapid technological development within medicine has added a great many difficult questions to medical ethics. There are now many more things that medical science can do, but it is less and less obvious *when* these techniques should be employed. Also, many people who would certainly have died in years past can now be kept alive (or at least functioning at some level). Is this always a good result, or are there times when we ought to limit the treatment we provide and let people die? There is a subtle shift here: new technologies become standard medical practice, and then we start thinking of them as treatments to which the patient is morally entitled.

Consider how the use of cardiopulmonary resuscitation (CPR) has changed since it was introduced in the 1960s. At first, it was intended only for a narrowly defined group of patients: those who were otherwise healthy but who had experienced sudden cardiac arrest. CPR was rapidly adopted by the medical profession, and its application was soon expanded. Today, it is used in nearly any case in which the patient goes into cardiac arrest, even if it is clear that the patient's condition is irreversible and he is dying. In many cases, medical professionals feel they are morally obligated to perform this procedure; failing to do so may be regarded as a form of neglect. The result is that this technology has become a sort of torture for many dying patients. Many objections have been raised in recent years to this new role of CPR; section 5 takes up this question in detail and considers what guidelines we should use in deciding which patients should be given CPR.

An older example of technological innovation in medicine also reveals the effect of cultural factors on our thinking. Although the use of anesthetics is now commonplace, there was a time when it was new and suspicious. In the 1840s, Dr. James Simpson began using chloroform in his obstetrical practice, but some saw this as a moral outrage. Quoting Genesis 3:16, they argued that pain was a necessary part of giving birth, put there by the Almighty for some good (although perhaps obscure) reason, and that any attempt to avoid this pain was impious and immoral.[2] The fact that this now strikes

---

2. Harvey Graham, *The Story of Surgery* (Garden City, N.Y.: Halcyon House, 1943), 325–28.

us as laughable is instructive: what appears to us as clear, reliable, moral common sense may in fact be the product of many unrecognized social, cultural, and psychological influences. Therefore, more cautious reflection and less confidence in our initial reactions would seem to be in order when we examine moral issues.

## An Overview of the Issues

This book approaches medical ethics by focusing on the questions that arise when patients are at the end of life. My experience as a member of a hospital ethics committee has been that the majority of the cases on which we consult involve patients who are approaching death. Therefore, a book on issues of medical ethics that arise at the end of life should address the topics that medical professionals, ethics committees, and patients and their families are worried about. Furthermore, addressing only end-of-life issues is a good way of making manageable the vast literature and breadth of medical ethics in such a way that inferences can be drawn concerning many topics not addressed explicitly. Thus, although there is no section on rationing medical resources, the section on medical futility has much to say about allocation decisions. And although there is no section on abortion, the discussion of treating seriously ill newborns takes up the hard questions of moral personhood, balancing the child's interests against those of the family, and so forth. Such an approach makes this text appropriate for a full-scale course on medical ethics.

The remainder of this chapter provides a brief outline of some of the prominent approaches to dealing with ethical issues. The sections that follow apply various of these ethical frameworks to many of the ethical questions that arise in providing medical care to those who are nearing the end of life. Sections 2 through 5 follow a common sequence of events that take place as a patient approaches death. The patient may refuse life-sustaining treatment (section 2), or a surrogate decision maker may do so on the patient's behalf (section 3). This often raises questions about whether the treatment at issue is beneficial to the patient or futile (section 4). As death approaches, decisions must be made about whether there will be any attempts to resuscitate the patient (section 5). The four remaining sections take up other issues that may arise in this sequence of events. These include assisted suicide (section 6), euthanasia (section 7), the treatment of seriously ill newborns (section 8), and the effects of managed care (section 9).

It is hoped that this book will be of value to health care professionals who are faced with these situations, to the patients and families at the center of these cases, and to students of medical ethics generally.

## Approaches to Addressing Ethical Issues

Although many different approaches have been suggested by philosophers for dealing with ethical issues, this section provides brief descriptions of those that have been the most influential in medical ethics.

## *Relativism and Objectivism*

One frequently hears it said that our moral evaluations are nothing more than expressions of emotion or opinion—that there can be no rational, objective basis for a moral judgment. Instead, it is suggested, every person, or perhaps every culture, devises its own set of moral standards, and it does so more or less arbitrarily. Thus, what is permissible according to one set of standards may be impermissible with respect to another, and any set of moral standards is just as good as any other. If this is true, then there can be no way of providing convincing evidence in support of a moral assessment of something and no rational way of settling moral disagreements. This position is referred to as *moral relativism*.

Opposed to this view is one that claims that moral evaluations, like most of our other assertions, are either true or false, and that this truth or falsity is determined by something other than our whims or preferences or cultures; in other words, moral standards are not created arbitrarily. Our claims that something is morally permissible (or impermissible, or obligatory, or whatever) are either correct or incorrect, and this is determined in some rational, objective manner. This is *moral objectivism*. An objectivist would say, for instance, that if lying is impermissible, this is a fact that we discover just as one might discover other facts about the world. Thus, anyone (or any culture) that believes that lying is generally permissible is mistaken.

It is important to notice that moral objectivism is *not* committed to the claim that moral standards are rigid or insensitive to circumstances. Instead, many moral objectivists believe that whether an action is morally permissible may depend in part upon circumstances. Although one is morally obligated to keep one's promises, for instance, there may be cases in which breaking a promise is permissible, perhaps because keeping the promise in the present circumstances would lead to great harm to others.

Moral relativism has been a rather widely held view—among non-philosophers—but the reasons offered in support of it have tended to be unclear and unconvincing. Two of the arguments offered in support of moral relativism are common enough to merit special attention. The point of looking at these arguments is to show that neither provides significant support for the conclusion that moral relativism is true.

The first of these arguments might be called the argument from moral disagreement. It begins with the observation that there are many deeply rooted moral disagreements among people. Some believe, for instance, that euthanasia and physician-assisted suicide are morally permissible, while others regard these actions as morally abhorrent. Although there has been a great deal of debate about these issues, we do not seem to be getting any closer to resolving them. The defenders of moral relativism take this to be very significant and claim that if there really were objectively correct answers to our moral questions, as the moral objectivists claim, we would have had more success in finding them. That is, our persistent failure to resolve our moral disagreements suggests that there *are* no objectively correct resolutions to be found. Instead, the moral relativists claim, we have only the moral standards that communities and individuals have created for themselves.

In responding to this argument, begin by noticing that in many cases the unresolved moral disagreements being discussed are not about *particular* actions (such as Dr. Jack Kevorkian's involvement in the first of his famous assisted suicide cases), but rather about *types* of actions (such as assisted suicide in general). This gives us a hint about why these disagreements might be so hard to resolve. Different particular cases of assisted suicide might involve different motives on the part of the person providing the assistance, might result in different consequences, might involve patients with differing prognoses and mental capacities, and so forth. Thus, it might be that some of these cases would be more readily defended than others. This makes it very difficult to defend either claim—that assisted suicide in general is permissible or that it is impermissible.

Does our failure to resolve moral disagreements really indicate that there are no objectively correct solutions? Probably not. To see why this is so, compare our moral disagreements with disputes in other matters. When scientists or historians disagree, it is generally taken for granted that there is a correct solution to the question. In these non-moral cases, it would not occur to us to be relativists. We would not say, for instance, that the earth is spherical for one culture and flat for another. (Certainly, it may be that in some cultures people *believe* that the earth is flat, but they are mistaken.) So why do we treat moral and non-moral disagreements differently? The moral relativist is likely to respond that factual disputes can be settled by examining the world to see who is right and who is wrong, but that this cannot be done to settle moral disputes; the claim here is that moral permissibility or obligation is not out there in the world to be examined.

But there is a problem with this response. The suggestion implicit in this line of argument is that if we are unable to find clear, empirical evidence to settle a dispute, then there must be no objective fact of the matter. This is false. Consider the number $\pi$. This is an irrational number; its decimal expansion, 3.14159 . . . , is infinite and non-repeating. This decimal expansion has been worked out to many thousands of places, but it should be clear that no matter how far we continue this project, there will still be infinitely many more decimal places left to calculate. Now consider this question: does the sequence "7777" appear anywhere in the decimal expansion of $\pi$? It has not come up in the part that has been worked out so far, but there is still an infinite sequence of digits left to be calculated. It may be that we will never know the answer to this question, but this does not imply that there is no fact of the matter. Either "7777" appears somewhere in the decimal expansion, or it does not; the fact that we will never know whether it does has no bearing upon this. Note that, as with moral questions, this is an issue about something abstract. Granted, people are unlikely to get very emotionally involved in a dispute about a number, but this should not make any difference to the question of truth and evidence. The point of this example is that we should reject the suggestion that if we are unable to answer a question, it must not have any answer. When we apply this to the relativists' remarks about being unable to settle moral debates, we can conclude that this inability does nothing to support the suggestion that there *is* no uniquely correct answer in these cases.

A second argument against moral objectivism focuses on its apparent arrogance and inflexibility. Objectivism is seen as inappropriately criticizing and rejecting other cultures and points of view and assuming that moral rules are to be applied without regard for circumstances. This is often turned into a defense of relativism and connected with accepting other cultures and other moral systems. The argument might go as follows: there are many cultures whose moral practices differ considerably from those of our culture; some cultures permit acts that we regard as impermissible, or prohibit acts that we regard as obligatory. However, there is no one uniquely correct culture, so we ought to be respectful of other cultures. Under objectivist moral theories, one judges other cultures by the standards of one's own, thus contravening this requirement for respect. Relativism alone yields the required acceptance, the argument continues, and therefore it must be correct.

There is something incongruous about this argument, and it is found in the claim that we ought to be tolerant of other cultures. When the relativists claim that this respect for other moral standards and ways of life is morally required, they do not seem to mean that it is required only if one is a member of a respectful group. Instead, being respectful is said to be incumbent upon all of us; if we are members of disrespectful groups, we have a moral responsibility to do something to change that. But although this may be what the relativists intend, it is not something their moral position entitles them to say. It is the cornerstone of their moral relativism that every moral judgment or principle must be made relative to a particular individual or culture. But their claim that tolerance is required seems to be made without reference to any particular person or group. Instead, it seems to be intended to apply to all people, whatever their moral views. Remember that only a moral objectivist could claim that tolerance is required, period. A moral relativist would have to say that respect is required *only if* you are a respectful person, or a member of a respectful culture, or something of that sort. This completely undercuts the argument presented above. The relativists are trying to show that moral objectivism is false, but in order to do so they have presented as true something (specifically, the rule that respect is required) that could be true *only if* objectivism is true and relativism is false. What moral relativism yields, then, is the absence of any universal moral requirement to be respectful of other cultures or values, not a moral injunction to respect others. In fact, in some cultures, respect itself would be morally prohibited, because in those cultures acting respectfully toward other groups would not be acceptable. Thus, an argument that began by noting the importance of respect ends up—inadvertently—permitting and even requiring disrespect.

We have seen that relativism does not perform as advertised; although it was supposed to promote respect for other cultures, it ends up either permitting or requiring disrespect. But what of the relativists' claim that moral objectivism leads to disrespect? It turns out that objectivism *can* require respect of other cultures, although there will be limits to how far this respect will extend. Unlike the relativists, the objectivists are entitled to the claim that there is a general objective moral obligation to be respectful—and many objectivists *do* claim that there is such an obligation. But how, you might ask, does the objectivists' claim that there is an objective fact of the matter about all moral issues leave room for this sort of respect? Would this not push the objectivists to reject any view inconsistent with the moral facts, and is not this rejection just a form of disrespect?

Well, yes and no. Moral objectivism does involve the claim that moral evaluations have some objective basis and that this basis is the same for everyone. Therefore, any culture or moral system that is inconsistent with these moral facts will be rejected by the realists as unacceptable. But this need not result in ethnocentrism, nor even in the rejection of any great number of other views. The moral facts will spell out which characteristics a culture must have and which it must lack in order to be acceptable, but this leaves a great deal of room for variation among cultures. Consider the analogy of nutrition. There is, one might claim, an objective fact of the matter about which foods are nutritious and which are not, and about which vitamins, minerals, proteins, and so on people need in order to be healthy. This places restrictions on what could count as a nutritious meal, and some meals will be rejected as not meeting these standards. But this does not leave us with just one acceptable meal. There are any number of different meals that meet the nutrition requirements.

Similarly, there are any number of ways of putting a culture together so that it meets objective moral requirements. These requirements might include treating people with respect and consideration, allowing for some degree of personal freedom, refraining from torturing the innocent, and so forth. Because lots of widely different cultures could meet these requirements, the objectivists can claim that there is no uniquely correct culture and that one ought to be respectful of these other ways of living. There is, however, a limit to this tolerance. Cultures that do not meet objective moral standards will be rejected as unacceptable. But there are better and worse ways of responding to this. It might be better to work to change the culture in question through friendly persuasion than through force, and respectful attitudes will be better than condescending or acrimonious ones. The point here, though, is that moral objectivism is better placed to be respectful of other cultures than moral relativism.

If moral objectivism is correct—and the remainder of this book will proceed on the assumption that it is—does it follow that for each moral issue there is exactly one morally acceptable solution? No. For one thing, many objectivist moral theories take the view that in a given situation there may be several different actions that are morally permissible. Therefore, when people disagree about what ought to be done, it does not automatically follow that anyone is recommending an action that is impermissible. They may have chosen different permissible alternatives.

More important, moral objectivism is quite consistent with the view that there is much we do not know about our moral obligations or the permissibility of actions. As in the sciences, there are limits to what we know, and we must learn to use the evidence available to us as well as we can. When engaging in a debate about a moral issue, it is very important that we strive to support our moral claims with evidence. Furthermore, we must consider carefully the evidence others provide in support of their views and try to determine what the preponderance of evidence indicates.

The remainder of this chapter presents a variety of ways of organizing the moral evidence and reasoning with it to arrive at a reasonable conclusion. These methods provide no guarantee that the answers we arrive at will be correct, but they do provide us with a means of ruling out many of the unacceptable alternatives.

## Basic Moral Principles

It is common for discussions in medical ethics to focus on a set of basic moral principles rather than on any particular moral theory. This allows one to avoid the task of settling disputes between theories and to concentrate instead on the common ground that most theories share. Moral theories still have an important role to play, however. For instance, they identify morally significant features of actions or situations and can help settle conflicts between moral principles. For this reason, knowing a set of basic moral principles is not an acceptable substitute for knowing a range of full-blown moral theories. Even so, a good deal of moral progress can be made by examining moral issues in the light of these basic moral principles.

One must first identify which moral principles are relevant to a situation or action. They indicate one's moral obligations. These, in turn, can be used to determine what one ought to do in that situation. It often turns out, however, that two or more principles are in conflict. In such cases, it is important to determine which of these principles overrides the others.[3] One must act in accordance with any moral principle that has not been overridden (in that situation) by other moral considerations. Typically, these considerations would be in the form of other moral principles. There are no clear, reliable guidelines for which principles will override which others, so one must generally work on a case-by-case basis, trusting to one's moral common sense and one's grasp of moral theories as guidelines. Even though moral principles do not provide a foolproof method for answering our moral questions, they perform a valuable service by drawing our attention to significant moral considerations.

Like all moral principles, the ones that follow are quite broad and general. For this reason, they can often be difficult to apply to practical situations. To aid in this, a number of more specific moral rules are linked with each principle; the rules make clearer when the principle would apply and what it requires of us.

*The Principle of Respect for Autonomy*   *You have a moral obligation to respect the decisions and actions of autonomous agents.* The first step in understanding this moral principle is to consider the concept of autonomy. To say that someone is autonomous is to say that she is capable of being a law unto herself. An autonomous agent is often described in terms of one's capacity and entitlement to make decisions and act as one sees fit. We each have an interest in making for ourselves any significant decisions regarding our lives and bodies. This is anchored in the notion that one makes one's own life and, to an important extent, creates oneself as a person. Respecting autonomy is also said to promote the well-being of autonomous agents.[4]

This concept implies a set of conditions one must meet in order to qualify as autonomous. To begin with, an autonomous agent must have a set of goals, values, preferences, and life projects. In addition to being free from coercion or undue influence, one must possess the capacity to reflect upon alternatives, recognize consequences, and consider their relevance to one's goals and projects. That is, one must be able to imagine what certain outcomes would be like and evaluate them in terms of one's goals and values. This implies that an autonomous agent must have adequate information

---

3. It is assumed that all of these moral principles are *defeasible,* that is, they are capable of being overridden by other moral considerations. An *absolute* moral principle is one that cannot be thus overridden; any moral principle with which it conflicted would be overridden. (There would be an exception to this last claim if two absolute moral principles were to conflict with one another. In such a case, the principles would deadlock and one would face a moral dilemma: no matter what one did, one would be violating a moral principle that was not overridden and would thus be acting in an impermissible way.)

4. See, for instance, John Stuart Mill, *On Liberty* (1859; reprint, Indianapolis: Hackett, 1959).

about the situation and about alternative courses of action and their probable consequences. As well as possessing information, one must have the ability to reason about it, enabling one to work out implications, spot inconsistencies, and so forth. When the information provided to the patient includes data on the likelihood of certain outcomes, an understanding of probabilities is also important to this process. Furthermore, a fully autonomous person will also have an understanding of risk and a strategy for dealing with it. This is linked to one's hierarchy of goals, indicating the trade-offs one is willing to make when not all of one's goals can be attained. An autonomous agent will also be free from coercion and other inappropriate influences. Each of these components admits of degree, and there does not seem to be any minimum threshold for meeting these conditions, so an agent can be autonomous to a greater or lesser extent.

An autonomous person is said to be entitled to act in ways that are likely to result in suboptimal or even disastrous consequences (as evaluated from that person's standpoint). Our moral responsibility, entitlement to create ourselves, and so forth are not limited to acting in prudent or rational ways. However, when the patient's decisions seem irrational or self-destructive, paternalistic intervention may be warranted, and questions about patient competency are sure to arise. This is an instance of the relevance of other moral factors. Before discussing competence, however, consider the moral relevance of autonomy.

Although a prominent requirement of the principle of respect for autonomy is that one refrain from interfering in the decisions and actions of autonomous agents, there is more to it than that. One also has a moral obligation to *foster* autonomy. If a patient's autonomy has been diminished in some way (by depression or coercion, perhaps), one has an obligation to restore that autonomy. Those who forget this move too quickly from the observation that a patient is no longer substantially autonomous to the conclusion that the principle of respect for autonomy has no force in the situation.

Applying this to the practice of medicine, the principle of respect for autonomy is sometimes said to imply that physicians ought simply to present medical facts and options without making recommendations or otherwise influencing patients' choices. This approach, which Wulff calls the "adviser model" of physician behavior,[5] fails to take into account the circumstances under which physicians and patients meet. Diagnosis, for example, is carried out in the understanding that the goal is to relieve the patient's suffering and (if possible) restore him or her to health. This, says Wulff, influences which tests are run, how information is interpreted, and so forth. Thus, certain values are built into the system that undercut the physician's ability to play the role of a value-free adviser. Also, the process of diagnosis and treatment does not involve a single decision. Rather, diagnosis and treatment are interwoven; the physician observes how the patient responds to a certain treatment and draws further conclusions about diagnosis. It simply is not reasonable to suppose that at each step the physician should present an array of information and ask the patient to make a choice. This is further complicated by the fact that patients are often confused, in pain, frightened, and so forth.

5. H. R. Wulff, "The Inherent Paternalism in Clinical Practice," *Journal of Medicine and Philosophy* 20 (1995): 299–311.

Respect for autonomy is evident in the requirement that voluntary informed consent be obtained for medical procedures. An autonomous person is one who is, among other things, adequately informed about alternatives and risks, which informed-consent policies are intended to ensure. A patient who has a clear understanding of his options is one who can evaluate outcomes and risks in light of his own values and then choose the course of action that best promotes those values. Related to this is the moral rule that medical professionals be truthful with patients. Withholding or distorting information relevant to a patient's decision undercuts that person's autonomy and is inconsistent with the requirements of the principle of respect for autonomy.

The concept of autonomy is very closely related to that of mental competence, although there are some important differences between the two. Determining whether one is autonomous differs in some respects from determining whether one is mentally competent. (The focus of this discussion is on the psychological, rather than the legal, conception of mental competence. From a legal standpoint, everyone who has reached the age of majority is assumed to be competent unless a judge has ruled otherwise.) A competent person is one who is capable of performing satisfactorily (although perhaps not perfectly) the various tasks that arise in the ordinary course of life. An action is performed competently when it is performed (deliberately) with a sufficient degree of skill or success. A competent person may, on a given occasion, fail to perform a task competently, but actions can be performed competently only by those who are competent, if only fleetingly. Such phrases as "sufficient degree of skill or success" in the definition of competence indicate that there is a good deal of vagueness here. Even so, the notion of competence has proved valuable (or at least popular) in law and policy.

Although there is some overlap between the concepts of autonomy and competence, they are distinct. The latter is narrower in that it leaves out any consideration of goals, preferences, or inappropriate influences. An autonomous person may not be competent to perform some task (perhaps because he or she lacks a relevant ability), and a task may be competently performed by someone who is not acting autonomously (perhaps because of coercion). Nonetheless, one's competence to make a significant decision about one's medical care is closely linked to one's capacity to act autonomously.[6]

Mental competence is used in law and policy as the practical link between autonomy (and the moral considerations associated with it) and the patient's role in medical decision making. Competent patients are generally regarded as autonomous agents (although this inference is faulty, as the preceding discussion reveals) and must be granted a central role in making decisions about their health care. Therefore, health care providers are said to have a strong obligation to refrain from interfering in the actions or decisions of competent patients and must ensure that their treatment meets the requirements of voluntary informed consent and so forth.

It is widely accepted that competence has to do with the *manner* in which one arrives at a decision and not with the *content* of the decision; that is, the concern is with the process rather than the product of decision making. Patients may have goals, values, religious beliefs, and so forth that others do not share and that may yield decisions that

---

6. Thomas L. Beauchamp, "Competence," in *Competency*, ed. M. Cardell Cutter and E. Shelp (Dordrecht: Kluwer Academic, 1991), 49–77.

appear inappropriate and even dangerous. But one should not slip into thinking that the only acceptable decision a patient can make is the one the physician recommends or the one that is generally accepted. When mentally competent patients arrive at decisions in a reasonable manner, there is a significant, albeit defeasible, moral obligation to respect those decisions.

It is worth noting that cultural factors have considerable influence on how much emphasis is put on the principle of respect for autonomy. In the United States, with its historical emphasis on individual liberty, this principle is given great weight and is said to override most other moral considerations that might conflict with it. In many other cultures, however, an individual's autonomy is seen as less significant than one's role in (and obligations to) one's family or community.[7] Moral objectivism implies that there is an objective fact of the matter concerning whether the American emphasis on individual autonomy is appropriate; it may well be that much less weight should be put on it.

*The Principle of Nonmaleficence   You have a moral obligation to refrain from causing harm.* The Hippocratic tradition adjures physicians to refrain from using the art of medicine to cause harm to patients, but the notion of harm, which is central to this principle, can be difficult to pin down precisely. It is important to note that harms are relative to goals or values; one person may regard a particular outcome as a harm, while another is indifferent to it and a third regards it as a benefit. To harm a person is to thwart one of that person's interests, damage something that that person values, take away that person's goods, or interfere with his or her opportunities. The seriousness of a harm is measured by its magnitude (the degree of damage done or the degree to which interests are thwarted) and whether the harm can be reversed or remedied. It is worth noting that one can be harmed without being wronged: some harms are inadvertent and could not have been foreseen, so the person who caused the harm may not be held morally accountable for it. (No small amount of the misunderstanding of medical malpractice arises when people confuse being harmed with being wronged.)

This connection between harms and goals or values should lead us to question some commonly accepted claims. Notably, we should ask ourselves whether death is always a harm. Certainly, death is *ordinarily* a harm; it prevents us from continuing our relationships with loved ones, interrupts projects that are important to us, and makes further pleasure and accomplishment impossible. But not everyone views death this way. There are those whose medical circumstances prevent them from experiencing pleasure, enjoying the company of loved ones, and so forth. For these people, death can be the only means by which they can escape suffering, and they may yearn for it. To insist that such persons undergo continued treatment that extends their lives may be regarded as causing unjustified harm. Bear this in mind when reading the sections on euthanasia and physician-assisted suicide.

Note also that the harms one must consider in making a moral evaluation of an action may go beyond harms to the patient involved. For instance, a medical professional may be harmed by being pushed into participating in something that he or she finds

7. See, for instance, L. J. Blackhall et al., "Ethnicity and Attitudes toward Patient Autonomy," *Journal of the American Medical Association* 274, no. 10 (1995): 820–25.

objectionable. A patient's family members might be harmed by having to spend their savings to pay for medical care or by being pressured into taking on the demanding role of long-term caregivers. There may also be harms toward individuals who cannot be identified at the moment. If an action uses scarce medical resources in an inefficient or wasteful manner, it might be claimed that this harms others who might have benefited from them but who now will not have access to them. Be sure that your moral evaluations take into account factors that go beyond the obvious and immediate details of the case.

Not every action that causes harm is morally unjustified. Causing a harm may be an unavoidable part of conferring some greater benefit. To take a simple example, consider giving a child an injection that will make him immune from a serious disease. The injection is painful, and the child hates it; thus, the injection causes harm. But, obviously, the injection is morally justified because of the greater benefit that the child then enjoys. In other cases, harms may be justified for reasons having to do with justice. A transplantable organ or a bed in an intensive care unit (ICU) may be withheld from a patient, even though the patient may be harmed as a result. The justification for this may be that giving this patient these resources would be unjust for some reason. The principle of nonmaleficence, like other moral principles, must be balanced against competing considerations.

*The Principle of Beneficence*   *You have a moral obligation to confer benefits upon others.* This is closely related to the principle of nonmaleficence; in fact, when nonmaleficence is relevant to a situation, the principle of beneficence is, too, and vice versa. However, the principle of beneficence is often regarded as having less moral force than the principle of maleficence. In other words, it is generally thought that our moral obligation to benefit others carries less weight than our obligation to refrain from harming them.

Just as harms are relative to one's goals and preferences, so what counts as a benefit will vary from one person or situation to another. If you give a blood transfusion to someone who is a devout Jehovah's Witness, you may believe that you have conferred a benefit upon the patient, while she believes she has been harmed. In most situations, it is the goals and values of the person on whom the benefit is conferred that should be used in evaluating outcomes.

It is important to remember that many medical attempts to confer benefits upon people involve risks. One should look to the patient's goals and values not only to determine which outcomes would count as benefits, but also to determine which risks are worth running. People have widely differing attitudes toward risk. Some are risk tolerant: they are willing to take considerable risks, provided that doing so gives them an opportunity to gain something they value. Others are risk averse: they would rather forgo the opportunity of gaining something of value than take the risks involved in the process of pursuing that outcome. There is no single, uniquely reasonable attitude toward risk. Therefore, any attempt to confer benefits upon another should be guided not only by that person's values, but also by his or her attitude toward risk.

The principle of beneficence often conflicts with the principle of respect for autonomy. When respect for autonomy is overridden in these cases, the result is a *paternalistic* action. To treat someone paternalistically is to act for that person's benefit without consent or even over his or her objections. This might involve making a choice on someone's behalf rather than letting that person choose, or withholding (or misrepresenting) information so as to influence that person's choice, or providing (or withholding) treatment despite that person's demands. Some paternalistic actions are justified, while others are not. In order to work out when and why paternalism is permissible, it is helpful to look at a couple of distinctions among paternalistic interventions.[8]

The first distinction that is relevant to its moral status is that between weak and strong paternalism. This has to do with the cognitive abilities of the person the paternalistic action is intended to benefit. *Weak* paternalism is the beneficent intervention in the actions or decisions of someone who has some significant cognitive deficit. *Strong* paternalism is the beneficent intervention in the actions or decisions of someone who has no significant cognitive deficit. An act of weak paternalism is more likely to be justified than an act of strong paternalism. There are two reasons for this. First, although both types of paternalism involve overriding one's moral obligation to respect the patient's autonomy, in cases of weak paternalism the patient is less autonomous, so one's obligation to respect autonomy is weaker. Clearly, a weak moral obligation can more readily be overridden by other considerations than a strong obligation. Second, the consequences of *not* intervening paternalistically are likely to be worse when the person one wants to benefit has a significant cognitive deficit. This deficit may prevent the patient from understanding alternatives, balancing long-term interests against short-term ones, evaluating outcomes in the light of one's values, and so forth. Simply put, someone with a serious cognitive deficit will be more prone to harmful errors than someone without a deficit.

The second distinction among kinds of paternalistic actions is that between hard and soft paternalism. This has to do with whose values, preferences, and attitudes toward risk are used in determining what would count as a benefit to the patient. *Soft* paternalism evaluates risks and outcomes from the patient's standpoint. *Hard* paternalism evaluates them using a set of goals and values the patient does not share. Soft paternalism is generally more readily justified than hard paternalism. Soft paternalism confers upon the patient something that he or she will regard as a benefit (involving what the patient regards as acceptable risk). Thus, it comes closer to respecting the patient's autonomy and avoids the anger and resentment often engendered by hard paternalism.

When one decides to act paternalistically, it is best to employ the least restrictive, intrusive, or humiliating interventions available.[9] Also, these interventions should be temporary, if possible. Every paternalistic action stands in need of a moral justification, and these guidelines will help one determine which actions are likely to be permissible and which are not.

*The Principle of Justice*   *You have a moral obligation to see to it that people are treated equally (unless there is some morally significant difference between them) and to distribute goods and opportunities in accordance with people's entitlements.* Several related

8. J. F. Childress, *Who Should Decide: Paternalism in Health Care* (New York: Oxford University Press, 1982).
9. Ibid.

moral concerns are grouped together under the heading of justice. These include *procedural justice,* which has to do with treating people and situations in an evenhanded manner (avoiding favoritism, for instance); *distributive justice,* which deals with giving each person an appropriate share of goods and opportunities; and *compensatory justice,* which requires that those who have been harmed receive appropriate compensation. There are also principles of retributive justice, which requires that people receive the punishment whose nature and severity is appropriate to their guilt, but this will not be dealt with here.

The principle as it is stated at the beginning of this section does not make clear what sorts of differences between individuals are morally significant or how goods should be distributed within a community if the result is to be equitable. The principle only presents the general structure or form of this moral guideline; for this reason it is called the *formal* principle of justice. When we fill in the details, providing substantive guidelines to be followed in acting justly, the result is a *material* principle of justice. There are many material principles of justice, and they address different types of moral situations and reflect different fundamental theories of justice. For instance, in deciding which of many patients should receive a transplantable organ, a material principle of justice might require that we consider each patient's past contribution to society, or that we try to estimate each person's probable future contribution, or that we compare their probable medical outcomes, and so forth. In many cases, rather than trying to determine which one of these material principles of justice is the correct one, we should regard them all as bringing to our attention relevant moral factors.[10]

*Principlism and Its Problems*   Although the moral principles described above highlight a number of morally significant factors, such as the importance of refraining from causing harm and of allowing autonomous individuals to shape their own lives, it has sometimes been suggested that these principles provide an adequate means of answering our questions about medical ethics. This view has become known as *principlism.* Cases in medical ethics are often discussed in terms of these principles, and attempts to resolve the moral problems they present often focus on citing one and applying it to the situation. This approach has, however, been the subject of criticism in the past few years.

One difficulty is that the principles being applied are quite abstract, and their separation from the details of a case often makes their application unclear. The principles of beneficence and nonmaleficence, for instance, set forth moral requirements having to do with harms and benefits, but it is often difficult to tell what would count, in a particular situation, as harmful or beneficial. Similarly, the principle of justice requires that resources be distributed justly, but it can be extremely difficult to tell whether a particular set of distribution decisions meets this standard.

A second objection is that although principlism is able to identify some of the moral conflicts involved in a situation, it does nothing to tell us how they ought to be resolved. For instance, it may be that in a particular case the principle of beneficence is

10. Tom Beauchamp and James Childress, *Principles of Biomedical Ethics,* 4th ed. (New York: Oxford University Press, 1994), 330.

in conflict with the principle of respect for autonomy, and there is no way of determining which of these principles ought to take priority in the situation at hand. Thus, as a method for identifying what one ought to do in particular cases, principlism is ineffective.

These criticisms highlight the fact that principlism is not a full-fledged moral theory and so cannot perform the functions of a theory, which include providing clear resolutions or direction when applied to cases. Attempts have been made to fill in some of the gaps and answer criticisms,[11] but these efforts have raised new objections, and no satisfactory principle-based approach seems to be available at present.[12] Even so, the four principles discussed earlier will play a significant role in this book. Even though they cannot be relied upon as a method for resolving all our moral questions, they still play an important role as a checklist of morally significant factors to be taken into account in our deliberations.

## Casuistry

*Casuistry*, a method of moral reasoning developed by medieval philosophers and theologians, has been gaining prominence in medical ethics, and it can be a valuable tool in working through moral issues.[13] It also points out that although we may often be uncertain about moral judgments, we can be more confident about them in some cases than in others. Unlike many moral theories, it takes our judgments about certain clear cases to be foundational and works from these toward general moral principles and toward solutions to cases that are more difficult. Casuistry has been defined as

> the analysis of moral issues, using procedures of reasoning based on paradigms and analogies, leading to the formulation of expert opinions about the existence and stringency of particular moral obligations, framed in terms of rules or maxims that are general but not universal or invariable, since they hold good with certainty only in the typical conditions of the agent and circumstances of action.[14]

This procedure for arriving at moral judgments in difficult cases begins with general moral principles and paradigmatic cases of their application. (These cases are selected as paradigms because here informed, thoughtful people agree that the principle in question is applicable and yields the appropriate moral judgment.) One works from a paradigm toward the case to be dealt with by considering a series of intermediate cases in which the circumstances are altered bit by bit. One might, for example, change the severity of a harm involved, the agent's motive or state of mind, the relationships among people, and so on. At each step in this process, one considers how the principle with which one began should be applied, whether new principles come into play, and how the changed circumstances bear upon the decision. The key tools here are

11. See, for instance, David DeGrazia, "Moving Forward in Bioethical Theory: Theories, Cases, and Specified Principlism," *Journal of Medicine and Philosophy* 17 (1992): 511–39.

12. See, for instance, Bernard Gert, Charles Culver, and K. Danner Clouser, *Bioethics: A Return to Fundamentals* (New York: Oxford University Press, 1997), 71–92.

13. Albert R. Jonsen and Stephen Toulmin, *The Abuse of Casuistry* (Berkeley: University of California Press, 1988). Although casuistry has long been regarded as a means of inappropriately manipulating moral judgments to suit our purposes, it is guilty of this only when misused. See Jonsen and Toulmin for a full defense.

14. Ibid., 257.

argument by analogy and one's practical wisdom in understanding situations and sensitively applying rules.[15] As these modifications take one further and further from the initial paradigm case, one's confidence in the resulting judgment will tend to diminish (which is what we should expect). Just how confident one is will depend in part upon whether different types of arguments (for example, pragmatic or legal considerations, or moral arguments employing different principles) converge upon a single judgment and in part on the strength of the analogies involved. When one acts upon such a judgment, one may not do what one ought (that is, one's moral judgment can be mistaken), but one will not have acted rashly or thoughtlessly; one can be "of good conscience."[16]

The judgments with which casuistry begins and the principles it finds appealing are heavily influenced by our moral traditions and common practices, a characteristic that has left casuistry exposed to criticism.[17] Among other things, we want an adequate moral theory to identify and weed out our biases and errors, but casuistry's dependence upon moral tradition makes it seem unlikely that it will do this effectively. The history of casuistry, however, provides examples of identifying and eliminating some cultural influences.[18] Furthermore, it may be that by requiring coherence among our moral theories and theories in other areas of philosophy and science, these biases can be identified and eliminated.[19] In any case, our uncertainty about the role of culture in our moral reasoning is (or ought to be) one of the sources of our diffidence in making moral judgments.

Although it has long been neglected, casuistry can make an important contribution to the debate about how value conflicts are to be resolved. As these examples reveal, this method allows us to take into account the human circumstances of the conflicts we encounter and yields results that better reflect the nature of the enterprise of ethics.

## *Moral Rights*

Although there is a great deal of talk about moral rights, one must be careful to understand rights-based moral theories correctly. The discussion of moral rights usually arises in the context of trying to determine whether a given action is morally permissible.

15. Casuistry's dependence upon reasoning by analogy accounts in part for its inability to render conclusions with certainty. It can be quite difficult to spot relevant points of disanalogy and to gauge the strength of analogies. This is particularly troublesome when a single case is analogous to two or more others that support conflicting judgments; no clear procedure is available for settling such conflicts.

16. Jonsen and Toulmin, *Abuse of Casuistry,* 251–56.

17. DeGrazia, "Moving Forward in Bioethical Theory."

18. See, for example, Jonsen and Toulmin, *Abuse of Casuistry,* chapter 11.

19. This has been described and defended by Norman Daniels, "Wide Reflective Equilibrium and Theory Acceptance in Ethics," *Journal of Philosophy* 76 (1979): 256–82. Notice that the goal here is not to eliminate *all* influences of culture upon moral judgments. Culture, after all, is part of the circumstances in which actions are performed and so should be taken into account in our judgments. (Remember that Mill's utilitarianism is sensitive to culture because culture has a bearing upon the consequences of actions.) The problem is that culture may strongly contribute to our feelings of certainty in what we take to be paradigmatic cases of the application of moral principles; when this happens, our judgments may be pulled away from the moral fact of the matter. A casuist might address this problem by requiring cross-cultural agreement on paradigm cases; it is unlikely that all cultures would bias people in the same way on a given case. But this requirement might well leave us without any paradigms.

What makes a rights-based approach to this question interesting is that it does not directly examine the action itself, the consequences of the action, or the motives of the person who performs the action. Instead, it focuses our attention on the moral entitlements of the people involved. Moral rights function by constraining how we are permitted to interact with others. People are morally entitled to expect certain kinds of treatment from others. If, for example, you have a right not to be caused unnecessary suffering, this places a constraint upon how I may interact with you; this right of yours does not permit me to use you as a dart board or a speed bump. Moral rights, then, can be spelled out in terms of the appropriate expectations one has regarding the sort of treatment one will experience at the hands of others. Not every such expectation constitutes a right, though. I may expect that you will pay the bills for all of my medical care, but I may not have a moral right to this treatment. Furthermore, I may have rights of which I am unaware; in such a case I would be entitled to expect certain treatment even though I do not actually expect it.

Our present concern is with *moral* rights, which must be kept carefully distinct from *legal* rights. Both sorts of rights spell out what expectations one can appropriately have about how one will be treated by others, but in various other respects these two types of rights differ considerably. Even so, these two types of rights are not completely unlike; in a number of cases, they correspond to one another. Many legal rights are based upon prior moral rights; that is, the law is sometimes designed to entrench moral requirements. For example, your moral right not to be killed by others is matched by your legal right not to be killed. There are, however, moral rights that have no corresponding legal right, and vice versa. You may have a moral right to someone's compassion and concern, but have no corresponding legal right. Similarly, you have a legal right to bring a lawsuit against someone, but (depending upon the circumstances) you may have no moral right to do so. Moreover, moral rights and legal rights can conflict; that is, in some cases it might be illegal to do what is morally right, or immoral to do what is legally permissible. Only moral rights will be discussed in what follows.

Moral rights can be grouped into several categories. Although not all of these will be discussed here, it is helpful to note the distinction between negative and positive rights. Negative moral rights put limits upon how others may behave toward the right-holder. More specifically, negative rights are those that make it impermissible for others to harm the right-holder or to interfere with his or her behavior in specified ways. There are two kinds of negative moral rights. *Liberty rights,* as their name suggests, prohibit others from interfering with one's actions; a person who has liberty rights may act as he or she pleases (provided that this behavior does not unacceptably interfere with the rights of others). For example, you have the liberty right to hold and express whatever opinions you please, to pursue whatever occupation you choose, to live where you like, and so forth. *Immunities,* the second category of negative moral rights, prohibit others from treating the right-holder in specified ways; in particular, immunities prevent others from harming the right-holder. Your right not to be killed is an immunity right.

For each negative moral right, there is a corresponding duty or obligation. In other words, if you have a negative right (of either sort), everyone else has a corresponding obligation regarding how they treat you. For example, if you possess the liberty right to hold and express any opinion you please, everyone else has a (negative) duty not to interfere with your doing so. Similarly, if you possess the immunity right not to be killed, everyone else has a (negative) duty or obligation not to kill you. Negative duties are always duties to refrain from doing something. Notice that the obligations that correspond to negative rights are had by all other people, not just a select few.

Positive moral rights entitle one to be treated in certain ways by others; typically, this amounts to an entitlement to the assistance of others. *Welfare rights* are the only class of positive moral rights that will be discussed here. It is often claimed that anyone who is in danger of an avoidable death is entitled to be rescued; this would be a welfare right. Similarly, if there is a right to adequate medical care, or to adequate food and shelter, these will also be welfare rights. It is interesting to note that although it is generally agreed that we have a number of negative rights, we seem to have far fewer welfare rights, and there is usually disagreement about what they are. The right to be saved from unnecessary death is perhaps the least controversial of these, but whether we have a welfare right to basic medical care is hotly disputed.

The question about corresponding duties arises once again with positive rights. This is a difficult matter. For example, if someone possesses the welfare right to be saved from an unnecessary death, who, if anyone, incurs an obligation to do the saving? Is it the person nearest to the action, or the one who is best trained to deal with such emergencies, or the one who has the fewest conflicting obligations, or is everyone equally obligated? To take a more controversial case, if people have a moral right to adequate health care, who, if anyone, is morally obligated to provide it (or pay for it)? Doctors? Hospitals? The patient's family or community? Some level of government? Unlike the duties that correspond to negative rights, those corresponding with welfare rights are generally thought to be held only by some limited group of people. Often the membership of this group is unclear or disputed.

Once we have settled which rights there are, the next question to address is this: Who (or what) has these rights? It is important to bear in mind that rights are not distributed haphazardly; rather, there are reasons why an individual possesses or lacks a specified right. These reasons or criteria for possessing a right will depend in part upon the nature of the right possessed. For each right that exists, we need to determine the criteria one must meet in order to possess it; these are called the *possession criteria* for the right. Again, this task cannot be completed haphazardly, nor can it be done by arbitrary stipulation. Suppose, for example, one is trying to determine which individuals possess the right not to be caused unnecessary suffering. It makes sense to say that only creatures that are *capable* of suffering would have this right. We can reasonably expect that different rights will involve different possession criteria. Therefore, individuals of different types may possess different sets of rights. For example, normal adult humans may have different moral rights from children. The criteria for possessing some rights (such as the welfare right to be fed and clothed) may be met by children but not by adults, and the criteria for other rights (such as the liberty right to determine one's lifestyle) may be met by adults but not children.

Once possession criteria have been worked out for each sort of moral right, one can determine which rights each individual has. This is done by simply comparing each individual's characteristics with the criteria for each moral right; if one meets the criteria, one has the right in question, but otherwise one does not. Some individuals may not meet the criteria for any rights and so would have no moral rights at all. It will probably turn out that human beings differ greatly in the rights they possess. For example, children may have some welfare rights (such as the right to be fed and clothed) that adults no longer have. And people who are rational probably have some liberty rights that irrational people lack. And normal adults probably have many rights not shared by those who are irreversibly comatose. It is highly unlikely that any individual possesses all the moral rights there are. This is because the necessary and sufficient conditions for possessing one right conflict with those for possessing some others. It is necessary for some rights (such as a child's right to be cared for) that one be vulnerable and inexperienced, but other rights (such as your right to live where you choose or to decide which risks are worth taking) require that you *not* be vulnerable or inexperienced.

Although many people talk about moral rights when they discuss ethical issues, what is said often indicates a misunderstanding of how rights work. Consider, for example, the claim that euthanasia is impermissible because it violates the patient's right not to be killed. Or the claim that making euthanasia illegal is impermissible because it violates the patient's right to have his or her decisions about life and health care respected. Each of these claims implies a misunderstanding of how rights function.

To see what the problem is in these statements, notice the pattern that they fit: in each case a moral evaluation is made (that is, some type of action is said to be permissible, prohibited, or obligatory, for instance), and this claim is supported by citing one of the moral rights involved. The problem here is that defending a moral judgment requires much more than this. When one mentions only a single moral right involved in the relevant situation, one leaves open the possibility that there are other rights involved as well and that one or more of these other rights override the one that has been mentioned. If the right that has been specified is overridden, then presenting it in this way does nothing to support the moral judgment in question.

Two rights are in conflict if one can respect one of these rights only by violating the other. An adequate theory of moral rights must provide an explanation of how these conflicts are to be resolved. One approach to resolving conflicts among rights is to say that one right takes precedence over (or overrides) the other. One does not do anything morally impermissible in violating a right if one does so in order to respect an overriding right. In order to work this out, though, we need a clear, principled way of determining which rights override which other rights. For example, one might claim that immunity rights always override liberty rights. It is very difficult, however, to come up with principles that will seem plausible. To take the conflict-resolution principle just suggested, although there are many cases in which immunity rights seem to override liberty rights, there also seem to be cases in which it is the other way around. (Think, for example, of how a theory of moral rights would explain why it is permissible to kill in self-defense.) Thus, this principle may need to be limited to account for these exceptions. Also, more principles would be needed to deal with conflicts that involved only immunity rights or only liberty rights. To date, no acceptable set of such principles has been formulated.

The upshot of this discussion of moral rights is that rights-based theories leave many important questions unanswered. We are not sure which rights exist, who has the duties that correspond to them, what the possession criteria are for each right, or how conflicts among rights are to be settled. Therefore, rights-based moral theories are unable, by themselves, to resolve moral issues clearly or authoritatively. Discussions of moral rights are most helpful as a means of reminding ourselves of moral considerations that ought to be taken into account.

## *Virtue Ethics*

Virtue-based approaches to ethics typically trace their roots back to the philosopher Aristotle (384–322 B.C.). Rather than focusing primarily upon the evaluation of particular actions, he asked instead about the sort of life a human being ought to lead. That is, instead of trying to formulate lists of permissible or prohibited actions, he focused on one's moral character. This begins with an account of the goal of human life and activity, which Aristotle argues is *eudaimonia;* this is rather like happiness or human flourishing (but is not to be confused with mere pleasure). A virtue is a characteristic that aids one in attaining this goal. A virtuous person is not simply someone who reliably follows moral rules. Aristotle points out that a virtuous person will sometimes break moral rules, so he requires wisdom to know when and how this should be done. Thus, virtue-based theories are much more than reformulations of principle-based theories.

Contemporary virtue theories often reject Aristotle's claim that there is a single goal appropriate for all humanity and that this goal is revealed by reason. Alasdair MacIntyre, for instance, has argued that each person develops his or her own conception of the good, a process that involves modifications and changes of direction throughout one's life.[20] A virtue, on this approach, is a feature of one's character that enables one to be successful in this search for happiness. Rationality is not the sole guide for this search. We also, MacIntyre suggests, draw meaning and pleasure from social practices and institutions that provide their own standards for success and failure.

A morally permissible action, according to a virtue-based approach, is the one that a virtuous person would perform in the circumstances. What *makes* an action permissible, however, is not that a virtuous person would perform it, but certain other characteristics of the act (such as being just or compassionate). The choices and actions of a virtuous person serve as indicators of permissibility but are not constitutive of it. A difficulty facing virtue theories has been explaining how a virtuous person determines what he or she ought to do. This is particularly difficult because there are situations in which particular virtues, such as being just or compassionate, are in conflict with one another. Do virtuous people have a reliable, non-arbitrary way of resolving these conflicts? If so, what is it? Could we use this method to determine the permissibility of actions without making any mention of virtues or the actions of virtuous people?

In addition to the general issue of moral character or integrity, some forms of virtue ethics address the virtues related to particular social roles or professions. For instance, there may be particular character traits—virtues—that would tend to make one a better physician or nurse. In medical ethics, virtue theories have played a role in examining the physician-patient relationship, using virtues as a basis for outlining how this relationship should be built and maintained.

20. Alasdair MacIntyre, *After Virtue* (Notre Dame, Ind.: University of Notre Dame Press, 1981).

## *Feminist Ethics*

Feminist philosophers have long been critical of the traditional approaches to dealing with ethical issues and have offered in their place an array of theories and considerations that change the ethical landscape profoundly. Several different approaches to ethics fall under this heading, and it is difficult to find a short description that will adequately cover them all.

One point on which most feminist ethicists agree is that abstract, principle-based approaches to ethics are unsatisfactory. One criticism of ethical principles is that they treat people as though we were all rational, autonomous, independent individuals meeting as strangers and interacting in ways that have more to do with contracts and exchanges than with caring relationships. But in fact, many people are being oppressed in one way or another and so cannot exercise their autonomy or interact with others in anything like the free and equal manner imagined by traditional moral theories. (What these theories really do, some feminists argue, is describe how white, socially influential, and economically powerful men interact with one another.) A second problem is that this model of human interactions leaves out much that is important morally: it downplays relationships, emotional commitments, and so forth. Although abstract rules and principles are readily used to control the behavior of others, some feminist ethicists argue that this should not be the primary goal of ethics.

Instead of dealing with abstract principles, feminist ethics generally places its emphasis on social and personal realities, taking particular note of how some groups or individuals subjugate others. The goal of ethics is to identify and eliminate these instances of oppression. Note that the focus of feminist ethics has come to extend beyond the oppression of women; it includes concern for *all* who are oppressed.

One feminist approach, the ethic of care, arises from the work of Carol Gilligan and others.[21] Gilligan argues that men and women follow different paths in their moral development, with men coming to focus on rights and justice, while women are more concerned with relationships and nurturing. The ethic of care is more flexible and more inclined to compromise and to avoid conflicts than traditional, male-dominated ethics are.

The ethic of care has been criticized by some feminists, however. They are concerned that caring might be seen as irrational and feminine and therefore inferior to masculine, principle-based moral reasoning. Another worry is that seeing caring as a female trait could endorse women's oppression in the medical professions. Most nurses are female and most doctors are male, and the ethic of care might be interpreted as endorsing this by saying that caring is the role of nurses and that women can do this best.

Care-focused approaches to feminist ethics have sometimes been contrasted with power-focused approaches.[22] The latter begin with a critical examination of the relationships between those who hold social or economic power and those who lack it, and of the ways in which traditional moral theories reflect the concerns and experi-

---

21. Carol Gilligan, *In a Different Voice* (Cambridge, Mass.: Harvard University Press, 1982).
22. Rosemarie Tong, *Feminist Approaches to Bioethics* (Boulder, Colo.: Westview, 1997), 37–38.

ences of those who have wielded this power (usually white males). This emphasis has led to the subordination or outright dismissal of the concerns and experiences of women and other oppressed groups. The correct response to this, it has been suggested, is not simply to move to a feminine ethic of caring, but to work to undermine and destroy many of the existing power structures, including the system of subordination incorporated in traditional ethics.

Applied to medical ethics, feminist moral thought begins with the observation that women have traditionally been, and continue to be, oppressed by medical institutions, medical practices, and the medical sciences in general. The central goal is to identify and eliminate these inequities. The history of birth control methods illustrates some of these issues. Traditional attitudes toward birth control have tended to be more concerned with men's experiences and concerns than with women's. For instance, the medical history of the development of birth control methods has shown startlingly little concern with such side effects in women as bleeding, depression, and sterility. The focus has been instead on whether these techniques are effective without causing medical problems that men regard as more serious (such as cancer). In addition, some feminists argue that the child-rearing role has been used to subjugate women to men, and so ready access to birth control methods and to abortion are essential if women are to be freed from this oppression.

Discussions in feminist bioethics have often dealt with topics that are of particular concern to women, such as birth control, abortion, reproductive technologies, and genetic counseling and therapy. It would be a mistake, however, to suppose that feminist ethics has nothing to say about other issues. There is also a broader concern with the physician-patient relationship, the role of nurses in health care, the nature and significance (or perhaps the impossibility and undesirability) of autonomous decision making, and so forth.

Because feminist ethics and feminist bioethics are so diverse, it is difficult to assess them as a whole. Some critics have argued that we do not need a *feminist* ethic to identify or correct oppression in society or problems in health care; traditional moral approaches are said to provide the same results when properly applied. The feminist rejection of the masculine "ethic of justice," with its attention to abstract principles, has been criticized for allowing too much capriciousness in handling ethical issues. Whatever the shortcomings of abstract principles, they are helpful in that they remind us of moral considerations that ought to be taken into account. They also yield a clearer means of arriving at decisions in difficult situations than, say, a care-based approach.

### Suggestions for Further Reading

MORAL THEORIES AND MEDICAL APPLICATIONS

Beauchamp, Tom L., and James F. Childress. *Principles of Biomedical Ethics.* 4th ed. New York: Oxford University Press, 1994.
   This book sets the standard for principle-based discussions of issues in medical ethics. Organized by moral principle, medical ethics issues are dealt with carefully and in detail.

Boss, Judith A., ed. *Perspectives on Ethics.* Mountain View, Calif.: Mayfield, 1998.
> This is a good introductory overview of the traditional positions in ethics. It also includes a detailed discussion of moral relativism and feminist views.

Clouser, K. Danner, and Bernard Gert. "A Critique of Principlism." *Journal of Medicine and Philosophy* 15 (1990): 219–36.
> This article presents a cogent argument against using a principle-based approach to trying to resolve ethical issues.

Crisp, Roger, and Michael Slote, eds. *Virtue Ethics.* Oxford Readings in Philosophy. New York: Oxford University Press, 1997.
> The essays in this collection explain the historical roots of virtue-based moral theories and present many of the innovations that have arisen in the past three decades.

Jonsen, Albert R., and Stephen Toulmin. *The Abuse of Casuistry.* Berkeley: University of California Press, 1988.
> Casuistry as a method for solving moral problems has long been misunderstood. Jonsen and Toulmin explain how the system works, why it is reliable, and how it should be applied.

Tong, Rosemarie. *Feminist Approaches to Bioethics.* Boulder, Colo.: Westview, 1997.
> A very good overview of the wide range of feminist approaches to ethics in general and medical ethics in particular. Tong carefully compares feminist and non-feminist theories.

Wolf, Susan, ed. *Feminism and Bioethics: Beyond Reproduction.* New York: Oxford University Press, 1996.
> This collection draws its articles from widely different feminist theorists, illustrating the broad range of approaches within feminism.

## COMPETENCE AND AUTONOMY

Beauchamp, Tom L. "Competence." In *Competency,* edited by M. Cardell Cutter and E. Shelp, 49–77. Dordrecht: Kluwer Academic, 1991.
> Beginning with an analysis of our concept of decision-making competence, Beauchamp considers in detail many of the practical methods used in determining patient competence.

Blackhall, Leslie, et al. "Ethnicity and Attitudes toward Patient Autonomy." *Journal of the American Medical Association* 274, no. 10 (1995): 820–25.
> Although individual autonomy looms large in North American discussions of patient care, many cultures find this objectionable. They may focus instead on the importance of the family or of the community. This empirical study sheds welcome light on this issue.

Inglefinger, Franz J. "Arrogance." *New England Journal of Medicine* 303, no. 26 (1980): 1507–11.
> Drawing on his own experience as a patient, Dr. Inglefinger discusses a sort of beneficial arrogance, a means of supporting patients when they are faced with difficult medical decisions.

# Section 2

# *Refusing Life-Sustaining Treatment*

## Introduction

Patients who refuse life-sustaining medical treatments present families and medical professionals with complex and heart-wrenching questions. Is the patient's decision the result of depression or exhaustion from the medical problems and treatments that have already been endured? Would it be wrong to override this decision and provide treatment against the patient's wishes? If treatment is stopped and the patient dies, will we ever stop wondering whether the patient would have reversed this decision or whether continued treatment would have been more successful than we expected?

Central to these and the many related questions that arise in these situations are the moral principles of beneficence and respect for autonomy. As was noted in the first section of this book, these principles frequently conflict, and to resolve such a conflict in favor of beneficence (that is, to conclude that the principle of respect for autonomy is overridden by the principle of beneficence) generally results in paternalistic actions. Each such action must be examined to determine whether it is morally acceptable.

In the case of a fully autonomous patient, there is a strong (but not necessarily overwhelming) obligation to respect the patient's decisions. Bear in mind, however, that as this autonomy diminishes, the obligation to respect it is more readily overridden by other moral obligations. In the previous section, it was pointed out that the standards for mental competence are task relative. That is, one must have a higher level of cognitive functioning in order to qualify as competent when the task is complex or risky than when it is simpler and safer. Thus, one may be competent to make one medical decision but incompetent to make another. Some theorists have argued that one implication of this is that a patient may be competent to accept a recommended treatment but incompetent to refuse that same treatment.[1] Accepting a recommended treatment is generally less risky than refusing it, and this may make a difference to the competence standards. According to this position, a patient is competent to refuse life-sustaining medical treatment only if he or she has a clear understanding of this choice and its alternatives.

It must be remembered that many things can influence and undercut one's autonomy and mental competence. Pain, depression, the effects of medications, mental illness, and other factors can play a significant role. Even the setting in which one is asked to make a decision can bear upon one's cognitive functioning. Some patients can think through choices and make them quite competently when at home but are easily confused when in the hospital. Similarly, there are those who are competent to make important medical decisions when family members are present to provide support but who are incompetent when they face choices alone.

Testing mental competence can be difficult and confusing. Two fairly simple methods for testing mental competency might seem plausible, but in fact they do not work very well. First, it cannot be assumed that any patient who refuses a recommended medical procedure is incompetent. Such a refusal may raise questions about the patient's competence but is not in itself evidence of incompetence.[2] Remember that decision-making competence has to do with the process by which one arrives at a decision, not with the outcome of that process. Regarding every patient who refuses treatment as incompetent to make medical decisions risks collapsing competence with simply doing what one's doctor recommends; but surely a competent person could disagree with his or her doctor (perhaps because doctor and patient have different sets of goals and values).[3] Second, determinations of competence cannot be made simply by determining whether the patient is mentally ill. While a diagnosis of mental illness may be relevant and significant, one cannot conclude that all and only mentally ill patients are incompetent to make decisions about their medical care.[4]

Furthermore, none of the battery of standard psychological tests is well suited to determining patient competence to make medical decisions.[5] These tests can determine the subject's orientation to time and place, basic reasoning skills, memory, ability to generate and understand language, and so forth. But as the preceding discussion reveals, competence to make medical decisions is far more complex than any of these components. Thus, one could score well on this sort of test and still be incompetent to make decisions about one's health care because of depression, denial, or other such factors.

1. Allen E. Buchanan and Dan W. Brock, *Deciding for Others: The Ethics of Surrogate Decision Making* (Cambridge and New York: Cambridge University Press, 1990).

2. Ibid.

3. President's Commission for the Study of Ethical Problems in Medicine and Biomedical and Behavioral Research, *Making Health Care Decisions,* vol. 1, *A Report on the Ethical and Legal Implications of Informed Consent in the Patient-Practitioner Relationship* (Washington, D.C.: Government Printing Office, 1982).

4. H. R. Searight, "Assessing Patient Competence for Medical Decision Making," *American Family Physician* 45, no. 2 (1992): 751–59.

5. Searight, "Assessing Patient Competence"; J. F. Scott and J. Lynch, "Bedside Assessment of Competency in Palliative Care," *Journal of Palliative Care* 10, no. 3 (1994): 101–5.

Some attempts have been made to develop straightforward clinical procedures for competency determinations, but success has been limited. This can be illustrated by considering briefly several representative attempts to come up with such a test: testing particular elements of the subject's cognitive performance,[6] interviews about hypothetical decisions,[7] and interviews about the subject's decisions about his or her own care.[8]

There are several problems with these approaches. First, none of them distinguishes between the subject's actual performance in making a decision and his or her abilities. Definitions of autonomy and mental competence are almost always put in terms of what the subject is *able* to do, but these tests focus on what the subject *does* do. Of course, there are many cases in which one's actual performance is not indicative of one's abilities. Second, these clinical instruments either fail to examine the process by which the subject's decision was made[9] or depend upon the subject's reports about that process.[10] The latter is a problem because the reasons the patient presents in the competency interview may not match the ones that were actually at work in his or her decision. This is not uncommon when people offer explanations of their behavior, even when these subjects believe they are being completely forthright in their reports.[11] When the interview focuses on a hypothetical case rather than on decisions about one's own care, this problem is compounded. One's reasoning about medical care in a hypothetical case about someone else may have too little resemblance to one's decision making about one's own medical care. For one thing, the former will have little of the emotive content or immediacy of the latter. One final problem with these approaches to determining competence is that none of them allows for the decision-relative nature of competence. It has already been noted that the threshold for competence is higher when there is more at stake, but there is little or no place for this variable in the clinical instruments to be found in the literature.

There does not seem to be any reliable method for testing mental competence to make medical decisions. There is, however, an approach that is probably as effective as any of the more complicated methods that have been proposed: simply ask the patient

6. G. Naglie et al., "A Randomized Trial of a Decisional Aid for Mental Capacity Assessments," *Journal of Clinical Epidemiology* 46, no. 3 (1993): 221–30; M. G. Weisensee, D. K. Kjervik, and J. B. Anderson, "A Tool to Assess the Cognitively Impaired Elderly," *Journal of Case Management* 4, no. 1 (1995): 29–33.

7. L. Weithorn, "Competency to Render Informed Treatment Decisions: A Comparison of Certain Minors and Adults" (Ph.D. diss., University of Pittsburgh, 1980).

8. G. Bean et al., "The Psychometric Properties of the Competency Interview Schedule," *Canadian Journal of Psychiatry* 39, no. 8 (1994): 368–76.

9. Naglie et al., "Randomized Trial of a Decisional Aid"; and Weisensee et al., "A Tool to Assess the Cognitively Impaired Elderly."

10. Weithorn, "Competency to Render Informed Treatment Decisions"; and Bean et al., "Psychometric Properties of the Competency Interview Schedule."

11. See, for instance, N. R. F. Maier, "Reasoning in Humans II: The Solution of a Problem and Its Appearance in Consciousness," *Journal of Comparative Psychology* 12 (1931): 181–94; R. Nisbett and T. Wilson, "Telling More than We Can Know: Verbal Reports on Mental Processes," *Psychological Review* 84, no. 3 (1977): 231–59; and T. Wilson, "Self-Deception without Repression: Limits on Access to Mental States," in *Self-Deception and Self-Understanding,* ed. M. Martin (Lawrence: University Press of Kansas, 1985), 95–116.

to explain how he or she arrived at the decision in question.[12] Although the patient's response may not provide an accurate picture of how that decision was actually made, it will at least show whether the patient has connected the relevant information with goals and values.

In addition to determining competence, one must also be very careful to investigate the reasons behind a patient's request that life-sustaining treatment be withheld. A patient's request that treatment be withheld might be an attempt to gain attention, a test to see whether physicians or family members care enough to talk the patient out of it, or something else. Thus, requests that treatment be withheld should not be taken at face value.

In this section, Sullivan and Youngner examine depression, a factor that can seriously undermine one's autonomy and prevent one from being competent to make important or risky medical decisions. They point out that depression is not a monolithic psychological phenomenon but has a number of components and can vary considerably from one case to another. They also argue that some depressed patients are still mentally competent to refuse lifesaving medical treatment, contrary to a standard interpretation of these cases.

Also in this section, Mark Yarborough considers a case in which a physician is asked to continue treating a patient who has refused further life-sustaining treatment. The central question in that case is whether the benefit continued treatment would have for the family—not the patient—could justify this. This could be described as a conflict between moral principles: the principle of respect for autonomy indicates that life-sustaining treatment should be withdrawn, but the principle of beneficence indicates that further treatment would benefit the family and should be continued. The principle of nonmaleficence might be relevant as well: continued treatment of someone who is not receiving any medical benefit from it and who has asked that the treatment be stopped could be construed as harming that patient. Yarborough also distinguishes between the moral justification of a particular action and the justification of a practice or policy. Because a policy would have different effects and implications from a particular action, the act might be justified, while the policy would not.

Jacquelyn Slomka takes up another matter that is the subject of much debate: should food and water (nutrition and hydration) be treated in the same way as respirators, surgeries, and other medical treatments when withholding treatment is being considered? Or is the provision of food and water not a medical treatment at all? Are there special obligations to provide food and water that do not apply to other forms of medical treatment? Slomka examines these questions and concludes that there is no significant difference between nutrition and hydration and other forms of medical treatment. Thus, a competent patient has the moral and legal authority to refuse food and water, regardless of the form in which it is administered.

In moral terms, this issue is usually linked with the principle of nonmaleficence. It is often argued that withholding nutrition and hydration causes the patient harm, and thus one has a moral obligation not to withhold them. But it would be a mistake to suppose that this settles the matter. For one thing, are we quite sure that withholding

12. Buchanan and Brock, *Deciding for Others,* 70–76.

nutrition and hydration causes harm? Whose goals and values are being employed when this conclusion is reached? Remember that what counts as a harm depends upon one's perspective, and it is the patient's perspective that ought to be employed here. Related to this are questions about exactly what happens when nutrition and hydration are withheld. It is often described as starving the patient to death, and the implication is that this withholding causes avoidable suffering. Slomka argues, however, this is mistaken. Even if withholding nutrition and hydration does cause harm, there is also the patient's autonomy to be considered. In which cases is a harmful act morally justified by one's obligation to respect the autonomy of the one who requested the action (and who is harmed by it)? There is also a fascinating question here about the social meaning of providing someone with food and water. Slomka's article considers this at length and clarifies the role of context in determining the social meaning of actions.

# Depression, Competence, and the Right to Refuse Lifesaving Medical Treatment

MARK D. SULLIVAN AND STUART J. YOUNGNER

*Objective:* The authors explore the possibility that psychiatrists inappropriately extend their views on suicide by the medically well to refusal of lifesaving treatment by the seriously medically ill. *Method:* The legal and bioethics literature on competence to refuse lifesaving treatment and the possible impact of depression on this refusal is reviewed. *Results:* Over the past 20 years, the burden of proof concerning the mental competence of seriously medically ill patients who refuse lifesaving treatment has shifted to the persons who seek to override these refusals. However, in psychiatry a patient's desire to die is generally considered to be evidence of an impaired capacity to make decisions about lifesaving treatment. This contrast between ethical traditions is brought into clinical focus during the evaluation and treatment of medically ill patients with depression who refuse lifesaving treatment. The clinical evaluation of the effect of depression on a patient's capacity to make medical decisions is difficult for several reasons: 1) depression is easily seen as a "reasonable" response to serious medical illness, 2) depression produces more subtle distortions of decision making than delirium or psychosis (i.e., preserving the understanding of medical facts while impairing the appreciation of their personal importance), and 3) a diagnosis of major depression is neither necessary nor sufficient for determining that the patient's medical

From the *American Journal of Psychiatry* 1994; 151 (7): 971–978. One paragraph has been omitted and notes 37–43 have been renumbered. Reprinted by permission of the American Psychiatric Association.

decision making is impaired. *Conclusions:* Depression can be diagnosed and treated in patients with serious medical illness. But after optimizing medical and psychiatric treatment and determining that the patient is competent to make medical decisions, it may be appropriate to honor the patient's desire to die.

IN THE CONTEXT OF SEVERE AND UNBEARable medical illness, refusals of medical treatment that hasten death are generally viewed as "allowing to die" or "letting nature take its course." In medical settings, legal competence to refuse life-sustaining treatment is presumed; the burden rests with the physician to prove otherwise. In psychiatric settings, a desire to die is not only considered prima facie evidence of mental disorder and critically flawed decision-making capacity but, by its very existence, provides a justification for treatment. In this article we explore the origins of these very different clinical and ethical perspectives and the moral assumptions that underlie them. We examine in depth one clinical phenomenon in which the clash between two perspectives comes into sharpest focus: refusal of life-sustaining treatment by patients with serious concurrent medical illness and depression.

## REFUSAL OF LIFE-SUSTAINING MEDICAL TREATMENT IN THE MEDICAL SETTING

Longstanding traditions in medicine and tort law have opposed treatment refusal that will result in the death of the patient. However, the past three decades have brought our nation to a medical, legal, and social consensus that under the right circumstances, all types of life-sustaining medical interventions may be withheld or withdrawn. The ideal circumstance is when a fully competent patient who refuses treatment after adding up the burdens and benefits, decides, all things con-

sidered, that death is the best of the available alternatives.

While patients' refusal of treatment may be questioned when health professionals are concerned about impaired decision-making capacity, among the medically ill, competence to make medical decisions is presumed until proven otherwise. The burden of proof concerning impaired patient competence is on the physician. Indeed, courts and legislatures across the country have articulated a "right to die" for seriously ill medical patients. This has been done through both court cases and natural death acts. While no absolute right has been recognized, no court has rejected the right to die in a wholesale fashion (1, p. 45).

The recognition of the right to die has taken place in the wake of advances in medical technology that make it possible to prolong life beyond the prospect of return to a satisfying and functional existence. The case of Karen Quinlan was exemplary. As legal scholar Alan Meisel has stated: "Prior to the *Quinlan* case, there was a great reluctance in case law to permit patients to refuse treatment when that refusal would probably lead to their death. *Quinlan* changed that by making clear to the courts what had long been apparent in the health professions, namely, that there is an increasing range of situations in which treatment will keep patients alive but not restore them to health" (1, p. 44).

Although legal precedent set by early cases such as *Quinlan* was limited to patients with extreme or terminal conditions, or to those who were being kept alive by "extraordinary" means (e.g., mechanical ventilators or renal dialysis machines), more recent cases have extended the right to refuse treatment. Courts have recognized treatment refusals by competent patients whose conditions were incurable but who were not near death—for example, patients with advanced neurological diseases such as amyotrophic lateral sclerosis or patients left quadriplegic after accidents who decided that their quality of life was unacceptable. Moreover, less extraordinary life-sustaining treatments such as tube feeding and hydration have become legitimate targets for treatment refusals (2). In all of these instances, the wishes of competent persons have been considered to be definitive, not the values of health professionals or health care institutions.

The court rulings that have legitimated patients' decisions to limit treatment have not framed these refusals as suicide. Although decisions to turn off ventilators or remove feeding tubes resulted in quicker deaths for patients, these decisions were almost universally characterized as allowing the patient to die or letting nature take its course. It was the disease process, not the decisions and behavior of patients, families, or health professionals, that "caused" the patient to die.

Some opponents of treatment limitation have regularly branded it as suicide or killing (3). Majority opinions in court cases have authorized treatment withdrawals and characterize them as allowing the patient to die, while some minority opinions angrily brand the same behavior as suicide and killing (4). Nevertheless, a clear prevalence of ethical and legal opinion now supports the right to refuse lifesaving treatment in the medical setting.

## REFUSAL OF LIFE-SUSTAINING TREATMENT BY THE PSYCHIATRIC PATIENT

While there have been important developments concerning the rights of psychiatric patients to refuse treatment in some circumstances, this has not generally included the right to refuse lifesaving treatment. Patients' wishes to die are still assumed to be rooted in psychopathology and are routinely characterized as suicidal on the basis of the wish (5).

Although legal competence traditionally has been considered a global property of persons, there has been a trend in the law toward a more specific understanding of competence. Alan Meisel commented: "The general incompetence approach has long been the dominant one used by the courts. However, it has fallen into disfavor in recent decades, spurred by both legislative changes and by litigation aimed at enhancing the rights of the institutionalized mentally ill and mentally retarded" (1, p. 188). For example, there is now a requirement for separate independent review (judicial in some states, administrative in others) of competence to refuse antipsychotic medication even after recognized procedures have permitted involuntary psychiatric hospitalization (6).

This trend toward a more specific understanding of competence has not, however, significantly changed the care of suicidal patients. For both involuntary commitment and involuntary treatment of the suicidal patient, the first priority remains preserving the life of the patient. In most states, a patient cannot be involuntarily hospitalized unless he or she is a danger to self or others. But for those patients who report suicide plans, the desire to die itself is considered prima facie evidence of mental disorder and impaired capacity to make decisions concerning the need for hospitalization and the value of therapeutic intervention.

There are substantial data to support these policies and attitudes. Post-mortem psychiatric investigations consistently reveal a high rate of psychiatric illness among persons who commit suicide (7). The thinking and judgment of suicidal patients are often distorted by depression. Persons who seek the help of psychiatrists or others are usually ambivalent about their wish to die.

Therefore, refusal of lifesaving psychiatric treatment is understandably seen as a symptom of an illness that psychiatrists treat, rather than the rational choice of an autonomous patient that should be respected. These observations have justified a temporary presumption of incompetence to refuse treatment for mentally ill patients who want to die. In psychiatry, when refusal of lifesaving treatment occurs, the burden of proof concerning competence is on the patient who desires to die; in internal medicine, the burden of proof concerning competence is on the physician who wishes to override the patient's refusal.

## THE *BOUVIA* CASE: CHALLENGING THE DICHOTOMY BETWEEN THE MEDICAL AND PSYCHIATRIC TRADITIONS

The case of Elizabeth Bouvia challenged the neat dichotomy between the medical and psychiatric perspectives. In this case, the patient's wish to forgo life-sustaining medical treatment was characterized by health professionals as suicidal. The patient was a young woman with severe cerebral palsy and pain who said that she was suicidal and was admitted to the psychiatric ward of a general hospital. She then refused tube feeding (she could not feed herself or swallow). The attending psychiatrist vehemently opposed this refusal by a patient who had been admitted because she was suicidal. Alan Meisel explained the appellate court decision that eventually upheld her refusal: "Although hoping that the forgoing of artificial nutrition and hydration, and indeed spoon-feeding, would not constitute suicide because the patient 'merely resigned herself to accept an earlier death, if necessary, rather than live by feedings forced upon her,' the court also stated that 'a desire to terminate one's own life is probably the ultimate exercise of one's right to privacy'" (1, p. 66). In this case, the court moved toward the view that the intent to die did not abrogate

one's right to refuse medical treatment: "If a right exists, it matters not what 'motivates' its exercise. We find nothing in the law to suggest that the right to refuse medical treatment may be exercised only if the patient's motives meet someone else's approval" (8).

Our legal tradition has relied on reference to intention and to causation in sorting out suicide from refusal of lifesaving treatment. The intention criterion appears to have been undercut by the *Bouvia* decision, at least insofar as it applies to patients' intentions. Analysis in terms of physicians' intentions persists in medical practice through the doctrine of "double effect": physicians' actions that cause death are not considered murder as long as relief of suffering, not death, is the intended goal of those actions. The causation criterion is also thrown into question by the *Bouvia* case. Ms. Bouvia was severely disabled by cerebral palsy but not at risk of dying of the illness in the near future. Her death, which would result from her refusal of tube feeding, was related to the illness that impaired her ability to swallow but was not "caused" by it. We are more comfortable with refusals of lifesaving treatment among the terminally ill, not simply because the death is "caused" by an illness but because the harm produced by honoring an incompetent refusal is limited, i.e., death occurs only a short time earlier than it would have without the treatment refusal. The *Bouvia* case, however, undercuts the legal grounds for limiting the right to refuse lifesaving treatment to patients who are about to die of their medical illness.

Scholars writing in the bioethics literature have increasingly questioned the validity of the distinction between allowing to die and suicide when the patient's intent in refusing treatment is to hasten death (9). We suggest that suicide should be a descriptive, not a normative, term. It describes a behavior as self-caused death; it does not tell us whether this behavior is morally right or wrong. If suicide is a behavior that intentionally leads to death, then some treatment refusals are suicide (10). We contend that the simple presence of the intention to die, of suicidal intent, does not invalidate the right to refuse lifesaving treatment. While it is true that some persons believe it is always wrong to refuse treatment if the intent is to die (3), the trend in clinical practice and the courts is otherwise.

Because of the moral baggage it carries with it, the term "suicide" is almost always reserved for situations in which physicians and courts reject the motives behind the wish to die. In the seriously medically ill, these motive are more likely to be accepted as reasonable under the circumstances and considered part of the process of allowing to die. In the psychiatric context, the choice of death is characterized as suicide, and the wish to die is most often seen as pathological, unreasonable, and ripe for preventive intervention. The clinical and moral pitfalls that attend each of these one-dimensional views is nowhere better revealed than in the evaluation and treatment of depressed patients who refuse life-sustaining medical treatment in the medical setting.

## DEPRESSION AND COMPETENCE TO REFUSE MEDICAL TREATMENT

As part of the Report of the President's Commission on the Protection of Human Subjects, Appelbaum and Roth (6) published the largest empirical study to date examining reasons for refusal of medical treatment. They considered all refusals of medical treatment, not just refusals of lifesaving treatment. The incidence of refusal ranged between one and 11 refusals per 100 patient-days. Refusal most often ended with ultimate acceptance of treatment, although this frequently appeared to be the result of serendipity rather than systematic effort. While no explicit count of refusals of lifesaving treatment was made, it appears that these were less than 10% of the total refusals of treatment.

Reasons for refusal were grouped into the following categories: problems in communication, problems in trust, psychological and psychopathological factors, hospital fatigue syndrome, other, and unknown. Of the 158 total refusals, 62 were ascribed to psychological and psychopathological factors. Identifying which refusals were "caused" by these factors was not always straightforward. Appelbaum and Roth explained, "Psychological factors are ubiquitous in treatment refusal. As noted above, refusal is almost always the result of extrinsic factors (e.g., impaired communication) acting on patients predisposed by their cognitive and affective states to reject the recommended procedures. To attempt to denote particular refusals as 'caused' by psychological factors, therefore, is difficult" (6, p. 431). This is a crucial issue, for only refusals that are "caused" by something other than autonomous choice should be overridden. We will return to this issue.

Psychiatric disorders were not specifically designated by Appelbaum and Roth as reasons for refusal. Among the psychopathological factors enumerated, two refusals were thought to be due to delusions, four to depression, six to denial, 22 to characterologic factors, 23 to other psychoses (including organic brain syndrome), and five to situational reaction.

Appelbaum and Roth made special mention of depression as a cause of treatment refusal that is particularly difficult to evaluate: "Of all the psychopathologic processes associated with refusal, depression is the most difficult to recognize, because it masquerades as, 'Just the way I would think if it happened to me.' It is also the most difficult to think causally about the refusal, because, unlike the grossly delusional patient . . . , the depressed patient is frequently able to offer 'rational' explanations for the choices that are made" (11).

Psychiatric tradition and clinical intuition hold that severe depression compromises patients' autonomy. Cautions, based on case reports, about accepting do-not-resuscitate orders from depressed psychiatric inpatients have been issued (12); some include the recommendation that a trial of ECT be used before accepting a do-not-resuscitate order for patients in whom the role of affective disorder is unclear (13). At least one study supports the traditional view that suicidal ideas, even among the terminally ill, are usually linked to psychiatric disorder (14). Thus, it is justifiable to assume that *some* medically ill patients desiring death are not acting autonomously.

However, psychiatrists may be inappropriately extending their views about suicide by the medically well to the refusal of treatment by the seriously medically ill. Beck et al. (15) demonstrated that hopelessness is a good predictor of suicide, but it is very difficult to distinguish realistic from pathological hopelessness among terminally ill patients. Psychiatrists tend to minimize the difficulty of this discrimination—sometimes to the point of denying that there can be an autonomous wish to hasten death. Determining whether someone with a serious (or especially, terminal) medical illness is competently assessing his or her quality of life can be exceedingly difficult. Alan Stone (16) has accused some psychiatrists of resurrecting the myth of the "omniscient psychiatrist" to combat the myth of the autonomous patient.

Clinical psychiatric wisdom may be overestimating the impact of mild to moderate depression on preference for life-sustaining treatment. In one study, mildly to moderately depressed elderly subjects did choose less aggressive treatment in hypothetical scenarios with good medical prognosis than did nondepressed elderly subjects. However, depression accounted for only 5% of the variance in responses, and its effect was limited to the good-prognosis scenarios (17). More important than depression in shaping treatment decisions was patients' assessment of their overall quality of life. In a follow-up study on this same group of subjects, recovery from mild to moderate depression was not associated with changes in preferences concerning life-sustaining treatment (18). These results are congruent with

results of other studies that have shown depression to be a poor predictor of preferences concerning life-sustaining therapy among the medically ill elderly (19–21). One recent study of the desire for life-sustaining treatments among patients over age 65 found that high depression scores were associated with the desire for more treatment during a hypothetical future illness (22). On the other hand, treatment of severely depressed patients who are initially without hope does not appear to increase their interest in life-sustaining medical treatment (Ganzini, personal communication).

Other factors, including race and social class, also appear to bear upon patients' decisions concerning lifesaving treatment. Studies have found black subjects to be more interested in aggressive lifesaving treatment (21) and less sympathetic to euthanasia (23). It has been hypothesized that persons who have been denied care without choice or who have been victims of legal discrimination are less likely to relinquish the right to any lifesaving medical treatment.

It would be a mistake to assume that depression—especially when severe—could not have a significant effect on the capacity to decide about medical treatment. But it also appears inappropriate to assume that depression, when present in the mild to moderate form common among medical patients, distorts patients' judgments about lifesaving treatment. Discriminating those cases in which depression impairs the capacity to make medical decisions from those cases in which it does not is best accomplished through a systematic approach to assessment of competence.

The clinical assessment of competence or capacity to consent to medical treatment has traditionally focused on cognitive capacities. Appelbaum and Grisso (24) have outlined four categories into which legal standards of competence fall. In order of increasing rigor, these are: communicating a choice, understanding relevant information, appreciating the current situation and its consequences, and manipulating information rationally. We will not go into detail here about the implementation of these tests. They are intended to assess the thought process behind a product of thought, namely, the treatment decision in question. According to the doctrine of informed consent, if the thought process is intact, then a refusal of treatment should be honored, even if the medical team disagrees with it.

In practice, the assessment of process and product are not this independent. Many authors have suggested that more stringent tests of competence are appropriate when the consequence of respecting a refusal will be serious harm to the patient. Appelbaum and Grisso proposed, "In life-threatening circumstances lower the threshold at which a determination of probable incompetence will be made" (24). Drane (25) has argued for a "sliding scale" of competence tests. Buchanan and Brock (26) have also proposed flexibility in their "process standard" of competence.

Such flexibility appears to be a reasonable way to protect patients' liberty and well-being. However, it can erode the independence of the competence determination from the specific medical treatment decision in question. Buchanan and Brock issued this cautionary note: "Treatment refusal does not reasonably serve to *trigger* a competence evaluation. On the other hand, a disagreement with the physician's recommendation or a refusal of a treatment recommendation is *no basis or evidence whatsoever* for a finding of incompetence" (26). Alan Meisel similarly condemned a finding of incompetence on the basis of treatment refusals as "paternalism in the extreme" (1, p. 198).

Charles Culver and Bernard Gert (27) claim that the concept of competence cannot withstand the flexibility required to make it responsive to the clinical consequences of treatment refusal. They argue that if the harm incurred by a refusal of treatment far outweighs the benefits, then the refusal is properly overruled regardless of an otherwise intact thought process. They argue that this harmfulness of the treatment refusal itself must be taken into account in determining whether the refusal should be honored.

It is specifically refusals of lifesaving treatment by depressed persons that prompt these debates about the concept of competence. Medical instinct rails against honoring refusals that will result in death or permanent impairment. However, finding a procedure that accords with clinical intuition concerning patients' welfare and protects patients' right to refuse treatment has been perplexing.

Evaluating the competence of the depressed patient has raised questions not only about the independence of the assessments of the process and product of thought but also about the traditional focus on cognitive aspects of competence. Bursztajn et al. succinctly stated that "patients with major affective disorders can retain the cognitive capacity to *understand* the risks and benefits of a medication, yet fail to *appreciate* its benefits" (28). Understanding medical facts in the abstract is different from understanding how they apply to your own life. It is this transition that is so often impaired in the seriously depressed patient.

Utilization of a competence standard that moves beyond assessment of the patient's abstract understanding of clinical facts (i.e., by asking the patient to paraphrase the clinician's statement of a treatment's benefits and risks) to assessment of the patient's concrete appreciation of the clinical situation (i.e., by asking the patient to describe how these facts count as pros and cons in his or her own life) is a reasonable response to the clinical challenge presented by the depressed patient who refuses treatment. This use of the "reasonable person" standard holds a risk, however, of invalidating the patient's values if these are different from those of the treating physician. Physician and patient may differ, for example, in the importance they accord to individual versus family well-being, the sanctity versus the dignity of life, or the value versus the futility of suffering. The doctrine of informed consent is intended to protect the right of patients to hold and exercise values different from those of physicians. James Childress phrased the problem as follows: "While false beliefs about a medical condition may be a reason for viewing a patient as an incompetent, false beliefs about goods are not" (29). We want to make sure that patients have their facts right about a life and death decision, but we must allow them to hold different values concerning life and death.

## THE ROLE OF PSYCHIATRIC ASSESSMENT AND TREATMENT FOR THOSE REFUSING LIFESAVING MEDICAL TREATMENT

There appears to be a substantial difference of opinion in the medical community concerning the role of psychiatrists in evaluating patients who are refusing treatment. In their study of medical treatment refusal, Appelbaum and Roth noted: "Psychiatric consultants were called upon to examine patients who had refused in two circumstances: first, when the patient had a known psychiatric history, and second, when the patient appeared to be suffering from an obvious psychiatric disorder and the refusal was potentially serious" (6, p. 450). This suggests that refusal of treatment should prompt more frequent psychiatric consultation. However, psychiatrists and other physicians have argued against more extensive involvement of psychiatrists with patients when there are problems obtaining informed consent (30). Gutheil and Duckworth (31) have warned against using psychiatrists as "informed consent technicians." They see a danger of the psychiatrist being consulted solely to facilitate the process of "getting the consent" or having the patient declared incompetent. This abrogates the appropriate role of the treating physician in establishing a consent dialogue with the patient and trivializes the diagnostic and thera-

peutic expertise of the psychiatric consultant. Greater attention by psychiatrists to depressed patients refusing treatment need not fall prey to this criticism, however.

Depression is especially common among the medically ill. Studies have also revealed that the most frequent precipitant for depression in the elderly is physical illness (32). Furthermore, the rate of depression has been shown to be higher in those who are more severely ill (33). This kind of data seems to indicate that these depressions are "reactive," in the sense that they are a reasonable response to such illness. Seeing serious depression in the face of severe medical illness as reasonable is one of the most common forms of "pseudo-empathy" against which physicians must be warned. Such interpretation of these depressions as purely reactive minimizes the value that psychiatric assessment and treatment might have in these cases.

The potential for successful treatment of major depression in the presence of serious medical illness is well documented. Antidepressants (34), psychostimulants (35), and ECT (36) have all demonstrated effectiveness in treating depression in medically ill patients. The efficacy of psychotherapy for the depressed medically ill has not been tested in controlled trials. . . .

## LIMITATIONS OF PSYCHIATRIC ASSESSMENT AND TREATMENT IN CASES OF REFUSAL OF MEDICAL TREATMENT

Psychiatric assessment and treatment have much to offer patients who are refusing lifesaving treatment or seeking to hasten their death by other means. However, important limitations of psychiatric expertise and therapeutic power must be acknowledged. While clinical severity of depression is generally well correlated with its impact on competence to make medical decisions, this is not always the case. The presence of a major depressive disorder is neither necessary nor sufficient for the impairment of competence. The symptoms that are the most important for the diagnosis of depression may not be the same as the symptoms that are most critical in determining the effect of the depression on competence. There is strong emphasis on vegetative symptoms in the DSM-III-R approach to diagnosis of depression. Although insomnia and anorexia may substantially decrease a patient's quality of life, they are less likely by themselves to impair competence to make medical decisions.

The depressive symptoms that are most likely to impair a patient's capacity to appreciate his or her medical situation accurately are the distorted assessments of self, world, and the future that typify depressive thinking (37). Depressive helplessness produces an underestimation of one's possible effectiveness in the face of serious illness. Guilt and worthlessness may make one believe that suffering and death are deserved and should not be forestalled. Anhedonia may make it impossible to imagine that life will offer any pleasures for which it is worth enduring the discomforts and indignities of medical illness. Depressive hopelessness can make it impossible to imagine that life will ever offer a better balance of pleasure and pain than it does at present. If some of these cognitive symptoms are present, competence to make decisions concerning life-sustaining medical treatment may be impaired although a full major depressive disorder is absent.

Even after clinical attention has been directed toward anhedonia, helplessness, hopelessness, and worthlessness, determining their status as psychiatric symptoms can be perplexing. It is less difficult to determine that these are mental distortions in the traditionally young and medically healthy psychiatric patient who has real future potential than it is in the intractably suffering, terminally ill patient. For the latter, activities providing pleasure may no longer be available. One may be unable to help oneself or others in any meaningful way. Intolerable symptoms may

in fact persist for the short remainder of one's life. One may have no real future.

It is essential for psychiatrists to accept that a seriously ill person's choice to die may be rational, especially in situations where the medical prognosis is very poor. However, acceptance of the desire to die as rational in any particular case is fraught with peril. Not only are the consequences serious and irreversible, but the temptations of pseudo-empathy are great. Physicians have been shown to underestimate seriously ill patients' quality of life and their desire for life-sustaining treatment (20). Physicians also neglect to explore adequately patients' reasons for refusing treatment. Appelbaum et al. issued the following caution: "Patients are sometimes initially reluctant to reveal their reasons for refusal, feeling embarrassed about having inconvenienced their physicians or fearful of some retaliation if their reasons are not good enough. Sometimes patients may even lack a conscious awareness of all the reasons. Physicians need to take the lead in identifying the bases for refusal" (38).

Reluctance to explore the reasons for refusal can be particularly dangerous when combined with a superficial adherence to the ideal of patient autonomy and respect for the "right" to refuse treatment (39). Inadequate exploration by the physician of reasons for the desire to die can turn situations that are remediable into unnecessary tragedies.

When hopelessness, helplessness, and worthlessness are not present or not clearly of pathological origin, the psychiatrist can be put into the uncomfortable position of validating a patient's request to die. The doctrine of informed consent implies that medical decisions have inescapable personal as well as medical elements. In a pluralist secular society such as our own, it must be assumed—unless proven otherwise—that adults are competent to evaluate their own quality of life as tolerable or intolerable. Assessing one's quality of life as intolerable is distinct from being depressed. We must learn to identify those refusals of lifesaving treatment that should be respected. The burden of proof concerning competence should be on the clinician who is seeking to override a refusal of treatment. The desire to die is by itself not adequate evidence of incompetence. As we have explained, a finding of incompetence cannot rest solely on the refusal in question.

There are some refusals in which the presence of depressive symptoms means that the refusal should not be respected. The boundary between these refusals and those that should be respected will not be clear because of the wide variability in values with respect to life and death that are present in our society. Christian values concerning the proper balance between the well-being of the individual and that of the family or community, between the sanctity of life and the dignity of life, and between redemptive and futile suffering tend to favor the prolongation of life. But this is not true of other legitimate religious and philosophical traditions. In the first century A.D., the Stoic philosopher and statesman Seneca stated, "The wise man will live as long as he ought, not as long as he can."

When depression compromises competence, it is advisable not only to treat the depression but also to consult advance directives and designated surrogate decision makers. A living will can verify that a current refusal is consistent with values and preferences expressed when depression was not an issue. Similarly, a family member can verify that a refusal is consistent with values held throughout a lifetime. These strategies are imperfect, however. When competence is questionable, it may not be clear when to defer to the advance directive, especially if it conflicts with currently expressed wishes. Advance directives often do not address the exact situation within which the refusal occurs (40). It is difficult to determine which differences in the actual situation would have changed the person's wishes and which would not. Families may not understand what the patient would have wanted or what the medical issues are (6, p. 464). While it is important to seek evidence of previously expressed wishes in order to verify that the desire to die is an authentic wish arising from the person rather than the depression, there will always be uncertainties that require the application of clinical judgment to the particular case.

As we have documented, depression can be treated in persons with serious medical illness. Before acceding to a wish to refuse lifesaving treatment, it is important to give optimal medical and psychiatric treatment. (It is not clear that this has been done for Dr. Kevorkian's patients.) Access to palliative and hospice care should be assured. Diminished severity of the medical illness (41) or of the pain associated with it (42) can improve psychiatric status. Both psychological and pharmacological treatment of depression can improve quality of life.

There are times when psychiatric treatment is not appropriate. This is clearly true when refusal of treatment is not associated with a treatable psychiatric disorder or symptoms. Aggressive psychiatric life support can paradoxically intensify suicidal ideas and behavior (43). Psychiatrists may also need to accept some depressions in the terminally ill as absolutely treatment resistant. These will be difficult decisions. How many different antidepressants must be tried? Are we willing to administer ECT to a terminally ill patient against his or her will? Gravely ill medical patients should not lose their right to refuse medical treatment simply because they have been transformed to a medical-psychiatric unit. Just as internists must at some point decide "enough is enough," so might psychiatrists at some point appropriately stop trying to intervene and let the dying process proceed. There may be a role for palliative psychiatric care (e.g., with benzodiazepines) of those for whom more definitive treatments for depression have not provided relief. There is always something that can be done to relieve suffering even if the disease cannot be cured or the life saved.

## CONCLUSIONS

Psychiatrists need to recognize that some treatment refusals that result in death are legitimate, even if they are accompanied by suicidal intent. Evaluating the role of depression in these refusals and determining the effect of depression on competence are difficult tasks. They are best accompanied on the basis of a clear distinction between diagnosis of depression and assessment of competence. We must not overestimate or underestimate the value of treatment of depression for patients with severe medical illness. It is often valuable to diagnose and treat depression in the seriously ill patient, but sometimes it is valuable to accept the patient's decision to die.

### REFERENCES

1. Meisel A: The Right to Die. New York, John Wiley & Sons, 1989.
2. Cruzan v. Director, 110 S Ct 2841 (1990).
3. Meilaender G: On removing food and water: against the stream. Hastings Cent Rep 1984; 14: 11–13.
4. Brophy v. New England Sinai Hospital, Inc, 398 Mass 417, 497 NE 2d 626, 1986.
5. Hendin H, Klerman G: Physician-assisted suicide: the dangers of legalization. Am J Psychiatry 1993; 150: 143–145.
6. Appelbaum PS, Roth LH: Treatment refusal in medical hospitals, in Report of the President's Commission for the Study of Ethical Problems in Medicine and Biomedical and Behavioral Research. Washington, DC, US Government Printing Office, 1982.
7. Pokorny AD: Prediction of suicide in psychiatric patients. Arch Gen Psychiatry 1983; 40: 249–257.
8. Bouvia v Superior Court, Number B019134 (Cal App 2d Dist April 16, 1986).
9. Brock DW: Voluntary active euthanasia. Hastings Cent Rep 1992; 22: 10–22.
10. Schaffner KF: Philosophical, ethical, and legal aspects of resuscitation medicine, II: recognizing the tragic choice: food, water, and the right to assisted suicide. Crit Care Med 1988; 16: 1063–1068.
11. Appelbaum PS, Roth LH: Competency to consent to research: a psychiatric overview. Arch Gen Psychiatry 1982; 39: 951–958.

12. Ganzini L, Lee MA, Heintz RT, Bloom JD: Do-not-resuscitate orders for depressed psychiatric inpatients. Hosp Community Psychiatry 1992; 43: 915–919.
13. Swartz CM, Stewart C: Melancholia and orders to restrict resuscitation. Hosp Community Psychiatry 1991; 42: 189–191.
14. Brown JH, Henteleff P, Barakat S, Rowe CJ: Is it normal for terminally ill patients to desire death? Am J Psychiatry 1986; 143: 208–211.
15. Beck AT, Brown G, Berchick RJ, Stewart BL, Steer RA: Relationship between hopelessness and ultimate suicide: a replication with psychiatric outpatients. Am J Psychiatry 1990; 147: 190–195.
16. Stone AA: Response to the article "Depression, self-love, time, and the 'right' to suicide" by Bursztajn et al. Gen Hosp Psychiatry 1986; 8: 97–99.
17. Lee MA, Ganzini L: Depression in the elderly: effect on patient attitudes toward life-sustaining therapy. J Am Geriatr Soc 1992; 40: 983–988.
18. Lee M, Ganzini L: The effect of recovery from depression on preferences for life-sustaining therapy in older patients. Am J Psychiatry (in press).
19. Cohen-Mansfield J, Rabinovich BA, Lipson S: The decision to execute a durable power of attorney for health care and preferences regarding the utilization of life-sustaining treatments in nursing home residents. Arch Intern Med 1991; 151: 289–294.
20. Michelson C, Mulvihill M, Hsu MA, Olson E: Eliciting medical care preferences from nursing home residents. Gerontologist 1991; 31: 358–363.
21. Uhlmann RF, Pearlman RA: Perceived quality of life and preferences for life-sustaining treatment in older adults. Arch Intern Med 1991; 151: 495–498.
22. Garrett JM, Harris RP, Norburn JK, Patrick DL, Davis M: Life-sustaining treatments during terminal illness. J Gen Intern Med 1993; 8: 361–368.
23. Caralis PV, David B, Wright K, Marcial E: The influence of ethnicity and race on attitudes toward advance directives, life-prolonging treatments and euthanasia. J Clin Ethics 1993; 4: 155–165.
24. Appelbaum PS, Grisso T: Assessing patients' capacities to consent to treatment. N Engl J Med 1988; 319: 1635–1638.
25. Drane JF: The many faces of competency. Hastings Cent Rep 1985; 15: 17–21.
26. Buchanan AW, Brock DW: Deciding for Others. New York, Cambridge University Press, 1989, p. 58.
27. Culver CM, Gert B: The inadequacy of incompetence. Milbank Q 1990; 68: 619–643.
28. Bursztajn HJ, Harding HP, Gutheil TG, Brodsky A: Beyond cognition: the role of disordered

affective states in impairing competence to consent to treatment. Bull Am Acad Psychiatry Law 1991; 19: 383–388.

29. Childress JF: Who Should Decide? Paternalism in Health Care. New York, Oxford University Press, 1982, p. 170.

30. Schneiderman LJ: Is it morally justifiable not to sedate this patient before ventilator withdrawal? J Clin Ethics 1991; 2: 129–130.

31. Gutheil TG, Duckworth K: The psychiatrist as informed consent technician: a problem for the professions. Bull Menninger Clin 1992; 56: 87–94.

32. Murphy E: Social origins of depression in old age. Br J Psychiatry 1982; 141: 135–142.

33. Berkman LF, Berman CS, Kasl S: Depressive symptoms in relation to physical health and functioning in the elderly. Am J Epidemiol 1986; 124: 372–388.

34. Rifkin A, Reardon G, Siris S: Trimipramine in physical illness with depression. J Clin Psychiatry 1985; 46: 4–8.

35. Masand P, Pickett P, Murray GB: Psychostimulants for secondary depression in medical illness. Psychosomatics 1991; 32: 203–208.

36. Dubovsky SL: Using electroconvulsive therapy for patients with neurological disease. Hosp Community Psychiatry 1986; 37: 819–825.

37. Beck AT: Thinking and depression, I: idiosyncrasy content and cognitive distortions. Arch Gen Psychiatry 1963; 9: 324–335.

38. Appelbaum PS, Lidz CW, Meisel A: Informed Consent: Legal Theory and Clinical Practice. New York, Oxford University Press, 1987, p. 196.

39. Jackson DS, Youngner SJ: Patient autonomy and death with dignity: some clinical caveats. N Engl J Med 1979; 301: 404–408.

40. Emanuel LJ: The health care directive: learning how to draft advance care documents. J Am Geriatr Soc 1991; 39: 1221–1228.

41. Kathol RG, Noyes R, Wald T: Criteria and symptom-based depression in cancer patients, in CME Syllabus and Proceedings Summary, 145th Annual Meeting of the American Psychiatric Association. Washington DC, APA, 1992.

42. Spiegel D, Sands S: Pain and depression in cancer patients. Ibid.

43. Pauker SL, Cooper AM: Paradoxical patient reactions to psychiatric life support: clinical and ethical considerations. Am J Psychiatry 1990; 147: 488–491.

# Continued Treatment of the Fatally Ill for the Benefit of Others

MARK YARBOROUGH

This paper examines the moral and professional issues present in cases involving continued treatment of fatally ill patients in order to benefit a third party. It is argued that such treatment can be justified in some cases from a moral point of view. Practical considerations make such cases difficult to identify at times. It is also argued on the other hand that professional concerns should rule out the permissibility of continuing such treatment. Thus, even though it may be morally permissible at times to continue treatment, it is not good medical practice to do so.

From the *Journal of the American Geriatrics Society* 1988; vol. 36 (1): 63–67. Reprinted by permission of the publisher.

MUCH HAS BEEN WRITTEN AND DISCUSSED recently concerning the discontinuation of treatment for the terminally ill elderly patient.[1-7] This debate is welcomed and greatly needed. However, one important area has been insufficiently discussed: those patients who are near death and are beyond benefit from therapy yet continue to receive treatment (e.g., intubation) for the emotional and psychological benefit of a third party such as a spouse or child. I want to evaluate this practice first from a moral point of view and then from a medical professional point of view. Do these perspectives preclude such unnecessary treatment? Or can a physician either morally or professionally continue treatment for the sole purpose of providing benefit to an involved third party? Before discussing the topic, I will briefly describe a case that brought the topic to mind.

## CASE STUDY

The members of the house staff at a community hospital in the West were both puzzled and upset by an attending physician's continued intubation and provision of other "aggressive" therapy for a patient they all considered beyond help. It was a classic case of "merely prolonging dying" and members of the house staff judged the attending physician to be practicing bad medicine in this case. The department head reported the complaints of the house staff to the attending physician. While the attending physician concurred with the clinical judgment of the house staff he still insisted continued treatment of the patient (whom I will call Mrs. Jones) was justified. His reason for continuing treatment was that her husband was not prepared for her death. In order to protect Mr. Jones, the treatment was being continued. This case raises the issues to be addressed. The details need not remain the same. One could discuss intravenously injected fluids and chemotherapy rather than intubation, or cardiopulmonary resuscitation for that matter, and the issues would remain largely the same. Can a physician treat a patient just to benefit an interested third party?

## CASE DISCUSSION

One could rightly question the treatment in this case at the outset from a moral point of view if Mrs. Jones had previously instructed her physician not to administer unbeneficial treatment at the time she became unable to make decisions for herself. By the same token, one could approve the actions of the physician from a purely moral point of view if he had sufficient reason, based on discussions with the patient, to determine that the patient would approve of the treatment if it was necessary to protect the spouse. The physician is, after all, the patient's advocate and is duty-bound to carry out, within certain limits, the decisions of the patient when the patient is unable to do so. (The limits will be discussed in a later section. Briefly, the interventions of physicians are limited by the professional obligation to practice good medicine and refrain from practicing what is judged to be bad medicine.) In some cases, however, the physician is insufficiently informed to make definitive judgments as to what the patient would want done. These are the scenarios the discussion will address.

I will begin by mentioning some of the emotions the physician is likely to experience. First of all, it is most likely the physician feels a sense of frustration and sadness that comes from having a patient dying and beyond help. Second, the physician may be confronted by a distraught family member who is emotionally wrecked from the ordeal and who desperately wants the patient to live. Indeed, the third party appears to gain some genuine emotional benefit and stability from the survival of the patient. Therapeutic interventions represent hope for this third party. Thus, the physician experiences some sense of contribution from treatment and it is therefore easier to decide to continue treatment.

## MORAL CONSIDERATIONS

Now what, if any, is the moral justification for these actions? To answer I will first address the issue in light of general moral obligations to determine if it can be morally justified. Because the actions are taken to benefit an interested third party, the purported justification would be benevolence. The physician's actions are undertaken with the intent to promote the welfare of the spouse. Yet the obligation to do no harm, nonmaleficence, is held to be morally prior by many to the obligation to promote welfare (i.e., beneficence).[8] It is generally thought that it is always, or almost always, wrong to harm others. In other words, we are morally required to refrain from harming others in all, or almost all, cases. However, it is a point of great controversy whether beneficent actions are ever morally required in the same manner. Many hold that actions of beneficence are not obligatory[9] for this reason: Actions that promote human welfare should admit of some discretion on the part of the agent because the importance of beneficence with other goods (e.g., liberty) must be weighed in light of the relationships that hold among the involved parties. A person has stronger obligations to a friend or family member than to a total stranger.[10] Given that there exist such degrees of obligation, it is difficult to prove that acts of beneficence are morally required of us in the same fashion that nonmaleficence is.[11] Because there is agreement at least on the duty not to harm others, one must determine if the continued treatment ought to be construed as harmful. Harm can be defined broadly or narrowly. If harm is restricted to physical harm, it will be true in many cases that therapy does not harm the patient. The patient's physical state may very well preclude the possibility of experiencing physical harm. This is true of comatose patients.

But as one moves from the obtunded to the incompetent patient, awareness will vary. Intrusive intensive care unit procedures could cause physical discomfort to the patient, even though the degree or intensity of harm may be difficult to ascertain. In these cases it would certainly be true that the patient would be physically harmed to benefit someone else. Such actions are a prima facie wrong from an ethical point of view. From a formalistic perspective, such actions are wrong in principle: To use the individual merely as a tool is judged to be a violation of the patient's personhood. And from a consequentialist perspective, that is, from a perspective that morally evaluates actions not by their intrinsic qualities but by their assumed good or bad consequences, it is difficult to justify a practice of harming patients in such a manner, regardless of the benefit judged to follow from isolated acts. By consequentialist standards, the benefits of such acts in isolation would not necessarily outweigh the erosion of the doctor-patient relationship resulting from a general practice of such acts.[12]

If the discussion is correct thus far the only possible candidates for morally permissible unnecessary treatment will be those patients who will not be able to suffer the pain associated with the procedures. These patients will be restricted, then, either to those who are sufficiently obtunded or comatose and fatally ill. But before one can approve unnecessary treatment, one must first conclude the discussion of the proper understanding of harm.

There is a strong case to be made that the fatally ill comatose patient deserves all the respect and dignity of any other person. I realize that, depending upon the extent of brain activity, there is a genuine philosophical debate as to whether such patients are in fact persons. Prudence would dictate treating them as such. After all, the patient has a history and continues to play an important social role in the community. So there is much to be said for the view that the patient is more than a nonviable biological organism.[13] Hence, certain prima facie claims for respect must be considered. Respect for dignity inclines us against using such patients as nonpersonal objects to be manipulated for the benefit of others. The formalist school of thought contends that respect for dignity not only inclines us against continued treatment, but that it categorically precludes continued treatment. Because the treatment is intended not for her well-being but for someone else's, the claim is that she is being relegated to the status of a nonperson in that she is being manipulated like an object and not treated like a subject or person.

But is it the case that Mrs. Jones is an "object being manipulated"? Is she being used as a "mere means"? It is not at all clear that she is. The argument can be made that since Mrs. Jones still is to be treated as a person with dignity, we can construe a willingness, in the absence of prior discussion, to undergo nonbeneficial procedures in order to promote the welfare of her spouse. Because Mr. Jones is her husband, she shares a special relationship with him that involves not only personal interests but shared mutual interests as well. In marriage generally there are actions thought to flow from vows made to support the other party. The word "generally" is used because not all marriages are faithful to this norm and because these promises can be present in nonmarital relationships as well. In the absence of reasons that would indicate their marriage falls outside the norm, one could reasonably infer a willingness by Mrs. Jones to help her husband. Mrs. Jones, the person, was (and still is, most would contend) the wife of Mr. Jones. To respect her inherent dignity and thereby avoid harming her is to recognize the interests implicit in her social roles.[14] The morally relevant role here is spouse (or mother, sister, etc.).

One cannot respect her as a person and at the same time ignore pertinent, fundamental aspects of her personhood. To contend that nonbeneficial treatment in the absence of verbal consent is immoral in principle and thus always is to abstract Mrs. Jones, possessor of rights, from her life-context. To extract a person from her life-context (i.e., community) is to rob her of her identity. And dignified treatment can be distinguished from undignified treatment only with reference to the identity of the person involved. This follows if we assume that actions are properly evaluated with reference to the ends they seek to accomplish. The end of the action in

question is the welfare of Mr. Jones. Mr. Jones's welfare, in turn, is an end inextricably linked with Mrs. Jones. Thus she is not being used as a means to someone else's exclusive end but to her own end as well. To recognize a duty to treat Mrs. Jones as a person with dignity is to accept a duty to investigate thoroughly the context of that personhood. When this investigation occurs it can be the case at times that continuing treatment is compatible with treating her with dignity. Hence, it is also compatible with refraining from harming her when harm is broadly defined. Therefore, the actions discussed can be justified by appeals to the principles of beneficence and nonmaleficence.

The preceding is the strongest moral argument one can give to justify the actions of the attending physician. One could take another approach that I will not pursue at length here. That approach would argue that the patient whom the physician must attempt to benefit and refrain from harming is, in this case, "the family." This view has adherents among family practitioners, and it can certainly be employed in this case. Briefly, the view holds that treatment decisions should be made in light of what will best promote the welfare of the family as a unit instead of focusing directly on the needs of an individual sick member of the family.[15] It assumes that illness and suffering are ascribable not just to the individual family member but to the family unit. Hence, the family unit must be "treated" along with the sick member of the family. However, this view will not be pursued here because in the final analysis it must make use of the previous argument. Regardless of how the patient is defined, it will still be necessary to refrain from treating one family member as a "mere object" to benefit the others. So the argument from the preceding paragraph will have to be forwarded to escape this charge. The moral permissibility, then, of the actions of the physician with respect to Mrs. Jones in this case rests on the strength of the argument presented.

One should note at this time the limits of this argument if it is found to be persuasive. It would be morally permissible to continue treating comatose, fatally ill patients for the benefit of others if there were sufficient evidence to conclude that such treatment would be "dignified" by the nature of the relationship between the patient and the benefited third party. These third parties must obviously be limited to those who shared such an intimate relationship with the patient that one can assume the patient identifies her interests and welfare with those of the third party. A spouse or some similar life-long partner would be the most prominent example of such a third party. Distant relatives and other "merely interested" parties such as the physician, for example, clearly would not qualify. Although these third parties may in fact share a close relationship with the patient, it is not reasonable to assume that the patient would relegate her own interests to those of these third parties as she would for a spouse. Thus, the physician would have to possess reliable information concerning the nature of the relationship between the patient and the third party in question before continued treatment could be judged morally permissible. To say that such actions are permissible on occasion is to say that it is not necessarily an abuse of the patient if treatment is continued beyond the point of therapeutic benefit. If the argument has been successful, it has only shown that such treatment is not wrong in principle, as those who would insist on explicitly verbal consent would contend.

## PRACTICAL CONSIDERATIONS

If such a practice is not morally wrong in principle, then would it be morally permissible in practice? First, as noted, the physician must have reliable knowledge about the nature of the relationship shared by the patient and the third party. If the physician does not have first-hand knowledge concerning this, she must be able to trust her sources. But this logistical problem is

not as formidable as a predictive one. The physician must also be able to make a reasonable inference that a prolonged death will benefit the third party. There may be benefit in the short run but, on balance, can the physician judge that greater benefit is achieved by a protracted dying? There could be occasions where a third party truly coped better by having one or a few more days to prepare for death. How, though, does one determine prospectively which cases these are? Are physicians' predictive abilities sufficient for the task? A final practical consideration involves economic matters. What will the expense of the life prolonging procedures be? What are the daily bed costs and physician fees involved? These costs could surely be considerable in many instances. They may also be passed on to the estate of the patient. All these considerations present quite a practical barrier to justifying unnecessary treatment.

It must be noted here that these practical problems would not occur in some cases if the physician adequately attempted to obtain the informed consent or refusal for treatment from the proxy (i.e., third party). When the physician judges treatment to be futile for the patient and entertains the wisdom of its removal, the spouse or other proxy should be informed of the recommendations and the reasons behind it. This is required by the two traditional standards of proxy consent, the substituted judgment standard and the best interests standard. The principle of substituted judgment requires that the proxy act on behalf of the patient in the same manner that the patient would if he were competent to do so. The best interests standard requires the proxy to act in such a manner that best promotes the patients' welfare without referring to the patient's own preferences.[16] The proxy would have to be sufficiently informed before he would be able to draw a reasonable conclusion following either standard of proxy consent. When the proxy is sufficiently (i.e., realistically) informed of the situation, one wonders what benefit the third party could enjoy from continued treatment. If Mr. Jones is adequately informed of his wife's irreversible condition, he may be less likely to benefit from continued treatment. So a thorough job of informing the third party, which is both morally and legally required, may bypass the problem altogether. Of course there will be those difficult cases, like our example, in which the third party is so emotionally distraught as to preclude effective cooperation between the physician and the proxy. Thus, appeals to informed consent cannot entirely rid us of the difficulty.

To summarize the discussion to this point, one can conclude that treatment continued for the benefit of others is sometimes a morally justified action among persons. These cases will be limited to those patients who are both either comatose or sufficiently obtunded to prevent them from experiencing the pain or burden of continued treatment and who are judged to be dignified by the treatment, given some morally important social role played by them. When these conditions are met and the various practical hurdles that may apply are overcome, then a strong argument supports the practice in question. Such instances do not constitute using patients as mere tools or means for the benefit of others. Instead, the treatment would promote a good end that is linked with the patient's own personhood in a morally significant manner.

## MEDICAL PROFESSIONAL CONSIDERATIONS

Nonetheless, serious difficulties with the practice still remain. These difficulties arise when one examines the practice from a professional point of view. First of all, to call continued administration of nonbeneficial medical procedures "treatment," may be stretching the term beyond its historical, professional boundary. Medicine is a "technique of healing" practiced in order to alleviate suffering and/or cure illness in the body in which either or both are located. The practice

of medicine is possible because there is firm empirical knowledge that directs patients "how to act according to what is the case and why it is the case." [17] When one acts against the suggestions of available evidence, one leaves the epistemological underpinnings and support of the profession behind. We may agree that the interventions are compassionate acts, but this is not necessarily the same as good medicine. Efforts to heal are still being made, but the technique is absent in that the evidence suggests the efforts will not result in healing. So a legitimate question is raised whether the types of practices we have been discussing are good medicine. The concerns of the house staff seem to be well-founded when viewed from this perspective. What the attending physician or others may do in similar cases can in fact be morally justified actions between persons, but good medicine is not being practiced when no therapy is involved: the need always to practice good medicine overrides the other previously discussed considerations. This follows because medicine is a social institution as well as a "technique of healing." The practice of modern medicine is possible in large part because of the subsidies it receives from society. Given the way we collectively value health and disvalue illness we direct a significant portion of our wealth to medicine to pursue these goals. Medical professionals are entrusted to act professionally in ways that promote health. So, physicians are stewards not only of the trust bestowed them by society but of the technology and funds bestowed them as well.

Unless it can be demonstrated that providing unnecessary treatment is consistent with responsible stewardship, the professional obligation to practice good medicine precludes the permissibility of providing unnecessary treatment to benefit third parties. It does not follow from this that physicians should ignore the emotional needs of family members. However, initiating and/or continuing useless treatments are not appropriate measures for attempting to meet these needs.

## CONCLUSION

Our conclusion then is this: Although offering unnecessary medical treatment to benefit an interested third party can be justified from a general moral point of view (i.e., it is not necessarily morally wrong), because it can be consistent with treating people with the respect and dignity they are due, it nonetheless is not justified as a professional practice.

### REFERENCES

1. Siegler M: Should age be a criterion in health care? Hastings Center Report, October 1984, pp. 24–27.

2. Childress JF: Ensuring care, respect, and fairness for the elderly. Hastings Center Report, October 1984, pp. 27–31.

3. Bloom G: Some thoughts on the value of saving lives. Theoret Med 5: 241–251, 1984.

4. Bayer R, Callahan D, Fletcher J, et al.: The care of the terminally ill: Morality and economics. N Engl J Med 309: 1490–1494, 1983.

5. Hilfiker D: Allowing the debilitated to die. N Engl J Med 308: 716–719, 1983.

6. Yarborough MA, Kramer AM: The physician and resource allocation. Clin Geriatr Med 2: 465–480, 1986.

7. Marsh FH: Refusal of treatment. Clin Geriatr Med 2: 511–520, 1986.

8. Frankena WK: Ethics, ed 2. Englewood Cliffs, New Jersey, Prentice-Hall Inc., 1973, p. 47.

9. Thomson JJ: A defense of abortion. Philosophy Pub Aff 1: 47–66, 1971.

10. Singer P: Practical Ethics. Cambridge, England, Cambridge University Press, 1979, pp. 168ff. [Singer provides an opposing point of view on the issue.]

11. Beauchamp TL, Childress JF: Principles of Biomedical Ethics. New York, Oxford University Press, 1983, pp. 148–160.

12. Rawls J: Two concepts of rules. Philsoph Rev 64: 3–32, 1955.

13. Englehardt HT Jr: The Foundations of Bioethics. New York, Oxford University Press, 1986, pp. 202–216.

14. McCormick RA: Proxy consent in the experimentation situation. Perspect Biol Med 18: 2–20, 1974. [Readers should note that my argument is similar in many ways to that employed by McCormick.]

15. Schneiderman LJ: My husband won't tell the children: commentary. Hastings Center Report, August 1984, p. 27.

16. Marsh FH: Refusal of treatment. Clin Geriatr Med 2: 517, 1986.

17. Pellegrino ED, Thomasma DC: A Philosophical Basis of Medical Practice. New York, Oxford University Press, 1981, p. 69.

# What Do Apple Pie and Motherhood Have to Do with Feeding Tubes and Caring for the Patient?

JACQUELYN SLOMKA

MEDICAL AND ETHICAL GUIDELINES STATE that the forgoing of artificial nutrition and hydration is no different from the forgoing of any other medical treatment. Yet a significant number of health care professionals believe that artificial nutrition and hydration must always be continued, even when the burdens of this treatment outweighed the benefits of prolonging life.

From the *Archives of Internal Medicine* (1995) 155: 1258–1263. Reprinted by permission of the American Medical Association.

I believe that health care professionals should accept the premise that artificial nutrition and hydration are medical treatment (which may be forgone under justifiable clinical and ethical conditions) rather than "basic care" (which morally cannot be forgone) because of (1) social meanings that create humans symbolically as "persons"; and (2) the permission medicine is given by society to touch the human body in various antisocial, but medically necessary, ways.

While any decision to forgo life-supporting treatment may cause anxiety and anguish for even the most experienced physician,[1] the withholding of artificial nutrition and hydration appears to be the most difficult kind of decision to make and carry out. Professional groups such as the President's Commission for the Study of Ethical Problems in Medicine and Biomedical and Behavioral Research,[2] the Hastings Center,[3] and the American Medical Association[4] have formulated guidelines that define artificial nutrition and hydration as medical treatment that, like any medical treatment, can be withheld or withdrawn when medically and ethically appropriate.

A recent study suggests that in spite of these guidelines, a significant number of health care professionals believe that artificial nutrition and hydration must always be continued, even if other life-supporting technologies are stopped. Furthermore, clinicians have demonstrated a reluctance to forgo medically supplied nutrition and hydration even when they recognized that the burdens of this treatment outweighed the benefits of prolonging life.[5] Other research has shown that in medical-ethical decisions to withdraw life support, tube feeding and intravenous fluids are the least preferred forms of therapy to be withdrawn.[6-8]

The reluctance of health care professionals, patients, and families to forgo burdensome artificial nutrition and hydration has been explained in several ways. Many persons fear that death from dehydration and/or starvation is a painful way to die, although current literature disputes this assumption.[9] Some state legislation charac-terizes artificial nutrition and hydration as different from other medical treatments and may require physicians to provide treatment in violation of their consciences.[10] But while legal fears sometimes appear to drive medical decision making, the majority of state laws permit, permit with restrictions, or are silent about the forgoing of artificial nutrition and hydration.[11,12]

The reluctance of clinicians, patients, and families to withhold or withdraw burdensome artificial nutrition and hydration has also been linked to the "symbolic" meanings associated with this treatment. While some authors recognize a difference between the physiological aspects of providing medical "nourishment" and the social aspects of eating and feeding, in both cases nourishment has been viewed as symbolizing faithfulness, love, nurturance, and care of both the living and the dying. Nourishing the patient has also been viewed as symbolizing community and communion and as parent-child relationships generalized to the physician-patient relationship.[13-16] However, other medical interventions may be symbolic of fidelity and caring, but are often less difficult to forgo than a feeding tube when the burdens of treatment outweigh the benefits.

Some of the difficulty and ambivalence in forgoing artificial nutrition and hydration may be related to the multiple meanings we assign to this therapy. Is a feeding tube "medical treatment" as most professional organizations and many individuals now define it, or is it "basic humane care" that is morally obligated by our unstated assumptions about and standards of human decency? While health care professionals may accept on an intellectual level the notion that a feeding tube is medical treatment rather than basic humane care, their actual practice suggests otherwise.

Why should we accept the premise that medically supplied nutrition and hydration are medical treatment? An important reason is suggested by Christakis and Asch[6]: "Biases about treatment modalities may prolong the patient's dying process, increase patient and family suffering, and waste health care resources." The continuing ambivalence of health care professionals and the public about artificial nutrition and hydration may interfere with the physician's desire and obligation to provide humane care for the dying patient.

To understand and resolve this ambivalence, it may be helpful to sort out the constellation of meanings associated with medically supplied nutrition and hydration. An extensive body of literature exists on how ethical decisions should be made in the forgoing of artificial nutrition and hydration.[17-23] A smaller body of literature supports the argument that this treatment should rarely or never be withheld or withdrawn.[24-27] I suggest that until we begin to understand the deeper meanings that drive our decision making, we will be unable to deal with the clinical paradox of a willingness to continue to provide artificial nutrition and hydration when the burdens of this treatment outweigh its benefits. Nor will we be able to resolve our own feelings and those of patients and families in dealing with this troubling issue.

## MULTIPLE MEANINGS OF FOOD AND FLUIDS

A particular image can evoke multiple meanings related to our different experiences. *Apple pie,* for example, represents a tasty desert, but it can also represent Americana, as in "motherhood, the flag, and apple pie" or in "as American as apple pie." In the first case, apple pie may not arouse any particular emotional meaning: it is simply something good to eat. Apple pie in the latter case may arouse certain emotions, e.g., patriotism, a pride in one's country. Apple pie may have other meanings: persons who are concerned about their personal appearance in terms of looking thin or who are concerned about their health in terms of eating healthy foods may des-

ignate apple pie as something bad to eat. This notion of the "badness" of apple pie may take on other moral dimensions if one "cheats" on one's diet or suffers guilt from eating too much pie.

Both the providing and the forgoing of artificial nutrition and hydration likewise evoke multiple and sometimes conflicting meanings that may account for our moral uneasiness when the question of forgoing or providing treatment arises. What are these meanings and how can we account for them?

Food and fluids are biologically essential to all living things. But humans in all cultures have assigned meanings to food and drink that extend far beyond physiological needs. Farb and Armelagos[28] have described how food and eating behaviors permeate the fabric of societies and how meanings associated with food and eating vary widely across cultures. Almost all social interaction involves food and drink, not simply to fulfill a physiological need, but to affirm the social bonds we have with other human beings. For example, in our own society, we offer coffee to a visitor as a mark of courtesy, we eat lunch with friends, or we have a family dinner together. Food is a part of ritual celebrations such as weddings, funerals, or the baptism or circumcision of a newborn. Special foods customarily are eaten on special holidays: hot dogs and hamburgers on the Fourth of July, turkey and pumpkin pie on Thanksgiving. These authors also note that food can be used to help define the boundaries of a social group, e.g., Catholics, who in the past refrained from eating meat on Fridays; Orthodox Jews, who refrain from mixing meat and dairy products at the same meal; or Italian Americans, many of whom eat spaghetti with their Thanksgiving turkey. Food habits and taboos thus help to create, define, and maintain the identities of and differences among social groups.

Farb and Armelagos[28] note additional social meanings attributed to the physiological need for nutrition and hydration. For example, the denial and provision of food may evoke the images of punishment and reward, as in the case of the prisoner who is given a diet of bread and water, a child who is sent to bed without supper, or good children who are rewarded with candy or dessert. Clearly, the provision and denial of food and drink have multiple meanings that may have little apparent direct relationship to physiological need.

The meanings of the provision and denial of food and drink are tied to other cultural images. The provision of food to those unable to feed themselves is viewed as an act of nurturing—the image that springs to mind is that of a mother breast-feeding her infant. But although mothers (and fathers) also feed their infant children by bottle-feeding them, the act of breast-feeding conjures up a more powerful image of nurturing than does bottle-feeding. The "milk of human kindness" is neither pasteurized nor homogenized. When a mother gives her breast to her child, she is quite literally giving of herself to her infant.

Underlying the image of feeding as nurturing is the assumption that the helpless child being nurtured will grow and thrive. The meaning of feeding here is further tied to our cultural and moral beliefs about motherhood: we believe that a "good" mother is one who nurtures her child by meeting his or her physical, emotional, and spiritual needs. Feeding the child symbolizes such nurturing. The denial or lack of food has the opposite image of nurturing: starvation and famine ensure that a child will not grow and thrive. A "bad" mother is one who neglects her child by failing to provide proper food, clothing, shelter, and emotional support.

The provision of artificial nutrition and hydration, usually in the form of what is called a *feeding tube* in the medical vernacular, certainly evokes images of food, feeding, eating, and nurturing. But while food and drink evoke *social* images of eating and feeding, a feeding tube evokes what might be called an *antisocial* image. The term *antisocial* implies that this therapy is different and distinct from the usual social methods of obtaining food and drink. In the past, for ex-

ample, tube feeding was commonly referred to as *forced feeding*. The antisocial aspect of artificial nutrition and hydration suggests one reason why this therapy should be viewed as an event with a physiologically based medical meaning, rather than as one imbued with the social meanings of food and drink. To further clarify this antisocial aspect of nutrition and hydration, it is necessary to examine some images underlying what it means, in a social sense, to be a person.

## SOCIAL PERSONHOOD

The usual meaning of *person* in bioethics is derived from a philosophical definition based on the individual possession of abstract criteria such as rationality, creativity, self-awareness, and autonomy.[29] On the other hand, social scientists tend to view the person as a "social" person by virtue of his or her participation in a social system. The anthropologist Jules Henry[30] says that in order to be part of a social system, an individual has to acquire and retain various symbols of "attachment" to the social system. He uses the example of a name as a symbol of such an attachment: we call each other by name in most ordinary social interactions. To refer to an individual as "the gallbladder in bed three" denies the person a status within the social system that a name provides. When persons are deprived of such symbols of attachment, Henry says, their personhood is diminished. They are depersonalized, i.e., treated in an "antisocial" manner.

This kind of depersonalization can occur in several ways in an institutional environment, according to Henry.[30] For example, he says, exposing one's genitals is considered a shameful act in our culture. To expose a patient or to allow him or her to be exposed unnecessarily is depersonalizing because we are treating the patient as if he or she were no longer a member of the social system in which breaking the taboo of exposure is a shameful act. Depersonalization also can occur by an inappropriate "mixing" of environments that are not normally mixed in everyday social life. Anyone who has worked with patients in a hospital has probably had the experience of entering a patient's room while he is eating, and finding a urinal on the table next to the patient's breakfast tray. The mixing of two such environments is not acceptable in the typical everyday interaction of persons. When such mixing is allowed to occur, the patient is being treated in a depersonalizing, antisocial manner, one that is contrary to the way we keep persons connected to our social system.

Another situation of depersonalization identified by Henry[30] occurs when an individual lacks the material objects to which a person is entitled in normal everyday interaction or when such objects are not used for the purposes for which they were intended. The use of nasogastric feeding tubes, intravenous lines, gastrostomy tubes, total parenteral nutrition, and other forms of artificial feeding can all evoke social images of nurturing and eating food. But they also evoke an antisocial, depersonalizing image: in our normal everyday interaction, a person eats with a knife and fork and drinks from a cup or glass, not through a tube inserted into a blood vessel or bodily orifice. The normality of our everyday actions and interactions, and the respect with which we treat each other, then, is what keeps us connected to the social system and what essentially (on a symbolic level) makes us persons.

The fact that artificial nutrition and hydration are supplied by a physician or nurse in a clinical setting, then, is not solely what defines this therapy as medical treatment. Nor does the fact that the technology of a plastic tube, a "tool," is being used define a feeding tube as a medical treatment. A fork, baby bottle, chopsticks, or even, in some cultures, certain fingers of the right hand are tools that are used for eating or feeding someone else. A normative, socially mandated way to eat or to feed someone exists in every society. It is this "normality" that helps to define us as persons and to keep us connected to our social system.

The use of a feeding tube or other forms of artificial nutrition and hydration, then, is not the "normal" social way of eating or of feeding someone—it is the "medical" way. To assign the social meanings of food and drink to a nasogastric or gastrostomy tube is to confuse these different levels of meaning. While most of the medical ethics literature tends to distinguish *nutrition and hydration* from *artificial nutrition and hydration* (at least theoretically, if not conceptually), often both the lay public and health care professionals tend to collapse these two meanings. I would argue against their collapse. Nutrition and hydration should be viewed as food and drink, with primarily a *social* meaning. Artificial nutrition and hydration should be viewed as medical treatment, with primarily a *physiological* meaning.

## WHY ARTIFICIAL NUTRITION AND HYDRATION ARE MEDICAL TREATMENT

Why should artificial nutrition and hydration be viewed as medical treatment, with an emphasis on physiological rather than social meaning? Certainly, we can attribute social meaning to a feeding tube as well as to food because all of medicine is part of the larger social realm. And, as was noted in the apple pie example, images or actions may have multiple meanings. One reason why the images of food and drink should be seen as distinct from those of artificial nutrition and hydration is that the collapsing of medical meanings with other social meanings is contrary to the responsibility that medicine has been given by society to define certain actions and things as *medical phenomena.*

Society traditionally allows physicians to touch the body in various antisocial ways when such touching is defined as a medical treatment or a medical necessity. The medical and societal definition of certain bodily intrusions as medical events justifies these intrusions. One does not, for example, confuse a gynecological examination with either an act of love or an act of rape.[31] All three acts involve vaginal penetration, but all three have very different meanings. The resulting psychological and emotional trauma that results in the rare instances when such confusion does occur demonstrates why the moral imperative to keep these meanings separate is so strong in our society.

The attribution of a medical meaning to artificial nutrition and hydration in some way justifies the antisocial or depersonalizing methods we use to fulfill the patient's basic physiological need for nutrition and hydration. But the use of these methods is not the same thing as the basic need, nor is it the same way of providing basic, supportive care for the patient through the use of more socially acceptable methods of feeding. Endowing a feeding tube with the social images of food and drink is comparable to equating someone's dislike of apple pie with a lack of patriotism or, to use Schneider's[32] example, to confusing "heartburn" with "heartache." As Geertz[33] (in paraphrasing Gilbert Ryle) has noted, the difference between an "eye twitch" and a "wink" lies in the meanings we attribute to them, rather than in anything "inherent" in these actions.

## MEANINGS OF CARING FOR THE PATIENT

This separation of the images of food and drink from those of artificial nutrition and hydration is important not only in the *forgoing* of artificial nutrition and hydration, but also in the *provision* of nutrition and hydration, i.e., food and drink. It may seem obvious to say that nutrition and hydration should always be offered to persons who can swallow, while the provision or forgoing of artificial nutrition or hydration is a clinical decision with ethical dimensions. But the problem here is not simply the collapsing of the images of food and drink with medical treatment; it also

involves the sorting out from these images the related images of what it means to care for the patient.

"Caring for the patient" can evoke many different meanings, from holding the patient's hand to providing a heart transplant. But in today's high-technology, bureaucratic health care environment, caring for the patient has come to be expressed, both concretely and symbolically, by action, i.e., medical treatment.

After World War II, as medical science and technology advanced, their results became more effective and predictable. In time, a bias toward treatment in cases of uncertain outcome became the norm, and eventually translated into an imperative to treat.[34] Society came to equate the meaning of *treating the patient*—providing the best medical care available (and this meant high-technology medical care)—with *caring for the patient,* a notion imbued with images of love, concern, and fidelity. Patients who embrace this meaning of *medical treatment* as *caring* may be compelled to demand treatments that are ineffective and incompatible with the legitimate goals of medicine because forgoing such treatments may symbolize abandonment by their physicians.[35]

But just as patients fear abandonment by their physicians, so too physicians fear abandoning their patients. The meaning of *caring for the patient* as *medical treatment of the patient* becomes explicit when physicians are heard to say, "We must do chemotherapy" or "We have to give the patient a transplant" because "We have nothing else to offer this patient." What health care professionals can offer is an alternative image of caring for the patient—that of keeping the patient connected to the social system until biological death alters those connections.

This shift in emphasis to maintaining connection to the social system has several implications for clinical decision making. It suggests that patients who can swallow should always be offered food and drink. For patients who have difficulty in swallowing or are unable to swallow, the decision to provide artificial nutrition and hydration should be subject to the same clinical and ethical criteria as would the provision of any other life-supporting treatment. In addition to medical criteria, the burden-benefit ratio will include weighing the depersonalizing meaning associated with the use of artificial nutrition and hydration against the patient's potential for having other ways of maintaining connection to the social system. Persons who have undergone surgical removal of a portion of the alimentary system, for example, may be willing to accept artificial nutrition and hydration permanently because they are able to maintain satisfactory social connections in other spheres of their lives.

For the elderly demented patient who is unable to swallow or who refuses to eat, the use of a feeding tube, often necessitating the use of physical or chemical restraints, could accelerate the process of depersonalization.[36] And because we find it difficult to watch a patient with a poor gag reflex choke or aspirate while eating, our instinct to provide the "simple technology" of a feeding tube may be hard to resist. Furthermore, the nurturing image associated with thriving and growing, an image that is sometimes associated with artificial nutrition and hydration, can be seen as inappropriate in the situation of an elderly person with an end-stage illness such as Alzheimer's disease. Such a person is in the process of loosening connections to the social system. "Caring for the patient" in this instance would mean enhancing those existing connections by continuing to offer food and drink, rather than by diminishing them through the use of a feeding tube.

## RECOMMENDATIONS

Meanings arise out of historical circumstances and the social and cultural experience of each individual. As such, they may not be subject to conscious control by the individual. But meanings may change over time and with education.

In dealing with decisions to provide or forgo artificial nutrition and hydration, the following directions of educational efforts are suggested:

1. Health care professionals should refrain from using the term *feeding tube* when providing artificial nutrition and hydration. The continued use of this term rather than others such as *stomach tube* or *gastric tube* may add to our uneasiness and confusion and is not helpful to patients and family members who may be struggling with the images that such a term evokes.

2. A decision to forgo artificial nutrition and hydration should involve the same clinical judgment, ethical justification, and soul searching that a decision to forgo any other life-supporting technology would receive; no less—but no more. Clinicians should become knowledgeable about state laws regarding treatment withdrawal, the physiological effects of starvation and dehydration, and the implications for caring for patients. The assumption that dehydration and/or starvation causes a painful death is unfounded based on numerous case reports, data from hospice caregivers, and a recent empiric study. The developing consensus is that (*a*) food and fluids not desired by dying patients do not add to the comfort of these patients; (*b*) artificial nutrition and hydration in terminally ill patients may increase pain, edema, respiratory congestion (and the need for suctioning), nausea, and vomiting; and (*c*) discomfort associated with dehydration results from thirst, which can be controlled with frequent mouth care, oral ice chips, and sips of fluids.[9,37-39] In addition, hospice care, which has been shown to have a higher rate of patient satisfaction (though not necessarily a lower cost) than conventional care, offers an opportunity to counter the image of abandonment that the withdrawal of therapy may evoke.[35,40]

3. We should avoid framing the ethical issues associated with artificial nutrition and hydration as individual moral choices of "basic care vs. medical treatment." Such a characterization collapses distinctions in meanings and obscures the clinical basis of decision making. Elimination is

as basic a human need as are nutrition and hydration, even though the social meanings of elimination, as opposed to those of nutrition and hydration, generally involve images of disgust and taboo. Yet health care providers view artificial forms of elimination, such as colostomies and urinary catheters, as medical treatments. For a health care provider to attribute to them the social meanings of disgust and taboo would be considered unprofessional. A shift in focus from this dichotomization to "social connection" ultimately may help in the clarification of treatment goals.

4. Health care providers should not be allowed or encouraged by institutional policies to "opt out" of caring for patients who forgo artificial nutrition and hydration any more than they would be allowed to opt out of assisting with or performing a gynecological examination because they failed to distinguish it from its other social meanings. (Nor should the decision to provide artificial nutrition and hydration be guided solely by family preferences, as has been suggested by some.[15,41]) The conceptual confusion inherent in the issue of artificial nutrition and hydration can be seen as similar to the confusion that both professionals and the lay public have about the concept of brain death. In such conceptual quandries, health care professionals should take the lead in educating the public and themselves and in developing a consensus of meaning.[42] While legitimate reasons of conscience may exist for refusing to participate in the implementation of a clinical decision, the failure to educate oneself about differences in meaning should not be such a reason.

5. Health care providers should not assume that because they are providing a medical treatment, they are fulfilling their obligation to care for the patient. The social meanings involved in caring for the patient may be more important than the medical treatment itself. It has been said that a society can be judged by how it cares for its very young and its very old. A failure of the health care system to care for the very young was demonstrated recently by an increase in the number of cases of infant dehydration in one midwestern city. Because of financial pressures for early hospital discharge and lack of adequate insurance coverage for home care followup, new mothers did not receive adequate training in feeding and caring for their infants, some of whom later were readmitted with dehydration (*Cincinnati Post*, May 14, 1994: A5, and *The Cincinnati Enquirer*, May 17, 1994: B1).

A failure to care for the elderly may result when health care providers equate caring for the patient with medically treating the patient. The conflating of the meaning of caring for the patient with the provision of a feeding tube is exemplified in some institutions where families perceive that feeding tubes are used because staff or family members are unavailable to assist the patient with eating.[43] When attendants cannot give elderly patients the time, attention, and coaxing necessary to help them feed themselves in the "normal" social manner, supplemental feedings by tube may be considered beneficent and caring because an elderly person is prevented from starving to death.

In such a situation, when the use of a feeding tube is given the meaning of caring for the patient, this aura of beneficence can shield us from finding out how far we, as a society, are willing to go in truly caring for others by according them full status—full equality—in the social system of which we all are a part. We can take the time, energy, and commitment needed to feed a helpless patient, or we can discharge our moral obligation by inserting a feeding tube. To discover that we are unwilling as a society to provide the means for doing the former would challenge basic beliefs about ourselves, our values, and our relationships with others. We would be presented with what Baumrind[44] calls "inflicted insight": we might learn something about ourselves that we really do not want to know and that could create anxiety for us. As we enter the age of health care reform, health care professionals increasingly will be challenged to ask and respond to these painful questions.

## ACKNOWLEDGMENTS

The author wishes to thank Rebecca Dresser, JD, Susan O. Long, PhD, Nancy Rosenberger, PhD, and Nadine Bendycki, MA, for their helpful comments on an earlier version of this article.

REFERENCES

1. Edwards MJ, Tolle SW. Disconnecting a ventilator at the request of a patient who knows he will then die: the doctor's anguish. *Ann Intern Med.* 1992; 117: 254–256.

2. President's Commission for the Study of Ethical Problems in Medicine and Biomedical and Behavioral Research. *Decisions to Forego Life-Sustaining Treatment.* Washington, DC: Government Printing Office, 1983: 43–90, 171–196, 275–297.

3. The Hastings Center. Guidelines on medical procedures for supplying nutrition and hydration. In: *Guidelines on the Termination of Life-Sustaining Treatment and the Care of the Dying.* Bloomington, IN: Indiana University Press, 1987: 57–62.

4. American Medical Association Council on Ethical and Judicial Affairs. Decisions near the end of life. *JAMA.* 1992; 267: 2229–2233.

5. Solomon MZ, O'Donnell LO, Jennings B, et al. Decisions near the end of life: professional views on life-sustaining treatments. *Am J Public Health.* 993; 83: 14–23.

6. Christakis NA, Asch DA. Biases in how physicians choose to withdraw life support. *Lancet.* 1993; 342: 642–646.

7. The Society of Critical Care Medicine Ethics Committee. Attitudes of critical care medicine professionals concerning forgoing life-sustaining treatments. *Crit Care Med.* 1992; 20: 320–326.

8. Rubenstein JS, Unti SM, Winter RJ. Pediatric resident attitudes about technologic support of vegetative patients and the effects of parental input: a longitudinal study. *Pediatrics.* 1994; 94: 8–12.

9. Sullivan RJ. Accepting death without artificial nutrition or hydration. *J Gen Intern Med.* 1993; 8: 220–227.

10. Hodges MO, Tolle SW, Stocking C, Cassell CK. Tube feeding: internists' attitudes regarding ethical obligations. *Arch Intern Med.* 1994; 154: 1013–1020.

11. *Artificial Nutrition and Hydration in Medical Durable Power of Attorney Statutes.* New York, NY: Choice in Dying Inc.; 1993.

12. *Artificial Nutrition and Hydration in Living Will Statutes.* New York, NY: Choice in Dying Inc.; 1993.

13. Capron AM. Ironies and tensions in feeding the dying. *Hastings Cent Rep.* 1984; 14: 32–35.

14. Carson RA. The symbolic significance of giving to eat and drink. In: Lynn J, ed. *By No Extraordinary Means.* Bloomington, IN: Indiana University Press; 1986: 84–88.

15. Miles SH. Futile feeding at the end of life: family virtues and treatment decisions. *Theor Med.* 1987; 8: 293–302.

16. Loewy RS. Commentary on the United States Bishops' Committee Statement on Nutrition and Hydration. *Camb Q Healthc Ethics.* 1993; 2: 349–352.

17. Lynn J, Childress JF. Must patients always be given food and water? *Hastings Cent Rep.* 1983; 13: 17–21.

18. Micetich KC, Steinecker PH, Thomasma DC. Are intravenous fluids morally required for a dying patient? *Arch Intern Med.* 1983; 143: 975–978.

19. Lo B, Dornbrand L. Guiding the hand that feeds: caring for the demented elderly. *N Engl J Med.* 1984; 311: 402–404.

20. Dresser R. When patients resist feeding: medical, ethical, and legal considerations. *J Am Geriatr Soc.* 1985; 33: 790–794.

21. Dresser R., Boisaubin EV Jr. Ethics, law, and nutritional support. *Arch Intern Med.* 1985; 145: 122–124.

22. Steinbrook R, Lo B. Artificial feeding: solid ground, not a slippery slope. *N Engl J Med.* 1988; 318: 286–290.

23. Scofield GR. The least restrictive alternative. *J Am Geriatr Soc.* 1991; 39: 1217–1220.

24. Callahan D. On feeding the dying. *Hastings Cent Rep.* 1983; 13: 22.

25. Meilander G. On removing food and water: against the stream. *Hastings Cent Rep.* 1984; 14: 11–13.

26. Siegler M, Weisbard A. Against the emerging stream: should fluids and nutritional support be discontinued? *Arch Intern Med.* 1985; 145: 129–131.

27. Rosner F. Why nutrition and hydration should not be withheld from patients. *Chest.* 1993; 104: 1892–1896.

28. Farb P, Armelagos G. *Consuming Passions: The Anthropology of Eating.* New York, NY: Washington Square Press; 1980.

29. van Melsen AGM. Person. In: Reich WT, ed. *Encyclopedia of Bioethics.* New York, NY: Free Press; 1978; 2: 1206–1210.

30. Henry J. Personality and ageing—with special reference to hospitals for the aged poor. In: *On Sham, Vulnerability and Other Forms of Self-destruction.* New York, NY: Vintage Books; 1973: 16–39.

31. Emerson JP. Behavior in private places: sustaining definitions of reality in gynecological examinations. In: Dreitzel HP, ed. *Recent Sociology No. 2: Patterns of Communicative Behavior.* New York, NY: Macmillan Publishing Co Inc.; 1976: 73–97.

32. Schneider DM. Conclusion. In: *American Kinship: A Cultural Account.* Englewood Cliffs, NJ: Prentice-Hall International Inc.; 1968: 107–117.

33. Geertz C. Thick description: toward an interpretive theory of culture. In: *The Interpretation of Cultures.* New York, NY: Basic Books Inc. Publishers; 1973: 3–30.

34. Scheff TJ. Decision rules, types of error, and their consequences in medical diagnosis. *Behav Sci.* 1963; 8: 97–107.

35. Schneiderman LJ, Faber-Langendoen K, Jecker NS. Beyond futility to an ethic of care. *Am J Med.* 1994; 96: 110–114.

36. Pearlman RA. Forgoing medical nutrition and hydration: an area for fine-tuning clinical skills. *J Gen Intern Med.* 1993; 8: 225–227.

37. Zerwekh JV. The dehydration question. *Nurs.* 1983; 13: 47–51.

38. Andrews M. Bell ER, Smith SA, Tischler JF, Veglia JM. Dehydration in terminally ill patients: is it appropriate palliative care? *Postgrad Med.* 1993; 93: 201–208.

39. McCann RM, Hall WJ, Groth-Juncker A. Comfort care for terminally ill patients: the appropriate use of nutrition and hydration. *JAMA.* 1994; 272: 1263–1266.

40. Kane RL, Wales J, Bernstein L, Leibowitz A, Kaplan S. A randomised controlled trial of hospice care. *Lancet.* 1984; 1: 890–894.

41. Waller A, Hershkowitz M, Adunsky A. The effect of intravenous fluid infusion on blood and urine parameters of hydration and on state of consciousness in terminal cancer patients. *Am J Hosp Palliat Care.* 1994; 11: 26–29.

42. Youngner SJ, Landefeld CS, Coulton CJ, Juknialis BW, Leary M. 'Brain death' and organ retrieval: a cross-sectional survey of knowledge and concepts among health professionals. *JAMA.* 1989; 261: 2205–2210.

43. Kayser-Jones J. The use of nasogastric feeding tubes in nursing homes: patient, family and health care provider perspectives. *Gerontologist.* 1990; 30: 469–479.

44. Baumrind D. IRBs and social science research: the costs of deception. *IRB.* October 1979; 1: 1–4.

## Discussion Questions

1. When Eric was twelve years old, it was discovered that the pains in his leg were the result of bone cancer. Although much of his leg was amputated, tumors began appearing in his lungs. Chemotherapy and surgery were tried, but the tumors kept showing up. Surgery has again been recommended for Eric, but he has refused, saying that he will never get better, so there is no point in going through all the misery of surgery. The oncologist admits the continual reappearance of tumors is a bad sign; even with surgery, it is not very likely that Eric will live for another year. He is thirteen now and has learned a lot in the last year about his cancer. The chemotherapy and surgeries, along with his many struggles to come to terms with his amputation, have left him exhausted and depressed. Eric's parents refuse to "give up hope" and insist that "everything possible be done" to save their son.[1]

    What should Eric's role be in making this decision about his treatment? Does his depression disqualify him from playing a central role? What about his age? How could one determine whether his parents have come to terms with their child's situation?

2. Dr. Edmund Howe describes a case in which he was trying to determine the treatment preferences of a patient with AIDS:

    When I initially asked him his preferences using the Medical Directive, he listed, rather dispassionately, the interventions he would want withheld, and described in some detail

1. Adapted from case no. 31 in J. Ahronheim, J. Moreno, and C. Zukerman, *Ethics in Clinical Practice,* 2d ed. (Gaithersburg, Md.: Aspen Publishers, 2000), 474–75.

his reasons. I then summarized for him what he had told me. He responded with in-
credulity. With much more fervor, as if he were another person, he stated that he
wanted all possible interventions, because at any time a new drug could be discovered
that would cure AIDS.[2]

What is the role of the principle of respect for autonomy in this case? With which other
principle(s) does it conflict? How should this conflict be resolved? In other words, should
the treatments first listed by the patient be withheld or not?

3. Slomka suggests toward the end of her article that when a medical professional's moral
standards would be violated by his or her participation in a medical procedure, opting
out of participation is permissible—but not if this opting out comes as a result of applying
moral standards that involve misunderstandings the medical professional should have
known about. This is a new twist on the widely accepted claim that medical professionals'
autonomy must be respected, that they must not be treated merely as tools patients use to
attain medical goals, and so forth. Is Slomka correct? How far should her view be pushed?
Do errors in working through one's own moral standards hinder one's autonomy to the
degree that the obligation of others to respect it is significantly undermined? Could it be
that all those who are on one side of the abortion debate (or any other hot moral issue)
hold moral views that are so seriously mistaken that their decisions about whether to participate in these procedures can be permissibly overridden?

## Suggestions for Further Reading

### ETHICAL ISSUES

Glick, Shimon M. "Unlimited Human Autonomy: A Cultural Bias?" *New England Journal of
Medicine* 336, no. 13 (1997): 954–56.

> The respect-for-autonomy justification usually offered for acquiescing in patients' re-
> fusal of treatment is challenged, using examples from other cultures in which this would
> not be acceptable.

Herr, Stanley S., Barry A. Bostrom, and Rebecca S. Barton. "No Place to Go: Refusal of Life-
Sustaining Treatment by Competent Persons with Physical Disabilities." *Issues in Law and
Medicine* 8, no. 1 (1992): 3–36.

> Beginning with a discussion of the Bouvia case, the plight of people who need the co-
> operation of others in order to die is examined.

Jackson, D. L., and S. J. Youngner. "Patient Autonomy and 'Death with Dignity': Some Clinical Caveats." *New England Journal of Medicine* 301, no. 8 (1979): 404–8.

> Treatment refusals need to be examined carefully to ensure that they are really exercises
> of patient autonomy rather than depression, cries for help, and so forth. The article
> considers several enlightening cases.

Majette, Gwendolyn Roberts. "An AIDS Patient's Right to Refuse Life-Sustaining Treatment." *American Family Physician* 58, no. 9 (1998): 2161 ff. *Infotrac Power Search
#A53476371.*

> This case raises interesting questions about competence and patient preferences.

---

2. Edmund G. Howe, "The Vagaries of Patients' and Families' Discussing Advance Directives," *Journal
of Clinical Ethics* 4, no. 1 (1993): 3–7, at 5.

Thomasma, David C. "Beyond Autonomy to the Person Coping with Illness." *Cambridge Quarterly of Healthcare Ethics* 4 (1995): 12–22.

It is claimed that respect for autonomy is widely misunderstood and misapplied in termination-of-care decisions. Rather than simply respecting patients' decisions, physicians should help patients reformulate goals when disease interferes with life plans.

Winslade, William J., and Judith Wilson Ross. *Choosing Life or Death: A Guide for Patients, Families, and Professionals.* New York: Free Press, 1986.

The authors use detailed case studies as a backdrop for considering the moral, medical, and psychological aspects of deciding whether to forgo life-sustaining treatment. Although the moral analysis is rather unsystematic and simplistic, there is much of value in this book.

## THE BOUVIA CASE

*Bouvia v. County of Riverside,* no. 159780. California Superior Court, Dec. 16, 1983.

In this landmark case, the court ruled that Elizabeth Bouvia, a woman with cerebral palsy, did have the legal authority to refuse nutrition and hydration, and that this was to be handled in the same way as the refusal of any other form of treatment.

Steinbock, R., and B. Lo. "The Case of Elizabeth Bouvia: Starvation, Suicide, or Problem Patient?" *Archives of Internal Medicine* 146 (1986): 161–63.

A summary and analysis of the Bouvia case bringing out its moral implications.

## MENTAL COMPETENCE

Cutter, M. Cardell, and E. Shelp, eds. *Competency.* Dordrecht: Kluwer Academic, 1991.

This collection of essays includes excellent discussions of the nature of competence, the relationship of competence to autonomy, and the methods for testing competence.

Grisso, Thomas. *Evaluating Competencies.* New York: Plenum Press, 1986.

Grisso considers the general nature of competence and the problem of making competence evaluations. There is a chapter on determining competence to make medical decisions.

# Section 3

## *Surrogate Decision Making*

## Introduction

As death approaches, many patients become less and less able to make decisions about
their medical care; this might be due to pain, dementia, the side effects of drugs, unconsciousness, or any of a number of other factors. Putting this in the terms introduced in the previous section, these patients become mentally incompetent to make
treatment decisions. However, these decisions must still be made, so, obviously, they
must be made by someone else: a proxy or surrogate, typically a member of the patient's family. This can be a particularly difficult task and a source of anguish to many
who find themselves burdened with this responsibility without being sure how to fulfill
it. When more than one treatment is available, how is a surrogate to determine which
would be best for the patient? And how is one to decide whether to pursue aggressive
medical treatment or to simply have the patient kept as comfortable as possible until
the end comes? One wants to make the right decision, but how is one to work out
what this is? The patient may have left instructions about what treatment he or she
would want, but they turn out to be much less helpful than one would have supposed.
This issue is explored here, considering the moral factors that are relevant, outlining
the problems to be faced, and offering principles to guide those who must decide
about others' treatments.

### *The Goals of Surrogate Decision Making*

The goal of surrogate decision making that has been most prominent in the literature is that of promoting and protecting patients' autonomy. We each have an interest in making for ourselves any significant decisions regarding our lives and bodies, and

decisions regarding medical care frequently fall into this category. As the significance of decisions increases, the importance of one's autonomy in making them increases also. Therefore, respect for autonomy is given added importance when the decisions involve the end of life. These should, when possible, be made by the individual whose life is in question; it has even been argued that no one else has a moral entitlement to intrude upon or override such decisions.[1] In the health care setting, the following are indications that the patient's autonomy is of particular importance:

1. when there are major differences in the kinds of possible outcomes (for example, death versus disability);
2. when there are major differences between treatments in the likelihood and impact of complications;
3. when choices involve trade-offs between near-term and long-term outcomes;
4. when one of the choices can result in a small chance of a grave outcome;
5. when the apparent difference between options is marginal;
6. when a patient is particularly averse to taking risks; and
7. when a patient attaches unusual importance to certain possible outcomes.[2]

In order to make a decision autonomously, one must have the capacity to reflect upon alternatives, recognize consequences, and consider their relevance to one's goals and projects. (A fuller explanation of autonomy and competence can be found in section 1.) Incompetent patients do not have these capacities to the required degree, and the surrogate's task is to make choices that best promote the patient's goals and interests. The patient may have provided instructions about medical treatment that indicate his or her preferences. These instructions are called advance directives; the most common sort is known as a living will. By following an advance directive, one can retain at least something of the competent patient's entitlement to participate in medical decision making. (Note that it is one's *former* autonomy that is respected when an advance directive is followed; when that stage is reached, the patient is, at least for the time being, nonautonomous.)

Respect for autonomy is not the only moral principle that is relevant here. The goals of surrogate decision making are also rooted in the principles of beneficence and nonmaleficence. The idea is that the overall results of treatment decisions will be better if these decisions are guided by the patient's own goals, values, life projects, and so on. People's goals and values can differ significantly, so a medical outcome that one person desires might be unacceptable to another. Surrogates are to make decisions that the patient would approve of, and respecting the patient's (former) autonomy generally promotes this. Note that guidelines such as "Do unto others as you would have them do unto you" sound like plausible rules for surrogates to follow, but considerable care should be exercised here. It is the *patient's* preferences—not the surrogate's—that are important here.

1. Ronald Dworkin, *Life's Dominion: An Argument about Abortion, Euthanasia, and Individual Freedom* (New York: Alfred A. Knopf, 1993).
2. J. Kassirer, "Incorporating Patients' Preferences into Medical Decisions," *New England Journal of Medicine* 330, no. 26 (1994): 1895–96, at 1896.

This effort to respect the patient's autonomy has also found expression in the Patient Self-Determination Act (PSDA), a piece of federal legislation that took effect in the United States in 1991.[3] It requires that patients being admitted to virtually any health care institution receiving federal funding must be asked whether they wish to record any treatment preferences to be followed in the event of incapacity; those who are interested in doing so must be offered assistance. These directives are then placed in the patient's medical record and can guide surrogate decision making should the patient become incapacitated. One difficulty is that although polls show strong support for this approach to decision making, relatively few people execute advance directives.[4] Therefore, there is often little clear indication of the patient's wishes to guide surrogates in their decisions.

When no formal advance directive is available, family members and others can provide information about what the patient probably would have wanted. The patient's conversations with others, history of past choices, and so on provide evidence of his or her goals and values and thus can serve as a sort of informal directive. Some courts, however, have been reluctant to accept decisions made on this sort of informal basis unless the patient's statements about treatment preferences have been persistent and clear; this is particularly true when the surrogate decides to withhold or withdraw life-sustaining treatment.[5]

The ethical challenge, then, is to find some way to accomplish the goal of surrogate decision making despite these barriers. To begin this task, consider the approaches that have been taken in guiding surrogates in their decision making.

## Advance Directives

An advance directive is a patient's indication of what medical decisions should be made in the event that he or she becomes incompetent. These directives might be either formal, such as a living will or some similar sort of document, or informal; the latter often takes the form of a conversation with a physician or potential surrogate. The other distinction used to classify advance directives has to do with whether the directive specifies particular treatments that are to be given or withheld in specified medical circumstances or simply indicates which person should undertake the responsibility of making treatment decisions on the patient's behalf. The former is an instructional directive, the latter a proxy directive.

## Instructional Directives

Instructional directives make clear the particular medical interventions the patient would want (or would want withheld) should specified medical situations arise while the patient is incompetent. Although the most common form of advance directive is

3. Omnibus Reconciliation Act 1990, title IV, section 4206, *Congressional Record*, Oct. 26, 1991.

4. H. Taylor, "Withholding and Withdrawal of Life Support from the Critically Ill," *New England Journal of Medicine* 322 (1990): 1891–92.

5. One prominent recent example of this is *Cruzan v Director Mo. Department of Health*, 497 US 110 Sup. Ct. 2841 (1990).

the living will, an instructional directive may cover many other matters as well. For instance, it might specify a preferred treatment for a certain medical condition or indicate which overall medical goals should be pursued in the patient's care.

Although instructional directives can be very useful, it is important to understand their strengths and weaknesses. Asking patients their treatment preferences and instructions seems very well suited to attaining the goals of respecting autonomy and being beneficent. After all, this is the patient's opportunity to communicate preferences and choices to the medical staff, and these instructions will be followed even if the patient becomes incapacitated. (There are, of course, limits to the instructions that can be followed. An instructional directive does not entitle patients to demand whatever drugs or treatments they may desire. Rather, patients' requests must fall within the limits of acceptable medical practice.) However, this approach faces a number of difficulties.

Perhaps the most obvious problem is that advance directives do not always make clear what the patient would have wanted in a specific medical situation. Living wills are frequently vague and incomplete, and even those who know the patient well can find it very difficult to work out what decision would be best in a given situation. Most physicians say that they have never had a case in which a living will clearly answered their questions about how the treatment of an incompetent patient should proceed. Furthermore, although physicians and family members may believe that they know the patient well enough to make medical decisions on his or her behalf, all too often they are mistaken. The numerous studies done in this area all point in the same direction: surrogates frequently make choices that are in conflict with what patients would want them to choose.[6] This unreliability may be rooted in part in the fact that the patient's life may present a confusing and perhaps inconsistent array of indications about what he or she would want, and surrogate decision makers tend to select only those components of evidence that fit with their own preferences.[7]

Even when advance directives are clear and relevant, there can be serious doubts about whether they ought to be followed. The treatment a patient requests might, for instance, be contrary to the patient's interests (even as the patient would view them). Medical science may have changed from the time the patient executed the directive in such a way that the treatment requested may no longer meet professional standards of care, or a treatment refused may no longer be as risky as it once was.[8] Instructional directives' emphasis on the patient's earlier statements also has an unfortunate tendency

6. See, for example, R. Steinbrook and B. Lo, "Decision-Making for Incompetent Patients by Designated Proxy," *New England Journal of Medicine* 310 (1988): 1598–1601; N. Zweibel and C. Cassel, "Treatment Choices at the End of Life: A Comparison of Decisions by Older Patients and Their Physician-Selected Proxies," *Gerontologist* 29, no. 5 (1989): 615–21; M. Danis et al., "A Prospective Study of Advance Directives for Life-Sustaining Care," *New England Journal of Medicine* 324, no. 13 (1991): 882–88; A. Seckler et al., "Substituted Judgments: How Accurate Are Proxy Predictions?" *Annals of Internal Medicine* 115, no. 2 (1991): 92–98; and T. Tomlinson et al., "An Empirical Study of Proxy Consent for Elderly Persons," *Gerontologist* 30, no. 1 (1990): 54–64.

7. D. Jackson and S. Youngner, "Patient Autonomy and 'Death with Dignity': Some Clinical Caveats," *New England Journal of Medicine* 301, no. 8 (1979): 404–8.

8. A. Brett, "Limitations of Listing Specific Medical Interventions in Advance Directives," *Journal of the American Medical Association* 266, no. 6 (1991): 825–28.

to de-emphasize that patient's current condition,[9] particularly if the patient is now moderately demented.[10] Because of all these concerns, we need to know how much leeway to give surrogates in interpreting patient's instructions. This concern is addressed by James Nelson in his "Taking Families Seriously," which is included in this section. He explains that families have goals and identities apart from those of particular family members and that these need to be given weight in the decision-making process.

Other complaints have been made about instructional advance directives. For instance, it has been said that it is difficult to predict from a patient's advance directive what he or she would want in situations not explicitly addressed in those instructions.[11] There is some evidence that people's treatment preferences are unstable, and advance directives are not well equipped to deal with these changes.[12] Furthermore, the medical circumstances may change in ways that invalidate the patient's directive.[13] For instance, the treatment the patient requests may no longer meet professional standards of practice and may have been replaced by some new, superior treatment.

It has been suggested by some that many of the difficulties outlined above arise from the advance directive's focus on particular medical interventions, which distracts our attention from the *reasons* patients have for giving these instructions.[14] That is, advance directives seldom reveal the goals patients are pursuing when they give these instructions to the medical team. Do they, for example, value the ability to live independently more highly than mere survival? A change in the emphasis of directives so that these reasons and preferences are drawn out could improve the usefulness of these documents. For instance, knowing a patient's goals would better enable physicians and surrogates to work out what treatments would be appropriate in any given set of circumstances.[15] This would also allow decision makers to take into account advances made in medicine since the directive was executed; this is not possible with directives that specify which treatments are to be used or forgone.

9. R. Dresser and P. Whitehouse, "The Incompetent Patient on the Slippery Slope," *Hastings Center Report* 24, no. 2 (1994): 6–12.

10. R. Morrison et al., "The Inaccessibility of Advance Directives to Transfer from Ambulatory to Acute Care Settings," *Journal of the American Medical Association* 274, no. 6 (1995): 478–82.

11. M. Everhart and R. Pearlman, "Stability of Patient Preferences Regarding Life-Sustaining Treatments," *Chest* 97, no. 1 (1990): 159–64. For a conflicting view, see L. Emanuel et al., "Advance Directives: Can Patients' Stated Treatment Choices Be Used to Infer Unstated Choices?" *Medical Care* 32, no. 2 (1994): 95–105. Although Linda Emanuel et al. argue that some predictions based on incomplete directives can be made with considerable confidence, they also point out that the information required to make these predictions is often absent from directives. In fact, the data most emphasized by most directives provide among the weakest bases for prediction.

12. See, for instance, J. Christensen-Szalonski, "Discount Functions and the Measurement of Patient Values: Women's Decisions during Childbirth," *Medical Decision Making* (1984) 4: 47–58; and L. Emanuel, "What Makes a Directive Valid?" *Hastings Center Report* (1994) 24 (6): S27–S29.

13. Brett, "Limitations of Listing Specific Medical Interventions in Advance Directives."

14. Brett, "Limitations of Listing Specific Medical Interventions in Advance Directives"; H. Taylor, "Withholding and Withdrawal of Life Support from the Critically Ill," *New England Journal of Medicine* 322 (1990): 1891–92; and A. Fade, "To Honor a Living Will," *Choice in Dying News* 3 (1993): 4.

15. R. Baergen, "Revising the Substituted Judgment Standard," *Journal of Clinical Ethics* 6, no. 1 (1995): 30–38.

Given the paucity of helpful information in the typical directive and the urgency of many situations in which treatment decisions must be made for incapacitated patients, one might allow physicians and surrogates considerable latitude in interpreting patients' instructions. A surrogate who is intimately acquainted with the patient would, it seems, be able to supplement the directive with a wealth of personal knowledge and thus make treatment decisions in such a way that the patient's autonomy is respected. This seems to offer a way around many of the difficulties noted above. There is evidence that this approach would be in line with what many (although not all) patients desire.[16]

There are, however, some dangers with this approach. Some physicians report that when they try to make treatment decisions for critically ill patients, considerations other than these patients' interests and desires creep in. Imbus and Zawacki, for instance, say that "[w]henever in the past we as caregivers tried to decide these matters for the patient, issues such as what was best for the morale of the nursing service, or for the solvency of the hospital, constantly clouded our judgment."[17] This is unlikely to be what patients have in mind when they turn decision-making authority over to their medical caregivers. Family members have also been known to use their decision-making authority inappropriately; this is discussed in John Hardwig's selection in this section.

Other problems with advance directives stem from the way in which they are handled once they have been completed. For instance, one study revealed that when patients were transferred from nursing homes to hospitals, their advance directives were sent to the hospital and included in their medical records only a little more than one-third of the time.[18] Another study revealed that only 26 percent of patients with advance directives had any clear reference to this document in the chart.[19] Also, it often seems that the directives receive little attention unless a patient advocate is there at the bedside to urge the medical team to follow the patient's instructions.[20] (This seems to be particularly true in nursing homes.[21]) Even when a strong patient advocate draws attention to a living will, there are cases in which it is still ignored by medical professionals who are sure they have the patient's best interests at heart.

Having said all of this, one should also keep these problems in perspective. When proper attention is paid to assisting patients in executing directives and care is taken in handling these documents, many of these difficulties can be minimized or eliminated. It is particularly helpful to have the patient communicate about the overall goals of treatment, rather than focusing only on lists of particular interventions to be provided or withheld.

16. A. Sehgal et al., "How Strictly Do Dialysis Patients Want Their Advance Directives Followed?" *Journal of the American Medical Association* 267, no. 1 (1992): 59–63; and J. Teno, H. Nelson, and J. Lynn, "Advance Care Planning: Priorities for Ethical and Empirical Research," *Hastings Center Report* 24, no. 6 (1994): S32–S36.

17. S. Imbus and B. Zawacki, "Autonomy for Burned Patients When Survival Is Unprecedented," *New England Journal of Medicine* 297, no. 6 (1979): 308–11, at 310.

18. Danis et al., "Prospective Study of Advance Directives for Life-Sustaining Care."

19. Morrison et al., "Inaccessibility of Advance Directives."

20. Fade, "To Honor a Living Will."

21. Danis et al., "Prospective Study of Advance Directives for Life-Sustaining Care."

## Proxy Directives

Proxy directives authorize a particular person to make medical decisions should the patient become incompetent. The most common sort of proxy directive is the durable power of attorney for health care (DPAHC). This sort of power of attorney is called durable because, unlike other sorts of power of attorney, which are invalidated when the principal becomes incompetent, the medical proxy's authority *begins* when the principal becomes incompetent. Thus, the power of attorney is durable in the sense that it endures despite the principal's incompetence. A DPAHC may include specific instructions to the proxy about what decisions he or she should make in specified medical circumstances; that is, a proxy directive can be combined with elements of an instructional directive.

Although virtually any competent person can be named as one's health care proxy, most people select family members (in the broad sense of "family," which includes all those with whom one has a continuing, committed, caring relationship). The idea here is that one will choose as a proxy someone who understands what one would count as a benefit or as a harm, who has one's interests at heart, and who will make treatment decisions accordingly.

One advantage of DPAHCs over instructional directives is that the former shift the focus in decision making from the patient's prior wishes to his or her current condition.[22] The nature of instructional directives, on the other hand, encourages one to do as the document says when the patient is incompetent, regardless of the details of the case.

DPAHCs share some of the problems facing instructional directives: family members often make decisions that are at odds with what patients want. For example, studies show that people are less likely to stop life-sustaining care for others than for themselves.[23] The reason for this seems to be that

> making life or death decisions for someone is psychologically stressful. . . . Thus, even if a patient's preferences are known, proxy decision makers may be hesitant to implement them, trying to avoid the moral and psychological responsibility for terminating life-sustaining treatments for a loved one.[24]

At the same time, there are also cases in which family members give instructions for less-aggressive treatment than the patient would have wanted; this may be due in part to the fact that proxies tend to underestimate patients' functional status.[25] Thus, in one way or another, many decisions made by proxies differ from those patients would have wanted and fail to promote the patient's well-being adequately.

22. Dresser and Whitehouse, "Incompetent Patient on the Slippery Slope."

23. See, for example, S. Steiber, "Right to Die: Public Balks at Deciding for Others," *Hospitals* 61 (1987): 72; and L. Emanuel, "Advance Directives for Medical Care: A Case for Greater Use," *New England Journal of Medicine* 324, no. 13 (1991): 889–95.

24. E. Emanuel and L. Emanuel, "Proxy Decision Making for Incompetent Patients: An Ethical and Empirical Analysis," *Journal of the American Medical Association* 267, no. 15 (1992): 2067–71, at 2068.

25. J. Magaziner et al., "Patient-Proxy Response Comparability on Measures of Patient Health and Functional Status," *Journal of Clinical Epidemiology* 33 (1988): 1065–74; and L. Rubenstein et al., "Systematic Biases in Functional Status Assessment of Elderly Adults: Effects of Different Data Sources," *Journal of Gerontology* 39 (1984): 686–91.

Other difficulties face the surrogate: anguish, guilt, denial, and other factors can interfere with good decision making. To further complicate matters, family members may disagree among themselves about who should act as surrogate or what the best decision would be. Physicians can find themselves in the middle of family feuds that threaten the patient's well-being. Molloy and colleagues call this the "daughter from California syndrome," and in their selection they explore it using a study of a representative case.

## Principles for Guiding Surrogate Decisions

*The Substituted Judgment Standard*    Various principles have been formulated to assist surrogates in arriving at decisions that will meet the constraints implied by these values. Perhaps the most significant of these is the substituted judgment standard (SJS). The fundamental idea underlying this principle is that the surrogate should make that decision which the patient would make in the circumstances were he or she competent to do so. Note that employing the SJS requires that the surrogate have considerable knowledge of how the patient would choose in the situation at hand. This information might be garnered from a living will or from conversations with the patient prior to his or her becoming incompetent. If this information is not available, the SJS cannot be used.

Although this approach looks promising, it is by no means clear that it would lead the surrogate to make appropriate decisions. As was noted earlier, advance directives and previous conversations with the patient may not provide the surrogate with enough detailed information to indicate exactly what the patient would want in the medical circumstances that actually arise; without this information, the SJS is useless. Also, the information the patient provides the surrogate reflects the former's preferences and choices from a time before he or she became seriously ill. These may poorly reflect that patient's goals, attitudes, and so forth as they are when that illness actually strikes. Changes in one's health can lead to changes in one's treatment preferences, as can experience with various forms of treatment. For example, experience with or education about CPR tends to decrease patients' preferences for this treatment.[26] Thus, the surrogate may have no clear idea what treatment the patient would want, even when a living will is available.

Even when the patient's wishes are known, they may not provide the surrogate with a consistent basis for decision making. The patient may, for example, value maintaining a high level of physical and mental functioning as well as avoiding pain. Unfortunately, there are clinical circumstances in which one of these goals would have to be sacrificed in order to attain the other. The surrogate will need to know what sort of trade-off would be acceptable to the patient, but this may not be clear; in fact, it may not be clear even to the patient.[27] When not all goals can be met, one can hope only

26. R. Shmerling et al., "Discussing Cardiopulmonary Resuscitation: A Study of Elderly Outpatients," *Journal of General Internal Medicine* 3 (1988): 317–21; and A. Wagner, "Cardiopulmonary Resuscitation in the Aged: A Prospective Survey," *New England Journal of Medicine* 310 (1984): 1129–30.

27. E. Howe, "The Vagaries of Patients' and Families' Discussing Advance Directives," *Journal of Clinical Ethics* 4, no. 1 (1993): 3–7.

to pick out a subset of prominent and mutually consistent goals and record these so that surrogates can guide physicians in working to attain them. (Some commentators add the constraint that the goals and values utilized by the surrogate should be fairly stable and should result from careful consideration on the part of the patient.[28])

*The Best-Interests Standard*   What should one do when faced with the responsibility of making medical decisions on behalf of a patient who has not executed a living will and whose goals and values one does not know very well? In such cases it is usually recommended that the surrogate employ the best-interests standard (BIS). In effect, this supplies the surrogate with a set of goals and values the patient is likely to have—or, some would say, with ones the patient *ought* to have. Contrary to what is often claimed, the SJS and the BIS share the same structure; they differ only in how the surrogate fills in information about the patient's values and goals. The surrogate who uses the SJS draws upon an advance directive and/or his or her knowledge of the patient to fill in the information required about the patient's values, while a surrogate using the BIS lacks this familiarity and must make educated guesses about the values the patient is likely to have. However this information about the patient is provided, the next step is the same: the surrogate should make medical decisions most likely to lead to the fulfillment of these goals. Of course, one's knowledge of the patient's goals, values, and so on will often fall somewhere in the middle; the greater this familiarity with the patient, the more evidence one has to support conjectures about what decision the patient would want to make in a particular situation.[29]

## Conflicting Interests

As was noted earlier, surrogates may well be caught in a conflict of interests; what would benefit the patient may harm the surrogate. In such a situation, should the surrogate be forced to ignore his or her own interests and simply act for the good of the patient? Or is it permissible for surrogates to take their own well-being into account when making decisions about the patient's medical care? Is it appropriate to take interests other than the patient's into account if the patient would not have done so if competent? That is, if the patient would have made treatment decisions with little regard for the consequences for others, should the surrogate do otherwise? Would this amount to forcing vulnerable people to be more virtuous than they otherwise would be?

It may be that it is permissible to override the patient's preferences if honoring them could put an unacceptable burden upon others. If we were to be guided simply by patients' preferences, the result could well be an unjust distribution of medical resources, the bankrupting of families, and so forth. This is related to the fact that the

28. Allen E. Buchanan and Dan W. Brock, *Deciding for Others: The Ethics of Surrogate Decision Making* (Cambridge and New York: Cambridge University Press, 1990).
29. Baergen, "Revising the Substituted Judgment Standard."

person responsible for making surrogate decisions is often faced with a conflict of interest. The surrogate may be financially responsible for the patient's care or pressed unwillingly into the role of long-term caregiver once the patient returns home. How are these conflicting interests to be balanced against one another?

Hardwig's selection offers a carefully reasoned but controversial answer to this question. He argues that moral considerations derive their force not from the fact that patients would have taken them into account if they had been competent, but from the nature of the considerations themselves. Apart from an unwarranted emphasis on individual autonomy, it is difficult to see why one would claim that the balancing of competing moral considerations should take place only if one of the people whose interests are involved in this conflict is now incompetent and would have undertaken this task of balancing had he or she been competent. Again, shifting our focus from autonomy to respect for persons is a step toward avoiding such errors. It should be noted that the balancing required in making treatment decisions is not simply an application of principles of justice. As these are traditionally conceived, they pay too little attention to the details of human relationships.[30]

30. A. Carse, "Justice in Intimate Spheres," *Journal of Clinical Ethics* 4, no. 1 (1993): 68–71.

# The Problem of Proxies with Interests of Their Own: Toward a Better Theory of Proxy Decisions

## JOHN HARDWIG

A seventy-eight-year-old married woman with progressive Alzheimer's disease was admitted to a local hospital with pneumonia and other medical problems. She was able to recognize no one, and she had been incontinent for about a year. Despite aggressive treatment, the pneumonia failed to resolve, and it seemed increasingly likely that this admission was to be for terminal care. The patient's husband (who had been taking care of her in their home) began requesting that the doctors be less aggressive in their treatment and, as the days wore on, he became more and more insistent that they scale back their aggressive care. The physicians were reluctant to do so, due to the small but real chance that the patient could survive to discharge. The husband was the patient's only remaining family, so he was the logical proxy decision maker. Multiple conferences ensued; finally a conference with a social worker revealed that the husband had recently proposed marriage to the couple's housekeeper, and she had accepted.

From the *Journal of Clinical Ethics* (1993) 4 (1): 20–27. Reprinted by permission of the publisher.

## THE CURRENT THEORY
## OF PROXY DECISIONS

Patient autonomy is the cornerstone of our medical ethics. Given this commitment to autonomy, proxy decisions will always strike us as problematic: it is always more difficult to ensure that the wishes of the patient are embodied in the treatment decisions when someone else must speak for the patient. Proxy decisions are especially disturbing when we fear that the proxy's judgment is tainted by his own interests, so that the proxy is covertly requesting the treatment *he* wants the patient to have, rather than the treatment the *patient* would have wanted. This problem of interested proxies is exacerbated by the fact that we seek out proxies who often turn out to have strong interests in the treatment of the patient. We do this for two reasons. (1) Those who care deeply for the patient are more likely than others to want what is best for the patient. (2) Those who are close to the patient are generally most knowledgeable about what the patient would have wanted. This familiarity allows us to apply the *substituted-judgment* standard of proxy decision making. Given a commitment to autonomy, substituted judgment is an ethically better basis for proxy decision making than the *reasonable-person* or *best-interest* standard.

The apparent alternative would be proxy decisions made by outsiders—physicians, court-appointed guardians, or ethics committees. We must learn to recognize that such outsiders also have interests of their own, and that their proxy decisions may also be influenced by these interests. The more common worry about outsiders is that they rarely know the patient as well as members of the patient's own family do, and outsiders' concern about the individual patient does not run nearly as deep. Proxies who are members of the patient's family have a difficult time ignoring their own interests in treatment decisions, precisely because they—unlike outsiders—are so intimately involved with the patient and have so much at stake.

Thus, it seems that our theory of proxy decisions has boxed us into a "Catch 22" situation. "Knowledgeable" about patient wishes usually means "close," but close almost always means having interests of one's own in the case. "Disinterested" usually means "distant," and distance usually brings with it less real concern, as well as lack of the intimate knowledge required to render a reliable substituted judgment.

I will argue that the reservations we have about interested family members and their proxy decisions are partly of our own making. The accepted theory of proxy decisions is deeply flawed and must be recast. Our medical practice is, I believe, often better than the conventional theories of proxy decision making. Nonetheless, some of our deepest worries about proxy decision makers grow out of the morally inappropriate instructions we give them.

If the current theory about proxy decisions for incompetent patients is mistaken, the accepted view of decisions by *competent* patients will have to be modified as well. However, I will be able to discuss decisions by competent patients only very briefly at the end of the article.

## CASE ANALYSIS: THE HUSBAND
## AND HIS PROXY DECISION

The husband in this case seemed a perfect scoundrel. The physicians involved in the case all believed that he should be disqualified as a proxy decision maker, due to his obvious conflict of interest and his patent inability to ignore his own interests in making decisions about his wife's care. There was no reason to believe that the patient would have wanted to limit her treatment, so the conclusion seemed inescapable that the husband was not faithfully discharging his role as proxy decider.

Both traditional codes and contemporary theories of medical ethics hold that physicians are obligated to deliver treatment that reflects the wishes or the best interest of the patient, and that the incompetence of the patient does nothing to alter this obligation.[1] There is similar unanimity about the responsibilities of a proxy decision maker: the proxy decision maker is to make the treatment decisions that most faithfully reflect the patient's wishes or, if those wishes cannot be known, the best interest of the patient.[2] If the proxy does not do so, commentators almost uniformly recommend that physicians reject the proxy's requests and have recourse to an ethics committee or to the courts.

Despite this impressive consensus of both traditional codes and contemporary theories of medical ethics, I was intrigued by this case and pressed the attending physician for more details. "Why is the husband in such a hurry? Perhaps he hopes that his wife will die, but she is dying anyway. Is he afraid that she might not die?" "No," the attending responded, "his worries are primarily financial. He is afraid that he'll lose his house and all his savings to medical bills before she dies. Since the housekeeper has no assets, they will then be left poverty-stricken."

To some, this seems even worse: the husband has not only allowed his own interests to override considerations of what is best for his wife, but he has let his own crass financial considerations predominate. If his decision is not altogether self-centered, it is only because he is concerned about his fiancée's future as well as his own. But married men are not supposed to have fiancées.

I do not necessarily want to argue that the husband made the correct decision. And I do not know enough about him to judge his character. But I do think his decision should not be rejected out-of-hand, as patently inappropriate. First, I do not believe that we can just assume that the presence of another woman means that he was insensitive to his wife's interests. I certainly know couples who have gotten divorced without losing the ability to care genuinely about each other and each other's interests. Second, while divorcing a long-standing wife simply

because she is now demented is difficult—"How can I abandon her at a time when she is so vulnerable?"—remaining married to an increasingly unreachable, foreign woman with Alzheimer's is difficult, too. His wife's dementia undoubtedly meant increasing isolation for him, as well as for her. And given that reality, his search for companionship does not seem unreasonable or morally objectionable. Third, the husband also had been the patient's primary caregiver for years without any prospect of relief or improvement. He probably longed for a chance to spend his few remaining years free of the burdens of such care. And, finally, supposing the husband to be an adherent of traditional values, he would be able to bring himself neither to simply "live with" the housekeeper, nor to consider himself no longer married while his wife was still alive, nor to accept medical care with no intention of trying to pay for it. Perhaps more "liberal" attitudes toward marriage and the payment of debts would have served his wife better. But we cannot be sure about that.

I doubt that the husband's proxy decisions were influenced by his own interests. Given the reasonableness and magnitude of the interests he had at stake, it is hard to see how he could ignore them. "How can *we* ignore his interests?" I wondered. "And how can we reasonably ask him to ignore them?" I do not think we can.

The attending physician and I got no further on this case than my suggestion that the husband's concern about his financial future was an appropriate consideration in deciding on a course of treatment for the patient. The physician was shocked that I thought this kind of consideration was relevant.

However, in today's society we limit treatment all the time in an effort to save money for the government or for a health maintenance organization. We develop theories of rationing and "costworthy" medicine to justify such decisions.[3] We regularly deinstitutionalize people, partly to limit the cost of the care that we, as a society, must provide. We limit the number of nursing home beds available for this man's wife and other Alzheimer's victims for the same reason. We thus force the burden of long-term care onto the families of the ill. And then we tell them that they must not consider their own burdens in making treatment decisions. I cannot make ethical sense of this.

We consider *our* pocketbooks, so how can we in good conscience tell proxies that they must ignore the impact of aggressive treatment on their personal financial futures? Financial considerations for a seventy-five-year-old with limited means are never trivial. We must recognize that for him, nothing less is at stake than the quality of the rest of his life, including, quite likely, the quality of his own future health care.

If we find it morally repugnant that proxies decide to limit treatment due to the burdens of long-term care on the family, then it is incumbent upon us to devise an alternative to our present system under which families deliver 75 percent of the long-term care. And until we have such a system in place, we dare not direct the husband to ignore the impact of treatment decisions on his own life. For *we* do not ignore the impact of such decisions on our lives. Moreover, the burdens of his wife's treatment to him may well outweigh any benefits we may be able to provide for her.

## THE MORAL RELEVANCE OF FAMILY MEMBERS' INTERESTS

There are, of course, many cases like this, in which optimal care for a patient will result in diminished quality of life for those close to the patient. This care can be a crushing financial burden, depriving other family members of many different goods and opportunities. But the burdens are by no means only financial: caring for an aging parent with decreasing mental capabilities or a severely retarded child with multiple medical problems can easily become the social and emotional center of a family's existence, draining away time and energy from all other facets of life. What are we to say about such cases?

I submit that we must acknowledge that many treatment decisions inevitably and dramatically affect the quality of more lives than one. This is true for a variety of very different reasons. (1) People get emotionally involved in others, and whatever affects the people we love affects us, too. (2) People live together, and important changes in one member of a living unit will usually have ramifications for all the others, as well. (3) The family is a financial unit in our culture, and treatment decisions often carry important financial implications that can radically limit the life plans of the rest of the family. (4) Marriage and the family are also legal relationships, and one's legal status hinges on the life or death of other members of the family. (5) Treatment decisions have an important impact on the lives of others, because we are loyal to one another.

Most of us do not believe that family and friendships are to be dissolved whenever their continued existence threatens one's quality of life. I know of a man who left his wife the day after she learned that she had cancer, because living with a cancer-stricken woman was no part of his vision of the good life. But most of us are unable or unwilling to disentangle ourselves and our lives from others when continuing involvement threatens the quality of our own lives.

This loyalty is undoubtedly a good thing. Without it, we would have alliances for better but not for worse, in health but not in sickness, until death appears on the horizon. It is a good thing even though it sometimes brings about one of the really poignant ironies of human existence: sometimes it is precisely this loyalty that gives rise to insoluble and very basic conflicts of interest, as measures to promote the quality of one life undermine the quality of others. If the husband in the case we have been considering had simply divorced his wife when she was diagnosed as having Alzheimer's, she would have died utterly alone. As such, only her own interests would have been relevant to her treatment. Her husband's loyalty—impure though it may have been—has undoubtedly made her life with Alzheimer's much better for her. But it also makes her treatment not simply her own.

Now, if medical treatment decisions will often dramatically affect the lives of more than one, I submit that we cannot morally disregard the impact of those decisions on all lives except the patient's. Nor can we justify making the interests of the patient predominant by claiming that medical interests should always take precedence over other interests. Life and health are important goods in the lives of almost everyone. Consequently, health-related considerations are often important enough to override the interests of family members in treatment decisions. But not always. Even life or death is not always the most important consideration. Thus, although persons become "patients" in medical settings, and medical settings are organized around issues of life and health, we must still bear in mind that these are not always the most important considerations. We must beware of the power of the medical context to subordinate all other interests to medical interests. Sometimes nonmedical interests of nonpatients morally ought to take precedence over medical interests of patients.

Because medical treatment decisions often deeply affect more lives than one, proxy decision makers must consider the ramifications of treatment decisions on all those who will be importantly affected, including themselves. Everyone with important interests at stake has a morally legitimate claim to consideration; no one's interests can be ignored or left out of consideration. And this means nothing less than that the morally best treatment in many cases will not be the treatment that is best for the patient.

An exclusively patient-centered ethics must be abandoned. It must be abandoned, not only—as is now often acknowledged—because of scarce medical resources and society's limited ability to meet virtually unlimited demands for medical treatment. It must be abandoned, as well, because it is patently unfair to the families of patients. And if this is correct, the current theory of proxy decisions must be rejected in favor of an ethics that attempts to harmonize and balance the interests of friends and family whose lives will be deeply affected by the patient's treatment.[4]

## REEXAMINING THE DOCTRINE OF SUBSTITUTED JUDGMENT

There is a second, related point. Arguably, there is a presumption that substituted judgment is a morally appropriate standard for a proxy decision maker. But this can be no more than a *presumption,* and it can be overridden whenever various treatment options will affect the lives of the patient's family. In fact, substituted judgment is the appropriate standard for proxy decision making in only two special (though not uncommon) situations: (1) when the treatment decision will affect only the patient, or (2) when the patient's judgment would have duly reflected the interests of others whose lives will be affected. In other situations, proxy deciders should make decisions that may be *at odds with* the known wishes of a formerly competent patient.

Consider again the case with which this paper began. I did not know the patient, and I have no idea what kind of person she used to be. Let us, then, consider two rather extreme hypotheses about her character. On one hand, suppose that the patient had been a very selfish, domineering woman who, throughout their marriage, had always been willing to subordinate her husband's interests to her own. If so, we can reliably infer that she would now have ignored her husband's interests again, perhaps even ridden roughshod over them, if she could have gotten something she wanted by doing so. Therefore, we can conclude that she would have demanded all medical treatment available, regardless of costs to him. We can even imagine that she would have relished her continuing power over him and her ability to continue to extract sacrifices from him. Obviously, her husband would know these facts about her. The substituted-judgment standard of proxy decisions would have us conclude that if that is the kind of woman she was, this would *increase* her husband's obligation to make additional sacrifices of his interests to hers.

Suppose, on the other hand, that this woman had always been a generous, considerate, unselfish woman, who was deeply sensitive to the interests of her husband and always ready to put his needs before her own. If that is the kind of woman she was, the theory of substituted judgment allows—strictly speaking, even *obligates*—her husband to sacrifice her interests once again by now demanding minimal care for her. After all, he knows that is what she would have done, had she been competent to make the decision. Even if he wanted to give her the very best treatment as an expression of love or gratitude for her concern for him throughout their lives, substituted judgment would require that he ignore those desires. Continued treatment is what *he* wants for her, not what she would have chosen for herself.

But surely that is exactly wrong. The theory of substituted judgment has it backwards. Loving, giving, generous people deserve to be generously cared for when they can no longer make decisions for themselves, even if they would not have been generous with themselves. And what do selfish, domineering, tyrannical people deserve? The answer to that question depends upon one's ethical theory. Perhaps neglect, maybe even retribution, are justified or at least excusable. Perhaps tyrannical behavior releases the family from any special obligation to care for the now incompetent tyrant. But unless one believes that good people should not be rewarded for their virtues, one will agree that caring, giving individuals deserve better care than domineering, self-centered individuals.

Where did we go wrong? What led us to widespread acceptance of the theory of substituted judgment? The major mistake is the one we have been considering—the mistake of believing that medical treatment affects only the life of the patient, or that its impact on other lives should be ignored. If the patient's interests are the only ones that ought to shape treatment decisions, those interests are best defined by the patient's point of view. Proxy deciders are, then, obligated to replicate that point of view insofar as possible. But most decisions we make affect the lives of others. That, of course, is the main reason why we have ethics. And the present incompetence of a patient should not obligate others to perpetuate the patient's former selfish ways.

It would, of course, be possible to modify and defend the doctrine of substituted judgment by reinterpreting the concept of autonomy.[5] Patient autonomy is, after all, the main reason we embrace substituted judgment, and we usually define patient autonomy as "what the patient would have wanted." But if we were to work instead with a truly Kantian notion of autonomy, we would arrive at a very different theory of substituted judgment. For Kant would insist that a domineering, selfish person would acknowledge that she deserves less generous care when she becomes incompetent than a more caring, giving person deserves. While she might not actually elect less generous care if she were able to choose for herself, the moral judge within her would recognize that she deserves less care from others due to the way she has treated them.

On Kant's view, then, the treatment she would choose for herself is not the appropriate standard of autonomy. Rather, her judgment about what is fair or what she now deserves would be the true meaning of autonomy. Kant would insist that the selfish, domineering ways of an individual are all heteronomous (subject to external influences), despite the fact that the person consistently chose them. He would further insist that a request for medical care that requires inordinate sacrifices from one's family is also heteronomous, even if the patient would have wanted that. This interpretation of autonomy and substituted judgment is clearly very different from the standard interpretation in medical ethics.

Barring a radical rethinking of the very concepts of autonomy and substituted judgment, the doctrine of substituted judgment must be rejected. At the very least, our standard view of substituted judgment must be replaced with a theory in which the interests of the incompetent are constrained by what is morally appropriate, *whether or not* the patient would have so constrained herself. Often, the patient would have been sensitive to the interests of the rest of the family. But not always. In any case, the interests of other members of the family are not relevant to proxy decisions *because* the patient would have considered them as part of her own interests; they are relevant *whether or not* the patient would have considered them.[6] It is simply not the patient's regard for the interests of her family that gives those interests moral standing. No patient, competent or incompetent, deserves more than a fair, equitable consideration of the interests of all concerned. Fairness to all includes, I would add, fairness to the patient herself, in light of the life she has lived and especially the way she has treated the members of her family.

The theory of proxy decision making must be rebuilt. While proxy deciders must guard against *undue* consideration of their own interests, undue consideration of the *patient's* interests is likewise to be avoided. Proxy deciders have been given the wrong instructions. Instead of telling them that they must attempt to put themselves into the shoes of the incompetent patient and decide as she would have decided, we must tell them that the incompetent patient's wishes are the best way for her to define *her* interests, but what she would have wanted for herself must be balanced against considerations of fairness to all members of the family.

## TOWARD A NEW THEORY OF PROXY DECISIONS

Fundamental changes in the theory of proxy decisions will need to be created and defended. And a view such as mine faces a host of important questions. I cannot develop an alternative theory in this article. Indeed, I cannot fully answer the most pressing questions about an alternative. Here, I can only provide suggestions about the way I would try to approach four of the most immediate questions about the theory of proxy decisions I would advocate.

First, if proxy deciders must avoid *undue* consideration of either their own interests or the interests of the patient, how is "undue consideration" to be defined? A full answer to this question would require an account of the family and of the ethics of the family. We can begin, however, by noting that, *prima facie,* equal interests deserve equal consideration. But what defines equal interest? Norman Daniels has developed the concept of a "normal opportunity range" for the purpose of allocating resources to different individuals and different age groups.[7] Perhaps this concept could be extended to problems of fairness *within* families by asking how different treatment options will affect the opportunity range of the various members of the family. If so, undue consideration could be partially defined as a bias in favor of an interest that affects someone's opportunity range in a smaller way over an interest that affects another's opportunity range in a greater way.

But even if this suggestion about the opportunity range could be worked out, it would represent only one dimension of an adequate account of undue consideration. Another dimension would be fairness to competent and formerly competent members of the family in light of the way they have lived and treated each other. Thus, as I have argued above, those who have been caring and generous to members of their families deserve more from them than those who have been selfish or inconsiderate.

Second, *whose* interests are to be considered? For example, what about the interests of family members who do not care for the patient or who have long been hostile to the patient? Lack of concern for the patient and even hostility toward the patient do not, in my view, exclude family members from consideration. Such family members still may have important interests at stake; moreover, we must not assume that the neglect or hostility is not merited. Neglect or hostility toward the patient would, however, diminish what fair consideration of their interests would amount to.

What of the interests of close friends or companions who are not members of the family? "Family," as I intend this concept, is not restricted to blood or marital relationships. Close friends, companions, unmarried lovers—all of these relationships may entitle persons to consideration in treatment decisions. Those who are distant—neither emotionally involved with the patient nor related by blood or marriage—will almost never have strong enough interests in the treatment of a patient to warrant consideration. (Health-care professionals may have strong interests, but they have special professional obligations to ignore their own interests and are usually well compensated for doing so.) I see no principled way to exclude consideration of anyone whose interests will be importantly affected by a treatment decision.

Third, wouldn't any theory like the one I propose result in unfair treatment of incompetent patients? After all, we do not require that competent patients consider the interests of their families when making treatment decisions. And if competent patients can ignore their families, doesn't fairness require that we permit incompetent patients to do so, as well? I have argued elsewhere that if we want to insist on patient autonomy, we must insist that patients have *responsibilities* and *obligations,* as well.[8] In many cases, it is irresponsible and wrong for competent patients to make self-centered or exclusively self-regarding treatment decisions. It is often wrong

for a competent patient to consider only which treatment she wants for herself. We must, then, try to figure out what to do when patients abuse their autonomy—when they disregard the impact of their treatment decisions on the lives of others. Sometimes, no doubt, we should seek to find ways to prevent patients from abusing their autonomy at too great a cost to their families.

Still, competent patients are almost always permitted to ignore the interests of their family members, even when this is wrong. We do not force them to consider the impact of their decisions on others, nor do we disallow their decisions if they fail to do so. How, then, can it be fair to incompetent patients to develop a theory of proxy decisions that will, in effect, hold them to a more stringent moral standard by requiring them to accept treatment decisions made in light of their families' interests? The answer to this question is, I think, that there are many actions that we are at liberty to take, but only so long as we do not need an agent to help us accomplish them. If we can file our own taxes, we may be able to cheat in ways that a responsible tax advisor will refuse to do. We may get away with shoddy deals that an ethical lawyer would not be a party to. Thus, the greater freedom of competent patients is only a special case of the generally greater freedom of action when no assistance of an agent is required.

And fourth, what about the legal difficulties of an alternative view of proxy decision making? They are considerable: it is presently *illegal* to make proxy decisions in the way I think is morally appropriate. The courts that have become involved in proxy decision making have almost all opted for exclusively patient-centered standards. I do not have the expertise needed to address the legal issues my view raises. My purpose here can only be to challenge the faulty moral foundations that undergird present legal practice.

However, it is possible that family law could provide a model for a revised legal standard of proxy decision making. Family law recognized the legitimacy of proxy decisions—for children, for example—that are not always in the best interest of the person represented by the proxy. It has to, if only because there are many cases in which the interests of one child will conflict with those of others. Nor does family law require parents to ignore their own interests in deciding for a child; instead, it defines standards of minimum acceptable care, with the hope that most families will do better than these minimum standards. Perhaps we should similarly separate the legal from the moral standard for proxy decisions. If no abuse or neglect is involved, the legal standard is met, though that may be less than morality requires of a proxy decision maker.

## CONCLUSION

All these issues—undue consideration, eligible interests, fairness between competent and incompetent patients, and the law of proxy decisions—may seem very complex. However, I do not believe they are unnecessarily complicated. Many important decisions within families are very complicated. In medical ethics, we have simplified our task by working with an artificially oversimplified vision of the interests and decisions of families in medical treatment. So, if my critique of the present theory of proxy decisions is correct, we all—medical ethicists, reflective health-care practitioners, legal theorists, lawyers—have a lot of hard work to do. The change I propose is basic, so the revisions required will be substantial.

I close now with a word of caution and a word of encouragement. The word of caution: we must recognize that even the necessary revisions in our moral and legal theories of proxy decisions would not resolve all the problems of proxy decisions. Proxy deciders with interests that conflict with those of the patient do face serious moral difficulties and very real temptations to

give undue weight to their own interests. Although the concepts of both "overtreatment" and "undertreatment" will have to be redefined in light of the considerations I have been advancing, pressure from proxies for inappropriate treatment will remain. I do not wish to minimize these difficulties in any way.

But we should not give proxies the morally erroneous belief that their own interests are irrelevant, censuring them for allowing their interests to "creep in" to their decisions. Instead, we must deal forthrightly with the very real difficulties arising from interested proxy decisions, by making these interests conscious, explicit, and legitimate. Then we must provide guidance and support for those caught in the moral crucible of proxy decisions. Not only would this approach be more ethically sound, but it would, I believe, decrease the number of inappropriate proxy decisions.

Finally, an encouraging word. The Alzheimer's case that I have cited notwithstanding, the practice of medicine is often better than our ethical theories have been. It has generally not been so insensitive to the interests of family members as our theories would ask that it be. Indeed, much of what now goes on in intensive care nurseries, pediatricians' offices, intensive care units, and long-term care facilities makes ethical sense *only* on the assumption that fairness to the interests of the other members of the family is morally required. To mention only the most obvious kind of case, I have never seen a discussion about institutional versus home care for an incompetent patient that did not attempt to address the interests of those who would have to care for the patient, as well as the interests of the patient.

Current ethical theory and traditional codes of medical ethics can neither help nor support health-care professionals and proxies struggling to balance the patient's interests with those of the proxy and other family members. Indeed, our present ethical theory can only condemn as unethical any attempt to weigh in the interests of the family. Thus, our ethical theory forces us to misdescribe decisions about institutionalization in terms of what is physically or psychologically possible for the family, rather than in terms of what is or is not too much to ask of them. If we were to acknowledge the moral relevance and legitimacy of the family's interests, we would be able to understand why many treatment decisions now being made make sense and are not unethical. And then we would be in a position to develop an ethical theory that would guide health-care providers and proxies in the throes of excruciating moral decisions.

## ACKNOWLEDGMENTS

I wish to thank Eric H. Loewy and especially Mary R. English for many helpful comments on this paper.

REFERENCES

1. L. Edelstein, "The Hippocratic Oath: Text, Translation, and Interpretation," *Bulletin of the History of Medicine,* supp. 1 (Baltimore: Johns Hopkins University Press, 1943), 3; World Medical Association, "Declaration of Geneva," *World Medical Journal* 3, supp. (1956): 10–12; World Medical Association, "International Code of Medical Ethics," *World Medical Association Bulletin* 1 (1949): 109–111; T. L. Beauchamp and J. F. Childress, *Principles of Biomedical Ethics,* 3rd ed. (New York: Oxford University Press, 1989); A. E. Buchanan and D. W. Brock, *Deciding for Others: The Ethics of Surrogate Decision Making* (New York: Cambridge University Press, 1989); J. F. Childress, *Who Should Decide? Paternalism in Health Care* (New York: Oxford University Press, 1982); Hastings Center, *Guidelines on the Termination of Life-Sustaining Treatment and the Care of the Dying* (Bloomington, IN: Indiana University Press, 1987); E. D. Pellegrino and D. C. Thomasma, *For the Patient's Good* (New York: Oxford University Press, 1988); President's Commission for the Study of Ethical Problems in Medicine and Biomedical and Behavioral Research, *Making Health Care Decisions: The Ethical and Legal Implications of Informed Consent in the Patient-Physician Relationship,* vol. 1 (Washington, DC: US Government Printing Office, 1982); R. M. Veatch, *A Theory of Medical Ethics* (New York: Basic Books, 1981).

2. Beauchamp and Childress, *Principles of Biomedical Ethics;* Buchanan and Brock, *Deciding for Others;* Hastings Center, *Guidelines;* Pellegrino and Thomasma, *For the Patient's Good;* President's Commission, *Making Health Care Decisions;* R. M. Veatch, *Death, Dying and the Biological Revolution: Our Last Quest for Responsibility* (New Haven, CT: Yale University Press, 1989).

3. See, for example, D. Callahan, *Setting Limits: Medical Goals in an Aging Society* (New York: Simon and Schuster, 1987); N. Daniels, *Just Health Care* (New York: Cambridge University Press, 1985); R. W. Evans, "Health Care Technology and the Inevitability of Resource Allocation and Rationing Decisions (pt. 2)," *Journal of the American Medical Association* 249 (1983): 2208–2219; E. H. Morreim, "Fiscal Scarcity and the Inevitability of Bedside Budget Balancing," *Archives of Internal Medicine* 149 (1989): 1012–1015; R. M. Veatch, "Justice and the Economics of Terminal Illness," *Hastings Center Report* 18 (August–September 1988): 34–40; L. C. Thurow, "Learning to Say 'No,'" *New England Journal of Medicine* 311 (1984): 1569–1572.

4. There are a few scattered references that acknowledge that the interests of the patient's family may be considered. At one point, the President's Commission states that "the impact of a decision on an incapacitated patient's loved ones may be taken into account," President's Commission for the Study of Ethical Problems in Medicine and Biomedical and Behavioral Research, *Deciding to Forgo Life-Sustaining Treatment: Ethical, Medical and Legal Issues in Treatment Decisions* (Washington, DC: U.S. Government Printing Office, 1983), 135–136. The Hastings Center *Guidelines* counsels consideration of the benefits and burdens to "the patient's family and concerned friends," but only in the special case of patients with irreversible loss of consciousness (p. 29). Buchanan and Brock devote one page of their impressive work, *Deciding for Others,* to the "limits on the burdens it is reasonable to expect family members to bear" (p. 208). But these are only isolated passages in large, systematic works and they do not inform the overall theory developed in these works. The discussion of neonatal care is the only place I know where the interests of members of the patient's family have received systematic attention. A good example is C. Strong, "The Neonatologist's Duty to Patients and

Parents," *Hastings Center Report* 14 (August 1984): 10–16. The fact that many ethicists seem willing to consider family interests in the case of newborns but not in the case of older patients suggests that we may not really consider newborns to be full-fledged persons.

5. I owe this point to an anonymous referee.

6. Thus, I am in substantial disagreement with even the one paragraph from the President's Commission's *Deciding to Forgo Life-Sustaining Treatment* that goes farthest toward something like the position I embrace. For the President's Commission would allow proxies to consider the interests of family members only if there is substantial evidence that the patient would have considered their interests. But in my view, this is not the reason that the interests of the members of the patient's family are relevant. If the patient was a selfish, inconsiderate person, this does not mean that the interests of her family somehow become morally illegitimate or irrelevant.

7. N. Daniels, *Just Health Care* (Cambridge, England: Cambridge University Press, 1985).

8. J. R. Hardwig, "What about the Family? The Role of Family Interests in Medical Treatment Decisions," *Hastings Center Report* 20 (March–April 1990): 5–10.

# Decision Making in the Incompetent Elderly: "The Daughter from California Syndrome"

DAVID W. MOLLOY, ROGER M. CLARNETTE,

E. ANN BRAUN, MARTIN R. EISEMANN, AND

B. SNEIDERMAN

DECISION-MAKING REGARDING THE CARE of the mentally incompetent patient is often complicated by legal,[1-7] economic,[8-12] and ethical factors[13-15] that affect case management. The incompetent patient requires an advocate, a responsibility that generally falls upon the family. If a conflict over a patient arises within the family, the result may well be inimical to effective patient management.

On June 25th, 1990, the United States Supreme Court issued its decision in Cruzan v. Director, Missouri Department of Health, the first case in which the high court considered the termination of life-prolonging measures for incompetent patients. In a 5-4 decision, the Court upheld the decision by the Missouri Supreme Court that the feeding tube of Nancy Cruzan, a patient in a persistent vegetative state since 1983 could not be removed at the request of her parents. The reason was that there was no 'clear and convincing' evidence that the patient when competent had specifically indicated that she would not wish to be tube-fed if she ever became irreversibly unconscious.

The narrow import of the decision in Cruzan must be stressed. The Court ruled that it is constitutionally permissible for a state to require that life-prolonging measures for an incompetent patient remain in place unless the patient had left behind a clear directive excluding such measures in the event of a future state of incompetence. The Court did not rule that such a state rule is mandatory but simply that a state may so rule if it chooses. The decision in Cruzan thus leaves

From the *Journal of the American Geriatrics Society* (1991) 39(4): 396–399.

intact the long line of cases, beginning with In the Matter of Karen Quinlan, in which state supreme courts have held that decisions to terminate life-prolonging treatment for incompetent patients should rest with the patient's family and physicians. The courts have further ruled that the courtroom should be the forum of last resort for decision-making involving the termination of life-prolonging treatment for incompetent patients.

In the view of the judges, however, they have a role to play when there is in-family conflict that cannot be resolved in the health care setting. In that event, judicial action is called for in which either the court makes the treatment decision or else vests that authority in a guardian appointed to act on the patient's behalf. (The trend in the more recent cases is to assign the decision to a guardian, not to the court itself.)

The "Daughter from California Syndrome" describes one such in-family predicament. In this case an adult daughter, who had not seen her mother for 5 years, appeared on the scene when critical health care options were being considered for her incompetent mother. Upon being confronted with her mother's condition, the daughter responded with acute denial as well as anger and resentment directed against the medical staff. She refused to come to terms with her mother's condition, demanded inappropriate aggressive care, and impeded the management of the case.

Health care directives[16-21] offer a plausible solution to these problems by allowing competent individuals to choose their own health care before they become incompetent. We report this case because it illustrates many of the features of this syndrome.

## CASE REPORT

The patient, Mrs. M., was an 83-year-old widow with a 5-year history of Alzheimer's disease. She had been cared for by her 60-year-old daughter who never married and had taken an early retirement. Mrs. M. was admitted to a nursing home 6 months before her hospital admission because the daughter was no longer able to care for her at home. At that time the patient was moderately demented, she no longer recognized her daughter, was incontinent of urine, and needed to be groomed, washed, and fed. Sometime later she fractured the neck of her left femur which necessitated surgical repair. Following surgery she refused to walk, was incontinent of urine and feces, and was a heavy two-person transfer.

After discussion with the daughter, a Do Not Resuscitate Order (DNR) was entered on the patient's chart and co-signed by her. Although the patient had not signed an advance directive, she had discussed termination of treatment issues with her daughter, who was confident that the DNR order would accord with her mother's wishes. The daughter further requested that we discontinue blood tests and provide palliative care in the event of a reversible or irreversible life-threatening illness. She also co-signed a request that medications be administered only for comfort and pain relief purposes.

When the second daughter arrived from California, it was quickly apparent that she had been unaware of her mother's recent deterioration. She was appalled at her mother's condition, and she accused her sister of institutionalizing their mother for financial gain. She demanded that the DNR order be withdrawn and that the mother receive whatever treatment was necessary to maintain life. She threatened to sue the hospital and all health care professionals treating her mother unless her mother was immediately transferred to the intensive care unit.

We arranged a meeting for the sisters with the medical staff. The daughter from California totally dominated the discussion. She took notes and threatened to sue everyone involved in her mother's care. There were follow-up meetings with the orthopedic surgeon, the internist, nurses, physiotherapists, occupational therapists, chaplains, and nutritionists. We spent considerable time with the daughter from California striving to deal with her denial, guilt, threats, and anger. She so intimidated her sister that the latter not only acquiesced in her demands but also ceased to come to the hospital. We accordingly withdrew the DNR order and directed that the patient be treated aggressively in the event of further deterioration.

Soon thereafter the daughter from California returned home. Her sister resumed her visits to the patient, and, at her written request, the DNR order and palliative care directions were reinstated. Mrs. M. died 2 weeks later. The daughter from California did not attend the funeral.

## DISCUSSION

The care of the incompetent patient poses particularly complex problems for clinicians who must consider the wishes of the patient, family, and other health care workers. On occasion the wishes of the patient and/or family conflict with the mission statement of the institution or with the ethical principles of staff members.[22] Legal, economic, ethical, and religious factors may add to the complexity of the situation. Such issues arise more frequently in geriatrics than in any other subspecialty. Indeed, few problem areas in medicine are more complex than decision-making for elderly incompetent patients.

Of course, the patient may have signed an instructional advance directive (i.e., living will) or a proxy advance directive (i.e., durable power of attorney for health care). What if, however, the patient while competent had not signed an advance directive or otherwise indicated treatment preferences to guide the decision-making process? Or what if there is an apparent conflict between the family's wishes and a living will direction or the views of a proxy nominated by the patient to make his/her health care decisions? In such cases, the hierarchy listed in Table 1 provides practical guidelines to facilitate decision-making for the incompetent patient.

The resolution of in-family conflict can be a difficult task. Resentment, grudges, rivalry, or long standing animosity within the family can impair its ability to reach a consensus sufficient to guide the incompetent patient's health care team. Denial, guilt, and anger among family members also impairs their ability to make rational decisions. In this case, the daughter from California was in an early stage of denial regarding her mother's illness. She may have hoped that her mother would recover to an extent enabling her to "make her peace" with her. The daughter's anger, guilt, and denial precipitated a crisis in management, disrupting a care plan that had been developed after considerable discussion and effort.

Strategies to deal with these situations include involving all those family members who wish to become involved in the discussions. It may be helpful to outline simply and exactly what decisions have to be made and give a consistent description of the patient's condition. It is important to allow the family to make all the major treatment decisions.

## Table 1   Hierarchy of Decision Making in the Incompetent Patient

1. If the patient while competent had signed an advance directive, then his/her wishes must prevail, even over the contrary views of family members.
2. If the patient has left no directive, it is necessary to turn to the family. An in-family discussion of treatment options is called for, although as a general guideline actual decision-making authority should be allotted in accordance with the following prioritized list: spouse, adult children, siblings, other family members. (The term "spouse" would include the patient's significant other.)
3. If there is unresolvable in-family conflict regarding case management of the patient, the court should be petitioned to appoint a guardian to act on the patient's behalf.
4. In the event that there is no one to speak for the patient, then the patient's health care providers should assume that role.

**Table 2     Strategies for Dealing with the Difficult Family**

1. Convene a meeting with all family members who wish to play a role in the decision-making process for the incompetent patient. All health care professionals involved in the patient's care (e.g., family physician, specialists, nurses, physiotherapists, occupational therapists, social workers, nurses and chaplains) should be invited to attend.
2. Provide the family with a consistent description in simple language of the patient's condition and prognosis. Use the same terms and responses because similar terms for the same condition may cause confusion and provoke the concern that there is disagreement within the medical team.
3. Outline in simple terms the areas wherein decisions must be made, e.g.,
   a) treatment in the event of cardiac arrest
   b) treatment in the event of acute reversible life-threatening illness (e.g., pneumonia)
   c) treatment in the event of acute irreversible life-threatening illness (e.g., stroke)
   d) nutrition (e.g., special diets, nasogastric tubes, gastrostomy tubes, total parenteral nutrition)
   e) routine blood work and further investigations.
4. Give over control to the family: advise the members that they must reach a consensus and then inform the health care team of their decision.
5. Nominate one family member to communicate with a team member (e.g., physician, head nurse, chaplain or social worker).
6. Give the family a deadline to provide a decision, arrange follow-up meetings for updates, provide a mechanism for the family to continue asking questions and to be kept informed of changes in the patient's condition.
7. If the family cannot arrive at a consensus, discuss their points of disagreement and follow-up with small group meetings to provide ongoing advice and information. If the family still cannot reach a consensus, then follow the wishes of the family members in accordance with the prioritized list provided in Table 1.
8. Finally, if all these measures fail, consult the Geriatric Service. Everyone else does.

Some of the strategies for dealing with the complex and time-consuming issues that can arise when there is in-family conflict regarding the care of incompetent patients are listed in Table 2.

In this case, interdisciplinary collaboration and support enabled the patient's health care givers to defuse anger and share the responsibility for dealing with this difficult, time-consuming problem. The views of the daughter from California did not accord with the previously expressed wishes of the patient as reported by the daughter who had lived with and cared for the mother. It was the latter who knew the mother's feelings about terminal care and who sought to promote her best interests. She was thus the appropriate surrogate decision-maker for her mother, and in honoring her wishes for the DNR and palliative-care-only order, the medical staff was fulfilling its legal and moral responsibilities to the patient.

According to the President's Commission for the Study of Health Problems in Medicine, "a health care professional has an obligation to allow a patient to choose from among medically acceptable treatment options . . . or to reject all options."[23] Although physicians are not morally (or legally) bound to provide treatment they regard as "countertherapeutic" or physiologically futile, it is nonetheless true that the threat of litigation (as in this case) cannot be taken lightly.[24] It is thus understandable that the medical staff complied with the daughter's demands for aggressive treatment.

This case illustrates the value of a patient's advance directives. If the patient had, while competent, documented her views regarding a DNR order and palliative care regimen, then the threats of the daughter from California could have been discounted. In other words, comprehensive health care directives completed by knowledgeable patients may serve to deflect conflict that can arise when the decision-making responsibility is laid upon family members. So long as incompetent patients have not left behind such directives, health care providers will be pressured into providing care against their better judgment because of the demands of family members like the daughter from California.

## REFERENCES

1. Curran WJ, Hyg SM. Court involvement in right-to-die cases: judicial inquiry in New York. N Engl J Med 1981; 305: 75.

2. Libow LS. The interface of clinical and ethical discussions in the care of the elderly. M Sin Med 1981; 48: 480.

3. McClung JA, Kamer RS. Implications of New York's do-not-resuscitate law. N Engl J Med 1990; 323: 270.

4. Glover JJ. The case of Ms Nancy Cruzan and the care of the elderly. J Am Geriatr Soc 1990; 38: 588.

5. Gasner MR. Cruzan v Harmon, and In the Matter of O'Connor; two anomalies. J Am Geriatr Soc 1990; 38: 599.

6. Bopp J. Reconciling autonomy and the value of life. J Am Geriatr Soc 1990; 38: 600.

7. Thomasma DC. Surrogate decisions at risk: the Cruzan case. J Am Geriatr Soc 1990; 38: 603.

8. Yarborough MA, Kramer AM. The physician and resource allocation. Clin Geriatr Med 1986; 2: 465.

9. Scitovsky AA, Capron AM. Medical care at the end of life: interaction of economics and ethics. Ann Rev Public Health 1986; 7: 59.

10. Bayer R, Callahan D, Fletcher J, et al. The care of the terminally ill: morality and economics. N Engl J Med 1983; 309: 1491.

11. Avorn J. Benefit and cost analysis in geriatric medicine. N Engl J Med 1984; 310: 1294.

12. Garber AM. Cost-containment and financing the long-term care of the elderly. J Am Geriatr Soc 1988; 36: 355.

13. Lynn J. Conflicts of interest in medical decision-making. J Am Geriatr Soc 1988; 36: 945.

14. Hilfiker D. Allowing the debilitated to die. N Engl J Med 1983; 308: 716.

15. Callahan D. Setting Limits: Medical Goals in an Aging Society. New York: Simon and Schuster, 1987.

16. Lazaroff AE, Orr WF. Living wills and other advance directives. Clin Geriatr Med 1986; 2: 521.

17. Davidson KW, Moseley R. Advance directives in family practice. J Fam Pract 1986; 22: 439.

18. Levenson SA, List ND, Zaw-Win B. Ethical considerations in critical and terminal illness in the elderly. J Am Geriatr Soc 1981; 29: 563.

19. Emanuel LL, Emanuel EJ. The medical directive, a new comprehensive advance care document. JAMA 1989; 261: 3288.

20. Eisendrath SJ, Jonsen AR. The living will, help or hindrance? JAMA 1983; 249: 2054.

21. Kelly JL, Elphick G, Mepham V, Molloy DW. Let Me Decide. Hamilton, Ont.: McMaster University Press, 1989.

22. Miles SH, Singer PA, Seigler M. Conflicts between patient's wishes to forgo treatment and the policies of health care facilities. N Engl J Med 1989; 321: 48–50.

23. President's Commission for the Study of Ethical Problems in Medicine and Biomedical and Behavioral Research. Deciding to Forgo Life-Sustaining Treatment. Washington, DC: US Government Printing Office, March 1983.

24. The Appleton Consensus: suggested international guidelines for decisions to forgo medical treatment. Lawrence University Program in Biomedical Ethics, Appleton, Wisconsin, May 1988.

# Taking Families Seriously

## JAMES LINDEMANN NELSON

IT HAS BECOME COMMONPLACE TO REMARK that advances in reproductive medicine do more than simply expand available options for form-ing families—allegations that they put pressure on such basic concepts as 'mother' and 'child', and threaten to distort fundamental features of

From the *Hastings Center Report* 1992, 22(4): 6–12. Reprinted by permission of the Hastings Center.

our most intimate ties, are widespread. For example, surrogate motherhood is criticized on the grounds that it illicitly substitutes a contractual model of obligation for duties that should be seen as flowing "naturally" from the biological fact of parenthood, or because it cuts a child off from natural kinship relations and hence imperils the sense of belonging that seems so important to children and other family members.[1] Prenatal diagnostic techniques are faulted for their contribution to the development of a "quality control-consumer choice" orientation toward infants; quite apart from whatever social harm might be involved in terminating pregnancies on grounds of, for example, cleft palates or femaleness, the attitudes underlying such practices seem out of keeping with the spirit of loving acceptance that we like to associate with families, and that may in fact be key to some of the important psychological work done within them.[2]

These arguments may seem unpersuasive, vitiated by their reliance on what may appear an unrealistically romantic view of families, by the vagueness of their causal claims, and by a lack of clarity concerning just what practical response they demand. (Are we supposed to abolish the offending practices, or simply modify them so that they become more "family friendly"?) There is justice in all these concerns; yet without endorsing every claim made in its name, I am broadly sympathetic to what might be styled a family-sensitive line of critique. In my view, in fact, the full critical potential of taking families seriously has not yet been tapped.

The interactions between medicine and families are deeper than those forged in an infertility clinic or a surrogacy brokerage; families and medicine interact not just when reproduction is a problem, but continually. Characteristically, the two systems appeal to each other at just the points of each others' greatest vulnerability. Families turn to medicine when domestic ability to provide appropriate care for sick members is strained or exhausted, when new members join at birth, and when members leave at death. Medicine, for its part, typically turns to families when its own store of expertise reaches its limit, when it is time to determine not simply what *can* be done for a patient, but what, finally, *ought* to be done. But despite this multifaceted and familiar pattern of interaction between two institutions, relatively little careful attention has been devoted to its ethical dimensions.[3]

Here, I attend particularly to how families are affected, not by reproductive technologies, but by day-to-day patterns of medical practice, decision-making in particular. Succinctly stated, what I find is this: standard accounts of medical ethics obscure what is particularly morally significant about families. Medical practice, influenced by those accounts as well as by its own traditions, can dishonor, sometimes possibly erode, those morally important features. What I will propose in response is a modification of the received view of how medical decisionmaking ought to occur that is sensitive both to the important values featured by current practice, and to values arising out of intimate relationships that current practice neglects. But the concerns I raise do have implications for reproduction, confidentiality, indeed for the whole way in which we tend to think about the role of families in healing.

Moral deliberation about families is more than usually difficult. In part this is because the mere idea of the family is very much a politically contested notion, and hence discussions of the idea are often productive of more heat than light. For many, to invoke "family values" is to summon up a deeply conservative agenda, hostile in particular to women and to homosexual people. This, I think, is a concern worth taking seriously, but it is appropriately directed only at deficient analyses of family values. There is a regrettable tendency to slide from the defensible conviction that there is something valuable about the kinds of intimacy that can prevail in families to the unsupported conclusion that such value can only be realized if Dad's in the workplace and Mom's in the kitchen; there are, moreover, those who see family values as overriding any other moral considerations with which they may happen to conflict. But nothing said here will support the claim that one kind of family is morally canonical, nor that family values—whatever they may turn out to be—are moral trump cards. Rather, I want to get a clear account of the special moral value of intimacy squarely on the bioethical table. Families tend to be contexts that support such value, and tend as well to be the site at which medicine most often encounters intimacy. But my interest is really in the values inherent in (many) families, rather than in families *per se*. Further, the remarks below also hold in principle for relationships that may not count as families, but that do count as intimate—enduring relationships in which people's interests are complexly entwined, and in which people care deeply about each other.

This aim introduces the second and more substantial reason why demonstrating the significance of families is hard: the methods through which we most commonly advance and assess ethical claims are clumsy at illuminating what's morally important about intimacy. Departing boldly from how people actually live and feel, standard theoretical approaches to morality—including the understandings of Kant and Mill that are still *au courant* in the varieties of bioethical theory with the most impact on practice—are resolutely impartial, of the "everyone counts for one, nobody for more than one" stamp. In their vision, every moral agent is, at base, symmetrically positioned with respect to every morally considerable being—everyone's needs and interests have precisely the same pull on everyone else.[4] Considerations of efficiency may dictate that I focus my efforts on those who happen to live in my vicinity, and that you do the same, but this is a mere happenstance. The standard theories are inherently suspicious of the notion that something as particular and contingent as intimate relationships could really be of any deep moral importance in themselves.

Viewed through the lenses of impartiality, the unvarnished fact that someone happens to be, for example, your husband could hardly be a good reason for him to count as "more than one"—or, for that matter, less than one—to you.[5]

Like the theories that have nurtured it, bioethics does not typically operate with a conception of the significance of our ties to kin and kith rich enough to see clearly or assess appropriately the full range of ethical tensions that arise in the relationship between families and medicine. Not that we should be surprised by this; in addition to the impartialism of its theoretical foundations, the moral traditions of medical practice are also rather remote from common intuitions. They are downright austere when it comes to attributing significance to familial intimacy. Medicine's traditional values, while not suspicious of "special relationships" as such, have a somewhat restrictive slant on which relationships count: the doctor-patient relationship certainly is morally special, but this privilege does not extend to those with whom the patient is most closely related. Families may be important as sources of information about the desires of incompetent patients, or even as reservoirs of emotional support, but fundamentally they remain only a means to the patient's ends.

Both theoretical medical ethics as now most widely understood and medicine's own ethical tradition are ruggedly individualist: the interests of the individual patient, in splendid isolation from her social context, are to a considerable extent privileged. To be sure, there are powerful reasons for this focus, rooted in our concern about defending the vulnerability and privacy of patients. Yet there is increasing reason to believe that this intensity of focus on patient interests—considered as the interests of splendidly isolated individuals—reflects a kind of moral obtuseness, and that we would do better to design a system of medical decisionmaking sensitive to a broader range of values.

## WHY FAMILIES MATTER

Their variegated forms notwithstanding, familial and other intimate relationships are typically crucial for attaining or protecting much of what is widely valued about human beings and their projects. In this respect, well-functioning families are analogous to Rawls's "primary goods": like basic liberties, a decent income, and self-respect, the significance of families stems in part from their being important to the successful pursuit of *whatever* more individualized conceptions of a good life a person may cherish.[6] But only in part. Families aren't simply more or less efficient means to some independently specifiable good ends; they are also (at least oftentimes) valuable in themselves. On this point we have the testimony not only of our intuitions, which is not altogether to be despised, but also of reflection, which reveals something uncomfortably close to a paradox: if we think of families *exclusively* as of *instrumental value,* we greatly attenuate their ability to produce that instrumental value.

We're well accustomed to the idea that a child whose parents withhold affection from her is less likely to do well in life than a child whose parents are openly loving. But imagine a child whose parents *act* affectionately toward her, but only so as not to spoil her chances of worldly success. That this is hard to imagine tells us something already, but with some effort we can think of these parents as having internalized the "each counts for one" view. They are thus motivated by a disinterested sense of justice, a notion that *everyone* ought to have an equal opportunity for a good life. Imagine further that, valuing candor, these parents are perfectly open about the reason behind their caring actions.[7] This may be a kind of benevolence, but it is surely not love, because it lacks the inherently preferential character of love. Being prized above others is essential to being loved; being respected as one end-in-herself among other such ends is something quite different, and quite unlikely to have the same psy-chological advantages for the child as love would have (provided, perhaps, that she doesn't succeed in deceiving herself that her parents actually do love her for her own sake).

The moral is that it is only if we are prized for ourselves that we can reap the instrumental goods of being prized. This point is central to understanding why the moral structure of family relationships cannot merely be subsumed by moral theories such as utilitarianism. While it's quite natural to suspect that the good consequences of love simply show that strong individual preferences are consistent with maximizing the good of everyone impartially considered, to love someone involves a disposition to advance her interests (at least marginally) beyond what would be consistent with advancing the general good. If you are disposed, instead, to respond to the general good as soon as that margin is crossed, then your claim actually to love that person is dubious.[8] Intimate relationships often are productive of very significant consequences, but their mechanism for doing so is caught up with our tacit awareness of the fundamentally non-consequential character of their value.

## THE VULNERABILITY
## OF FAMILIAL VALUE

The morally distinctive features of life in families and other settings of intimacy are vulnerable in part because they express themselves in relationships whose structure is different from nonintimate relationships, and it is those nonintimate relationships that serve as the model for our moral reflections on how all relationships ought to be conducted. One of the features of family life—familial partiality, or our tendency to love our own children more than other people's, our own parents and spouses more than the parents and spouses of others—is both so familiar and so conspicuously out of step with standard moral theories that it has garnered a fair amount of attention.[9] But families also typically embody other departures from standard accounts of moral matters. By way of illustration, consider how "unpaternalistic" most parental behavior is. "Weak" paternalism, as typically treated in the literature, permits us to make judgments for incompetent others, even against their will. But such judgments must always be made strictly in the best interests of the affected party and are wound about with other safeguards: for example, the intervention must encroach as little as possible upon the dignity of the patient.[10] But in real life, parents often make decisions for their kids that are not endorsed by those children, many of which will have little or nothing to do with the children's best interests. Parents often, for example, expose their children to small risks of serious harm for the parents' ends, not the children's—recall the last time you made your toddler accompany you on a car ride through snowy streets to pick up wine for dinner guests. Nor is the "paternalism" always of a "weak" variety: we may insist that our children attend a certain church with us, or avoid a certain kind of entertainment, but we cannot justify this because they are incompetent to understand their own interests in the matter, at least as "understanding interests" would be taken in a "secular" context. Are we really in any position to demonstrate that there is indeed a God, and that God is willing for children to be bored for an hour every Sunday? Or that watching MTV erodes character more seriously than peer acceptance bolsters it? Rather, parents intervene in their children's lives on the basis of undemonstrable views that there are things that matter apart from a child's own interest, and this is often precisely what they are trying to convey by means of the intervention.

These may seem trivial illustrations, but they do serve to show that families not only generally prize their members above others, but also distribute burdens and benefits to their members in ways that differ from the strictures imposed by a more general morality. They also prepare us to appreciate a conflict with patterns of medical practice.

In families, the interests of some members sometimes give way to the interests of others, or to the interests of the family as a whole. Put thus, this observation may seem just a condition of social living, and nothing having much special to do with families at all. In fact, it may seem a simple consequence of finitude: *individuals* often have different and incompatible desires and interests, some of which have to give way to others. But what's interesting is how our response to this fact differs from context to context.

Social distribution of benefits and burdens, duties and opportunities, must accord with some defensible conception of distributive justice. Assigning personal resources and priorities to one's own interests is a different matter. The difference is that in the first-person case I may pattern my own distribution to pursue ends that would not be chosen by everyone behind a veil of ignorance, or that do not maximize utilities; my decisions about what to do with my life may reflect practices and projects that appeal to me quite individually. This point is most often supported by appeal to how our own fundamental projects serve as sources of meaning, definition, and character. As Bernard Williams has maintained, "There can come a point at which it is quite unreasonable for a man to give up, in the name of the impartial good ordering of the world of moral agents, something which is a condition of his having any interest in being around in that world at all."[11] A life in which a person directs all her energies at maximizing the overall utility, or indeed at any general aim, is a life seriously depleted in ways we regard as profoundly important. It is a life without any deep loyalties, and without the personal commitment that is central to love.

So too, the way in which families choose their projects, distribute their energies, and assign their burdens and benefits may serve goals other than those picked out by general theories of justice: these particularities constitute how families distinguish themselves, how they become more than simply units of economic transfer. They express what might be regarded as familial character, as those reasons for which people have the deep and abiding interest they do in forming and maintaining families. For instance, a family may encourage and support music lessons but not karate lessons, despite the ostensible injustice in the circumstance that all the girls like music and the boys like karate, on the grounds that family traditions and convictions elevate music over martial arts.

This is not, it should be underscored, an argument that within families anything goes, that whatever kind of abuse a family might practice could be justified if somehow it could be related to "traditions" or a family's "sense of itself"; neither would Williams argue that considerations of personal character and integrity allow an individual to act as a thoroughgoing egoist. But it does bring to our attention an important and commonly shared part of life that has an ambiguous relationship with much of standard moral thinking—we might call it the importance of the intimate. Recognizing that the concerns of intimacy can have a legitimate call upon the way a person lives makes of morality a messier thing, but if that mess were cleaned up, much of significant human value would be lost.

## MEDICAL DECISIONMAKING AS IF RELATIONSHIPS MATTERED

I want now to discuss how recognizing the importance of the intimate should make medical decisionmaking a messier thing as well. John Hardwig began this project in an important paper in which he underscores the significance for medical ethics of a plain but oddly neglected fact: families—and intimates in general—share important interests. A major decision affecting the lot of one is very likely going to redound in important ways on the lot of others. Given this incontrovertible fact, how can physicians, medical ethicists, lawyers justify officially excluding those others from playing a significant role in decisionmaking?

Hardwig's work makes it very plausible that the presumption in favor of patient-centeredness, despite its dogmatic status, faces a heavy burden of proof. As he says, "I am a husband, a father, and still a son, and no one would argue that I should or even responsibly could decide to take a sabbatical, another job, or even a weekend trip, *solely* on the basis of what I want for myself. Why should decisions about my medical treatment be different?"[12]

The answer to this question that first comes to mind is this: Patients are especially vulnerable. They are ill, and they have been extracted from their homes and inserted into an institutional, unfamiliar context; they are not in a position to defend their own interests fairly. (What has already been said about the complexity of balancing familial and individual interests only adds to this problem.) Further, the consequences of treatment decisions affect them in a particularly concrete and vivid way; if a given treatment is withheld in favor of another more acceptable to the family as a whole, or in favor of no treatment whatever, the patient will suffer the consequences, not solely in her pocketbook or in her feelings, but in her body.

Hardwig has sensibly replied that while such considerations underscore the significance of fairly and fully representing patient interests in decisionmaking, they do not disenfranchise the interests of others. That has to be allowed, I think—which makes one wonder what kind of considerations *might* effectively disenfranchise other stakeholders.

It might be alleged that there is a difference in kind, not just in degree, between the interests of the patient and those of her intimates, and that such a difference justifies disenfranchising the family. Consider that if familial authority is extended to the point at which treatment can be imposed on a patient, then we must set aside our particularly strong moral aversions to penetrating a person's body without her or his own consent.

Perhaps this is just the point at which any reasonable attempt to insert the family more centrally into medical decisionmaking should temper its ambitions. For practical, as well as ethical reasons, a patient's own consent to an offered treatment will be necessary; only in the most unusual circumstances could it be justifiable to force treatment on a competent patient who flat-out rejects the intervention. But the proposal to allow significant familial input into authorizing or refusing offered treatment that is desired by the patient, while reserving to her the right to refuse unwanted interventions, is not so tidy as it may at first appear.

Imagine a patient suffering from a kidney stone. She would prefer to have the stone removed via lithotripsy, a benign, noninvasive, but very expensive procedure; her family, whose insurance does not cover lithotripsy, is certainly anxious that she receive the best care, but is also very concerned about the $12,000 or so the procedure would cost. While the money is in the bank to be drawn upon, it represents many joint sacrifices over a period of years to save up for a downpayment on a house in a neighborhood distinguished by the quality of its schools—education has always been an important family priority. Insurance will cover the more traditional procedure, which is safe and effective but does involve anesthesia and the insertion of a catheter through the urethra. If the family's interest in enhancing educational opportunity is allowed to prevail over the patient's interest in lithotripsy, then it is hard to say that the patient's acceptance of the violation of her physical integrity is an instance of a fully free and informed consent. Cases like this somewhat blur the distinction we might be tempted to make between a family's special

stake in authorizing treatment that will have negative effects on the family as a whole, and the patient's special prerogative to refuse any unwanted intervention in her body.

In my view, the moral significance of both Hardwig's argument and these considerations about vulnerability and personal privacy and integrity must be acknowledged; in theory, neither clearly trumps the other. But it is hard to figure out just what this should come to in practice. Ought we to stick with the status quo, or might Hardwig's view be bolstered until the balance is tipped in its favor?

Note that Hardwig's position makes no special appeal to the kinds of arguments that formed the opening sections of this paper. Can looking at family relationships not simply as an aggregate of overlapping and mutually affecting interests, but in their character as contexts of intimacy, add weight to the claim that medical decisionmaking ought to include family interests more explicitly?

Adding intimacy concerns expressly brings another player to the table: we have not only a potential clash of individual concerns (this, indeed, is arguably the case in any medical intervention, given the present climate of fiscal scarcity), but also a clash between the interests of individuals and the interests they share as members of a family. Whatever decision is arrived at will say something about what the involved parties think about the importance of their familial intimacy and of the projects, aims, and traditions in which it is expressed.

As the economic character of the lithotripsy example may obscure the significance of the "family traditions" point, let's return to our family that values music over martial arts and add some substance to its story. The significance they see in music is not a mere preference; if anything brief could capture what music means to this family, it might be the motto Bach inscribed in his *Little Organ Book:* "To the greater glory of God, and that my neighbor may be benefited thereby." Part of this family tradition, which spans several generations, is the making of *Haus-musik,* at which they are very skilled. Unfortunately, there is also a history of breast cancer in the family, and it is calculated that the women face an above normal risk of developing the disease themselves—say, along the order of 4 chances in 1,000 per year. This makes them eligible to enroll in a randomized clinical trial of tamoxifen, a drug that has been useful in treating postmenopausal women with breast cancer and whose prophylactic properties are currently under investigation. Barbara, now a junior in college but still much involved in family life, is inclined to accept the invitation to participate in the trial, but there is a side effect that is of special concern to her family—tamoxifen may cause vocal changes, lowering pitch by as much as one octave. Enrolling in the trial, therefore, could spell the end of her pivotal role in the family's music-making.[13]

The considerations of honoring family values and traditions that emerge in this case seem to me to strengthen Hardwig's contention that the patient generally has a moral duty to consider the impact of treatment options on the family: there is a sense in which families, as well as family members, have interests affected by what will happen as a result of treatment or similar decisions, and these interests are such that the patient has a special moral reason to consider them. The value of music to this family is not an aggregate of the value that each member places on it; rather, part of the reason they value music is as an expression of what is significant and distinctive about what they share in common. If a family member takes steps to remove herself from this shared endeavor, the value of what's left is reduced by a disproportionate degree. This of course does not amount to a strict prohibition for members of this family of anything inimical to music, but it does suggest what kind of harm to others is involved in the action being contemplated; the character of the family, not merely the individual interests of family members, is at risk.

But what remains to be determined is the impact of this line of reasoning on how the structures and procedures of health care should be shaped. Should the urologist, in explaining the lithotripsy procedure, require that the patient get her *family's* explicit consent before the procedure can occur? Should an IRB mandate that families of research subjects also agree to their participation in protocols?

The critical point of such questions can be felt more vividly if we return to Hardwig's illustrations: no one, he tells us, would think him morally responsible if he decided simply to take another job without involving his family in the decision. And that, I think, is clearly right, although different members of the family would be involved in different ways. But imagine two conclusions to the interview. In one, the dean of the university offering Hardwig a chair says, "Of course, we understand that you may not be able to let us know before you've talked things through with your family." In the alternative scenario, the dean says, "Of course, you'll have to have your family's consent before we can officially allow you to accept the job."

Of course, deans don't act that way—why ever should doctors? The difference is that medicine's intolerance of intimacy, unlike that of other institutions, strives to disenfranchise families, challenges their standing, and teaches them that their efforts to balance their rich array of values is inappropriate. Were Hardwig, against his own strong inclinations, to decline the chair, citing familial considerations, the dean would have no choice but to accede; academic ethics does not officially regard familial interests as impertinent. But if the urologist's patient were to say, "I'd much prefer lithotripsy, but my family is so against using the money that way that I guess I'll have to go along with the surgery," it is far from clear that the urologist has what counts as a free and informed consent, and therefore lacks what her professional ethics construes as the authorization for an invasive procedure. The message that familial interests are strictly out of bounds is even stronger if someone serves as a proxy decisionmaker for an incompetent family member.

Whether medicine can reverse this message then becomes a question of whether structures can be developed that more appropriately accommodate the values of affected intimates while at the same time preserving to an acceptable degree the values protected by patient-centeredness. Hardwig favors moving the locus of decisionmaking in such cases from the patient to the "family conference"; presumably, given his account, deliberations there would be guided by a "presumption of equality" in which "the interests of patients and family members are morally to be weighed equally."[14] While I certainly endorse such conferences, the rub comes when mutual exploration of differences and attempts at persuasion, consensus, or compromise fail. Letting families decide becomes problematic if they cannot find a single voice.

In such instances, it is reasonable for health care providers to presume that the consent of the patient is necessary and sufficient to authorize offered treatment; as a rule, her interests will be most at stake, and her position most vulnerable. But the importance of the interests of intimates strongly suggests that the presumption ought to be regarded as defeasible, rather than absolute. If mediation is unavailing, then a family should have the option of challenging patient authorization; this, of course, necessitates that there be some mechanism for assessing the challenge.

Such mechanisms do not presently exist, although ethics committees might be regarded as their embryonic versions. Changes in law, as well as institutional structure, would be necessary if a patient's treatment authorization were to be regarded as no more than a rebuttable presumption in her favor. But health care workers shouldn't wait on the law; they face the same moral challenge now as they would should such changes be made. Family interests are not impertinent to medical decisionmaking; they ought to be heard

and paid due heed, and conflicts met with efforts to mediate, to facilitate consensus, or to forge acceptable compromise. This sort of change in the culture of health care doesn't go far enough toward taking families with appropriate seriousness, but it's a significant step along the way.

## INCOMPETENCE AND INTIMACY

A fully realized theory can't be provided here, but the outlines of what taking families seriously might mean in cases where patients lack the ability to represent themselves in decisionmaking can be sketched. The prevailing orthodoxy is that the preferences of incompetent patients, as memorialized in treatment directives or entrusted to specifically designated surrogates, should prevail. In the absence of explicit directives, the appeal is to substituted judgment, in which patient preferences are reconstructed from general knowledge of patient desires, beliefs, and character. If neither avenue is open, then decisionmakers must fall back on a "best interests of the patient" standard. But despite the broad consensus on this view of the matter, criticism has not been wholly absent.

Nancy Rhoden has argued that the families of decisionally incapacitated patients who lack advance directives ought to be presumed to have authority to make treatment decisions, without having to shoulder the burden of demonstrating that termination decisions meet substituted judgment or best interest criteria. However, she stops short of allowing any role to interests of families or family members that might conflict with patient interests.[15] Hardwig argues that the interests of family proxy decisionmakers are perfectly pertinent to decisionmaking even for incompetent patients who possess advance directives.[16]

My own view is that Rhoden is too timid and Hardwig a shade too bold; the preferences of a patient, as expressed in an advance directive, ought to enjoy the same rebuttable presumption of authority, and hence, in principle, to be open to the same process of challenge and response, as would the contemporaneous decisions of the competent patient. The difficulty, of course, is fairly conducting such a process in the absence of the patient as a participant. However, as matters currently stand, conflicts between incompetent patients and their families, like conflicts among family members, should be mediated to the extent possible, with the interests of the incompetent patient being represented by an advocate, preferably the patient's own chosen proxy. It would be the advocate's task to represent her principal as a person, not simply as a self-interest maximizer, and hence as someone capable of some degree of compromise and altruism, and as someone whose interests are not necessarily altogether estranged from those of her family.

As contrasted with persuasion and compromise, directly overturning clear patient preferences, while justifiable in theory, probably needs to be preceded by the evolution and testing of mechanisms designed to make such adjudications in the case of competent patients. While there is a tendency to regard the interests of the incompetent as attenuated, thus leaving more "room" for familial and social interests to operate,[17] it must also be borne in mind that not all incompetent patients lack robust interests, and that they are particularly vulnerable to what others do. If, after all, the patient's vulnerability is one of the chief props of the "patient-centered" view, we should be hesitant about starting major revisions in the current system with decisionally incapacitated—and hence particularly vulnerable—patients.

If the patient had not executed any explicit advance directive, and family members are charged with providing a sense of what the patient's expressed preferences would have been, it is reasonable to encourage them to try to distinguish between what the patient would have wanted for herself and what is in the best interests of the family, without telling them that the family considerations need be identified only to be dismissed. If there is a divergence between patient and family preferences, then the incompetent patient, like the competent, ought to enjoy a rebuttable presumption in her favor. While the primary motivation for this system is to honor all the legitimate interests involved in treatment decisions, it shouldn't be overlooked that it could well more fully protect the interests of incompetent patients than does the current procedure. If families are encouraged to identify their own stake in treatment decisions, and promised help in ameliorating conflicts, any tendency to couch family-regarding considerations in individual-patient centered terms may be lessened.

## ASSESSING THE FAMILY-SENSITIVE PROPOSAL

The restructuring of medical decisionmaking proposed here clearly presupposes a certain picture of both family and patient: disagreeing without being sundered from each other; able to deliberate about disagreement, and to share decisionmaking. Many families involved in health care will fit this picture tolerably well, but many won't, and a full-blown theory of the role of families in medical decisionmaking would need to take carefully into account the variety of ways in which families and patients diverge from this paradigm. And the proposal surely has its liabilities: it is a less simple system than one that privileges the patient, and it trusts to human judgment matters that may be of great consequence for vulnerable people, and that may hinge on subtle factors. It is, I suppose, also arguable that the very knowledge that a patient's advance directive might be overturned by the interests of others could exert a chilling effect on the use of such mechanisms at all (although it could still be asserted that the advance directive offers the patient as much assurance that her decisions will be enacted against family dissent as would be the case if she were competent).

At the same time, the system has a great advantage: it does not simply turn its back on concerns of great moral significance. And seen against the background of an overall attempt on the part of medicine to regard a patient's intimate relationships as more than merely instrumental, it may actually nourish a sense on the part of patients that their encounter with medicine need not be so "unfamiliar," that the emotional ties that sustain us in health can follow us into the domain of illness, where, if anything, we need them more than ever.

## ACKNOWLEDGMENTS

Members of the Hastings Center project on the Family and Bioethics have been extremely helpful to me in working out the themes of this essay; I am particularly grateful to John Hardwig, William Aiken, Jeffrey Blustein, and Hilde L. Nelson. The project on the Family and Bioethics was supported by a grant from the Esther A. and Joseph Klingenstein Fund, Inc.

### REFERENCES

1. See, for example, Ruth Macklin, "Artificial Means of Reproduction and Our Understanding of the Family," *Hastings Center Report* 21, no. 1 (1991): 5–11, for an overview of concerns; Sidney Callahan's "Ethical Challenge of the New Reproductive Technology," in *Medical Ethics: A Guide for Health Care Professionals,* ed. John F. Monagle and David C. Thomasma (Frederick, Md.: Aspen Publishers, 1987), pp. 26–37, for concerns about children of the new reproductive technologies being alienated from their heritage; and Hilde Lindemann Nelson and James Lindemann Nelson, "Cutting Motherhood in Two: Some Suspicions Concerning Surrogacy," *Hypatia* 4, no. 3 (1989): 85–94, for concerns about the contractual character of parental obligation assumed in surrogacy arrangements.

2. See, for instance, Barbara Katz Rothman's *Tentative Pregnancy: Prenatal Diagnosis and the Future of Motherhood* (New York: Viking-Penguin, 1986).

3. Among the several writers who are taking the family seriously as a bioethical category of analysis, Ferdinand Schoeman, John Hardwig, and William Ruddick are prominent. See, for example, Schoeman's "Parental Discretion and Children's Rights: Background and Implication for Medical Decision Making," *Journal of Medicine and Philosophy* 10 (1985): 45–61; Hardwig's "What About the Family?" *Hastings Center Report* 20, no. 2 (1990): 5–10; and Ruddick's "Are Fetuses Becoming Children?" in *Biomedical Ethics and Fetal Therapy,* ed. Carl Nimrod and Glenn Greiner (Calgary: Wilfrid Laurier University Press, 1988), pp. 107–18.

4. For an interesting discussion of "equal pull" versus "differential pull" moral theories, see Christina Hoff Sommers, "Filial Morality," *Journal of Philosophy* 83, no. 8 (1986): 439–56.

5. See Bernard Williams's well-known discussion of the man who decided that impartial morality allowed him to save his wife in preference to others on the grounds that she was his wife, and it is permissible in such situations for husbands to save their wives first. In Williams's view, this man had a "thought too many." The discussion occurs in his "Persons, Character, and Morality," in *Moral Luck* (Cambridge: Cambridge University Press, 1981), pp. 1–19.

6. Rawls discusses primary goods throughout *A Theory of Justice* (Cambridge, Mass.: Harvard University Press, 1971); the notion is introduced on page 62.

7. See Lawrence Blum's discussion of the goods conveyed by the altruistic emotions in his *Friendship, Altruism and Morality* (Boston: Routledge and Kegan Paul, 1980).

8. This point is discussed in greater detail in James Lindemann Nelson, "Partialism and Parenthood," *Journal of Social Philosophy* 21, no. 1 (1990): 107–18.

9. See, for instance, John Cottingham, "Partialism, Favouritism and Morality," *Philosophical Quarterly* 36 (1986); 357–73.

10. For an excellent discussion of these conditions, see James F. Childress, *Deciding for Others* (New York: Oxford University Press, 1982).

11. Williams, "Persons, Character and Morality," p. 14.

12. Hardwig, "What About the Family?" p. 6.

13. Adapted from the account of British tamoxifen trials related in Richard H. Nicholson, "Paternalism No Problem," *Hastings Center Report* 22, no. 2 (1992): 4–5. See also "MRC to Go Ahead with Con-

troversial Tamoxifen Trial?" *Bulletin of Medical Ethics,* no. 72 (October 1991), pp. 3–5.

14. Hardwig, "What About the Family?" p. 7.

15. Nancy Rhoden, "Litigating Life and Death," *Harvard Law Review* 192, no. 2 (1988): 375–446. See especially n. 114.

16. John Hardwig, "The Problem of Proxies with Interests of Their Own: Toward a Better Theory of Proxy Decisions," *Journal of Clinical Ethics* (1993) 4 (1): 20–27.

17. See, for example, Rebecca Dresser, "Life, Death, and Incompetent Patients: Conceptual Infirmities and Hidden Values in the Law," *Arizona Law Review* 28, no. 3 (1986): 373–405.

# Sample Statement of Patient's Preferences [1]

To my Doctor:

While I have been at _____, I have discussed my wishes concerning my medical treatment in the event that I become extremely ill. I did this in the hope that if I made my wishes known beforehand, it would be easier for my doctors to know my preferences at a time when I am unable to express them.

If I become critically ill:

I want to be hospitalized.
I want to go into intensive care.
I want to have my heart revived if my heart stops.
I want to have surgery.
I want to be put on a breathing machine.

If I become terminally ill:

I want to be hospitalized.
I want my family members to decide whether I shall go into intensive care after they talk with my doctor.
I want my doctor to decide whether to revive me if my heart stops.
I want my family members to decide whether I shall have surgery after they talk with my doctor.
I want my family members to decide whether I shall be put on a breathing machine after they talk with my doctor.

If I am in an irreversible coma:

I want to be hospitalized.
I want my family members to decide whether I shall go into intensive care after they talk with my doctor.
I want my doctor to decide whether to revive me if my heart stops.
I want my family members to decide whether I shall have surgery after they talk with my doctor.

1. From M. Danis et al., "Prospective Study of Advance Directives for Life-Sustaining Care."

I do not want to be put on a breathing machine.

I want my family members to decide whether I shall be fed through a tube after they talk with my doctor.

If I am unable to make decisions for myself, I would like the following person to make necessary decisions on my behalf:

1. Name (relationship):
Address:
Phone: (home)        (work)

If you cannot reach _____, I would like the following person to make necessary decisions on my behalf:

2. Name (relationship):
Address:
Phone: (home)        (work)

There will be a time when I want my doctor to stop keeping me alive.

I have provided this information in the hope that it will be easier to respect my wishes about my medical care at a time when I am unable to express them.

Patient (name printed)     (signature)     (date)
Witness (name printed)    (signature)     (date)

# Durable Power of Attorney[2]

[Explanations and instructions omitted.]

1. CREATION OF DURABLE POWER OF ATTORNEY
   FOR HEALTH CARE
   By this document I intend to create a durable power of attorney by appointing the person designated below to make health care decisions for me as allowed by the California Civil Code. This power of attorney shall not be affected by my subsequent incapacity.
2. DESIGNATION OF HEALTH CARE AGENT
   (Your attorney-in-fact, i.e., your agent, must be an adult and a California resident. Insert the name, address, and telephone number of the person you wish to designate as your agent to make health care decisions for you. None of the following may be designated as your agent: (1) your treating health care provider, (2) an employee of your treating health care provider, (3) an operator of a community health care facility, or (4) an employee of an operator of a

2. Excerpted from the California Civil Code, sections 2410–2443; reproduced in Buchanan and Brock, *Deciding for Others,* 374–86.

community health care facility. For example, your agent may not be your physician, your nurse, an employee of your nursing home, or an operator of a board and care home.)

I, _____, do hereby designate and appoint:

    Name:

    Address:

    Telephone Number:

as my agent to make health care decisions for me as authorized in this document.

3. GENERAL STATEMENT OF AUTHORITY GRANTED

If I become incapable of giving informed consent with respect to health care decisions, I hereby grant to my agent full power and authority to make health care decisions for me including: consent, refusal of consent, or withdrawal of consent to any care, treatment, service, or procedure to maintain, diagnose, or treat a physical or mental condition, and to receive and to consent to the release of medical information, subject to the limitations and special provisions, set forth in Paragraph 6 below.

4. CONTRIBUTION OF ANATOMICAL GIFT

(You may choose to make a gift of all or part of your body to a hospital, physician, or medical school, for scientific, educational, therapeutic, or transplant purposes. Such a gift is allowed by California's Uniform Anatomical Gift Act. If you do not make such a gift, you may authorize your agent to do so, or a member of your family may make a gift unless you give them notice that you do not want a gift made. In the space below you may make a gift yourself or state that you do not want to make a gift. If you do not complete this section, your agent will have the authority to make a gift of all or part of your body under the Uniform Anatomical Gift Act.)

If either statement reflects your desires, sign the box next to the statement. You do not have to sign either statement. If you do not sign either statement, your agent and your family will have the authority to make a gift of all or part of your body under the Uniform Anatomical Gift Act.

(_____) Pursuant to the Uniform Anatomical Gift Act, I hereby give, effective upon my death:

☐   Any needed organ or parts; or

☐   The parts or organs listed: _____

_____

(_____) I do not want to make a gift under the Uniform Anatomical Gift Act, nor do I want my agent or family to do so.

5. SPECIAL PROVISIONS AND LIMITATIONS

(By law, your agent is not permitted to consent to any of the following: commitment to or placement in a mental health treatment facility, convulsive treatment, psychosurgery, sterilization, or abortion. In every other respect, your agent may make health care decisions for you to the same extent that you could make them for yourself if you were capable of doing so. If there are any special restrictions you wish to place on your agent's authority, you should list them in the space below. If you do not write in any limitations, your agent will have the broad powers to make health care decisions on your behalf which are set forth in Paragraph 3, except to the extent that there are limits provided by law.)

In exercising the authority under this durable power of attorney for health care, the authority of my attorney-in-fact is subject to the following special provisions and limitations:

6. DESIGNATION OF AN ALTERNATIVE AGENT

(You are not required to designate any alternative agents but you may do so. Any alternative agent must meet the requirements set forth in Paragraph 2 above. Any alternative agent you designate will be able to make the same health care decisions as the agent designated in Paragraph 2 above in the event that he or she is unable or unwilling to act as your agent. Also, if the agent designated in Paragraph 2 is your spouse, his or her designation as your agent is automatically revoked by law if your marriage is dissolved.)

If the person designated in Paragraph 2 as my agent is unable to make health care decisions for me or is disqualified by law from so doing, then I designate the following persons to serve as my agent to make health care decisions for me as authorized in this document, such persons to serve in the order listed below:

    A. First Alternative Agent
       Name:
       Address:
       Telephone Number:
    B. Second Alternative Agent
       Name:
       Address:
       Telephone Number:

7. DURATION

I understand that this power of attorney will exist for seven years from the date I execute this document unless I establish a shorter time. If I am unable to make health care decisions for myself when this power of attorney expires, the authority I have granted my agent will continue to exist until the time when I become able to make health care decisions for myself.

(Optional) I wish to have this power of attorney end before seven years on the following date: _____.

8. PRIOR DESIGNATION REVOKED

I revoke any prior durable power of attorney for health care.

(YOU MUST DATE AND SIGN THIS POWER OF ATTORNEY)

I sign my name to this Durable Power of Attorney for Health Care on

_____ (Date) at _____ (City),

_____ (State).

_____ (Signature)

THIS POWER OF ATTORNEY WILL NOT BE VALID FOR MAKING HEALTH CARE DECISIONS UNLESS IT IS EITHER (1) ACKNOWL-EDGED BEFORE A NOTARY PUBLIC IN CALIFORNIA OR (2) SIGNED

BY AT LEAST TWO QUALIFIED WITNESSES WHO PERSONALLY
KNOW YOU AND ARE PRESENT WHEN YOU SIGN OR ACKNOWL-
EDGE YOUR SIGNATURE.
[Statements of notary public and witnesses omitted.]


## Discussion Questions

1. In their discussion of the "daughter from California syndrome," Molloy and colleagues offer suggestions about how decisions should be made for an incompetent patient. In the first item in their Table 1, they make no reference to instances in which an advance directive can be overridden. Others have argued, however, that advance directives may sometimes be overridden by other considerations. Think about what these considerations might be and rewrite the first item in Molloy and colleagues' Table 1 to reflect this.
2. Suppose a young and very athletic woman has an accident in which her foot is so badly crushed that it must be amputated. The patient refuses this amputation, however, insisting that her foot somehow be saved. The physician is unable to convince her that saving the foot is impossible; meanwhile, the surgery has been delayed, and the crushed foot is now dangerously infected. If the patient does not accept treatment soon, her entire leg may be lost; if this standoff continues, her condition could even become life threatening. And yet she refuses all treatment except that which is intended to save her foot; she says that if she cannot participate in all her accustomed activities, life would not be worth living. At this point the toxins from the infected foot render her delirious, and a family member is asked to make medical decisions on her behalf. What should the surrogate do? What moral obligations conflict with the obligation to respect autonomy in this case?
3. Strokes, dementia, and other medical circumstances can greatly change a patient's personality, preferences, and so forth; in fact, there seems to be some significant sense in which such a patient is no longer the same person he or she used to be. Even so, an advance directive executed by the patient's "former self" would continue to guide the medical care for the "new self" this patient has become; this would be the case even if the treatment specified in the directive is not in accordance with this "new person's" wishes. Could such changes in personhood ever provide an adequate justification for disregarding an advance directive? How much authority do you have to decide about what will happen to the person you may one day become?


## Suggestions for Further Reading

### FORMAL ADVANCE DIRECTIVES

Emanuel, L., and E. Emanuel. "The Medical Directive: A New Comprehensive Advance Care Document." *Journal of the American Medical Association* 261, no. 22 (1989): 3288–93.
  This presents a common format for advance directives, along with instructions about how these documents are to be used.
Emanuel, L., et al. "Advance Directives: Can Patients' Stated Treatment Choices Be Used to Infer Unstated Choices?" *Medical Care* 32, no. 2 (1994): 95–105.
  This empirical investigation reveals ways in which some of the limits of advance directives can be overcome. The best predictors of unstated choices turn out to be things frequently omitted from directives.

Hastings Center Special Supplement. "Advance Care Planning: Priorities for Ethical and Empirical Research." *Hastings Center Report* 24, no. 6 (1994): S1–S36.

>Twelve articles by various authors consider the strengths and shortcomings of advance directives and pose questions we must address in making headway in advance care planning.

Robertson, J. "Second Thoughts on Living Wills." *Hastings Center Report* 21, no. 6 (1991): 6–12.

>Advance directives often lead surrogate decision makers to ignore the patient's present interests; this article explains how one's interests change when competence is lost and shows how living wills can undermine them.

## PATIENT SELF-DETERMINATION ACT

Emanuel, E., et al. "How Well Is the Patient Self-Determination Act Working: An Early Assessment." *American Journal of Medicine* 95 (1993): 619–28.

>This report of an empirical study shows how patients' planning for health care has been changed by the PSDA. Important shortcomings in this legislation are explained.

Hastings Center Special Supplement. "Practicing the PSDA: Selected Resources in Patient Self-Determination." *Hastings Center Report* 21, no. 5 (1991): S1–S16.

>Ten articles by various authors explore how physicians, patients, and ethicists regard this important legislation. Many of the practical difficulties with the PSDA are noted, and related ethical issues are discussed.

## SURROGATE DECISION MAKING

Blustein, Jeffrey. "Choosing for Others as Continuing a Life Story: The Problem of Personal Identity Revisited." *Journal of Law, Medicine, and Ethics* 27, no. 1 (spring 1999): 20 ff. *Infotrac Power Search #A54700011.*

>The article addresses general guidelines for surrogates to follow and the nature of personal identity.

Buchanan, Allen E., and Dan W. Brock. *Deciding for Others: The Ethics of Surrogate Decision Making.* (Cambridge and New York: Cambridge University Press, 1990).

>This detailed examination includes discussion of the ethical underpinnings of surrogate decisions, as well as a consideration of competence, guidance principles, exceptions, and common problems.

## CONFLICTS OF INTEREST

Bopp, James, and Richard Coleson. "A Critique of Family Members as Proxy Decisionmakers without Legal Limits." *Issues in Law and Medicine* 12, 2 (Fall 1996): 133–65. *Infotrac Power Search #A18880085.*

Jecker, N. "The Role of Intimate Others in Medical Decision Making." *Gerontologist* 30, no. 1 (1990): 65–71.

>In an attempt to bring our emphasis on individual autonomy back into proper balance, Jecker argues that families have a significant role to play in making treatment decisions.

Lynn, J. "Conflicts of Interest in Medical Decision-Making." *Journal of the American Geriatrics Society* 36, 10 (1988): 945–50.

>Conflicts within the family, patient and physician ambivalence, and conflicts with the health care system are all discussed, and suggestions are made for resolving them.

Nelson, J. "Taking Families Seriously." *Hastings Center Report* 22, no. 4 (1992): 6–12.

>When making treatment decisions, patients have a moral obligation to bear in mind the needs and interests of family members.

GENERAL

Brock, D., and S. Wartman. "When Competent Patients Make Irrational Decisions." *New England Journal of Medicine* 322, no. 22 (1990): 1595–99.

The authors argue that even the irrational choices of competent patients must be respected if the patients cannot be persuaded to change them.

Powell, Tia. "Extubating Mrs. K.: Psychological Aspects of Surrogate Decision Making." *Journal of Law, Medicine, and Ethics* 27, no. 1 (Spring 1999): 81 ff. *Infotrac Power Search #A54700018.*

President's Commission for the Study of Ethical Problems in Medicine and Biomedical and Behavioral Research. *Deciding to Forgo Life-Sustaining Treatment.* Washington, D.C.: Government Printing Office, 1983.

The decision to forgo treatment is given closer attention. Competence, legal authority, medical complications, and other issues are discussed.

President's Commission for the Study of Ethical Problems in Medicine and Biomedical and Behavioral Research, *Making Health Care Decisions.* Vol. 1. *A Report on the Ethical and Legal Implications of Informed Consent in the Patient-Practitioner Relationship.* Washington, D.C.: Government Printing Office, 1982.

All of the important aspects of surrogate decision making are covered, including the legal and ethical underpinnings and standard procedures. The President's Commission tends to be rather conservative and allows no room for compromise between the patient's interests and the interests of family members.

# Section 4

## *Futility and Fighting Death*

## Introduction

There are times when patients, families, or physicians ask themselves whether a certain medical intervention will really do any good. They might ask whether its benefits outweigh its harms, or whether there is a good enough chance that it will yield the desired outcome, or whether that outcome is really worth pursuing. These and related questions are often framed in terms of futility, and judging that a treatment is futile is generally used as a reason for withholding or withdrawing that treatment. This issue is surprisingly complex, however, and is linked in vital ways to the goals and values that underlie one's medical care.

### *Futility Is Relative*

Defining futility is complicated. To begin with, we can say that a futile treatment is one that does not work or is not worth trying. Notice, however, that this brings up the question of what one is trying to accomplish with the treatment and what chances one thinks are worth taking. One important consequence of this is that one cannot determine on purely medical grounds whether a given treatment is futile in a given case. In fact, it is possible for there to be two patients in the same medical circumstances who receive the same treatment and get the same results (as described in medical terms), but the treatment will have been effective in one case and futile in the other. This is because these patients may have widely different goals. One patient's goal may have been to avoid further declines in her medical status, and the treatment

101

may have achieved this (making it effective with respect to this goal). But the other patient may have wanted to return to her pre-morbid level of functioning, and the treatment may have had little or no chance of bringing this about (making the treatment futile with respect to this goal).

Strictly speaking, treatments are never simply futile, period; rather, they are always futile (or effective, which is the flip side of futility) with respect to some goal.[1] Just what this goal is can differ greatly from one person to the next. One common goal is being returned to health and a high level of functioning; others include being free of pain or disease, or perhaps just continuing to breathe and have a pulse. Thus, a treatment may be effective in one respect but futile in another. For instance, a ventilator used in caring for a patient in a persistent vegetative state (PVS) would be effective with respect to the goal of keeping that person's body warm and tissues pink, but futile with respect to the goal of returning that person to consciousness. The patient, family, and physician may have different goals in mind for the patient's treatment and so may disagree about whether a particular intervention is futile.

A common goal of medical treatment is to restore the patient to health, but in cases of chronic illness, this goal needs to be revised. Then medicine's goal becomes assisting the patient in accommodating him- or herself to the disease, a process that in the case of degenerative diseases involves frequent adjustments. Thus,

> healing involves restoring, or preserving, a sense of equanimity and personal integrity in the face of the many and varied disturbances in living that are necessarily caused by illness. In the context of chronic illness, this means learning to live well in the presence (rather than absence) of physical or mental incapacity, recognizing that such disorder is a way of life.[2]

It is important to bear this set of goals in mind with respect to which treatments of patients with chronic illnesses might be effective or futile.

Because values and goals play this central role in determinations of futility, futility judgments are not purely empirical claims. Stuart Youngner points out that

> [a]side from rare instances in which clinical studies identify treatment interventions that have no chance of achieving the physiologic ends for which they were designed, futility determinations will inevitably involve value judgments about: (1) whether low probability chances are chances worth taking; and (2) whether certain lives are of a quality worth living.[3]

## Quantitative Futility

Futility can be given a quantitative definition. Taking a position that is summarized in the first selection in this section, Schneiderman and colleagues suggest that "the noun

---

1. R. Truog, A. Brett, and J. Frader, "The Problem with Futility," *New England Journal of Medicine* 326, no. 23 (1992): 1560–64.

2. S. Toombs, "Chronic Illness and the Goals of Medicine," *Second Opinion* 21, no. 1 (1995): 11–19, at 13.

3. S. J. Youngner, "Applying Futility: Saying No Is Not Enough," *Journal of the American Geriatrics Society* 42, no. 8 (1994): 887–89, at 887.

'futility' and the adjective 'futile' be used to describe any effort to achieve a result that is possible but that reasoning or experience suggests is highly improbable and that cannot be systematically produced."[4] Institutional policies and professional standards require a clear threshold of futility, so these authors propose that any treatment that has less than a 1 percent probability of bringing about its intended consequence should be regarded as quantitatively futile.[5] Other factors may play a role in determinations of futility: "[i]n the clinical setting, such judgments also would be influenced, of course, by considering such tradeoffs as how cheap and simple the intervention is and how serious or potentially fatal the disease."[6] For instance, if treatment $x$ is the patient's only chance for survival, and $x$ is inexpensive and readily available, the fact that $x$ has not worked in the last 100 similar cases should not stop the physician from trying it. In such situations, respect for the patient's autonomy (or the family's wishes) may override the fact that the requested treatment is futile.

Although this has been described as being a quantitative definition of futility, it must be recognized that there is a central qualitative component here as well. Whether a treatment provides a benefit in any of the last 100 cases depends upon what counts as a benefit. Thus, what is distinctive about the quantitative definition is the role it gives to probabilities, not any neglect of qualitative factors. Notice that this leaves open just how these qualitative issues are to be settled.

This quantitative definition has been the target of considerable criticism. Working out the effectiveness of a treatment in the last 100 cases does not leave any room for taking account of the differences between patients and their conditions.[7] Another difficulty with this approach is that determinations of the probability of success can involve judgments (or guesses) about such things as future patient compliance. How, for instance, would one estimate the likelihood of medical success for a liver transplant for an alcoholic patient, or the replacement of heart valves for a patient who abuses intravenous drugs and has bacterial endocarditis?[8]

There has also been criticism of the 1-percent-effectiveness threshold set by Schneiderman and colleagues:

> But what about something that has a 0.05% chance of success; what about 0.1%, 2%, or 5%? Who then decides what is futile? The authors [Schneiderman et al.] suggest that this ought to be a "medical" (i.e., made by health-care professionals) decision. This is where we disagree. . . . We think that such decisions are legitimate decisions that can profitably be decided by the community (with critical collaboration and advice by physicians, but not merely by physicians).[9]

4. L. Schneiderman, N. Jecker, and A. Jonsen, "Medical Futility: Its Meaning and Ethical Implications," *Annals of Internal Medicine* 112, no. 12 (1990): 949–54, at 951.

5. Ibid., 949.

6. Ibid., 952.

7. Truog et al., "The Problem with Futility."

8. J. Lantos et al., "The Illusion of Futility in Clinical Practice," *American Journal of Medicine* 87 (1989): 81–84.

9. E. Loewy and R. Carlson, "Futility and Its Wider Implications: A Concept in Need of Further Examination," *Archives of Internal Medicine* 153 (1993): 429–31, at 430.

In other words, setting a threshold for futility judgments involves making value-laden choices about which low-probability chances are worth taking. Thus, working out institutional policies and professional standards regarding futile treatments should be done in such a way that we are clear about which values are being employed and why.

## Qualitative Futility

There is also a qualitative definition of futility. Robert Pearlman distinguishes between this understanding of futility and the previous one thus: "[i]n quantitative futility, the value judgment rests in the meaning and value of the probability. In qualitative futility, the value judgment rests in the meaning and value of the existence."[10] That is, the focus shifts from whether it is sufficiently likely that a certain outcome will be attained to whether attaining that outcome would be worthwhile. Schneiderman and his colleagues argue that the failure to bring about an adequately good result renders a treatment futile.[11] For instance, suppose treatment x can, in six cases out of ten, restore kidney function in patients who are (and remain) in a persistent vegetative state. Although a medical effect—in fact, a medical improvement—has been brought about, the result is still not good enough, and the treatment is qualitatively futile in such cases.

Qualitative futility has also found a place in doctors' thinking. One study revealed that nearly 10 percent of patients in the intensive care units studied had orders to withhold or withdraw life-sustaining care, and in virtually all of these cases, futility was cited as an explanation; this is a sharp increase from the findings of a study done five years earlier. Furthermore, "futility was never defined through objective probability estimates and was rarely interpreted quantitatively."[12]

The fact that a treatment has a medical effect does not answer the question of whether that treatment is futile. Effects are not the same as benefits, and as Schneiderman and Jecker argue in their article in this section, a non-futile treatment must confer some benefit. This is where goals and values come in: whether an outcome counts as a benefit depends upon one's values and goals. Because people often differ on these matters, one person might regard an outcome as beneficial while another does not. Of course, it is the patient's goals and values that are of the greatest significance here, but it may be that these do not trump all other moral considerations.

It is important to see that patients and physicians not infrequently disagree about the goals of treatment; this generally arises because they place different values on certain outcomes. For instance, some patients with laryngeal cancer prefer radiation therapy to surgery, even though the latter treatment has a significantly better probability of five-year survival.[13] The reason for this is that the surgery would deprive patients of their normal voice, and some value their ability to speak more than they value longer survival. To take another sort of example, a physician may regard as beneficial a treat-

10. R. Pearlman, "Medical Futility: Where Do We Go from Here?" *Journal of the American Geriatrics Society* 42, no. 8 (1994): 904–5.
11. Schneiderman et al., "Medical Futility: Its Meaning and Ethical Implications."
12. T. Predergast and J. Luce, "Withholding and Withdrawal of Life Support from the Critically Ill," *American Journal of Respiratory and Critical Care Medicine* 149 (1994): A576.
13. Lantos et al., "The Illusion of Futility in Clinical Practice."

ment that would allow the patient a few more days' survival in ICU, while the patient might regard this outcome as not worth the suffering and other costs it would involve and conclude that the treatment is futile (or vice versa).

When a treatment simply maintains a patient in a PVS, it is difficult to see this medical effect as counting as a benefit to the patient.[14] However, it would be too hasty to conclude (as many do) that it is impossible to benefit or harm an irreversibly unconscious patient. (In the final paper in this section, Robert Veatch and Carol Spicer make this assumption without clearly defending it.) The nature of harms and benefits is less clear than this suggests, and one need not be aware of something in order for it to qualify as a harm or benefit. To take a simple, nonmedical example, I can harm you by stealing from you, even if you never discover your loss. Also, if it is correct (as many people believe) that at least some of one's interests survive one's death, then it seems highly likely that these interests persist when one is in a PVS. And if one has interests, then one can be harmed or benefited, so the question of whether such treatments are futile would still be open.

Another question is this: Is a treatment futile if it generates a benefit for someone other than the patient? Consider, for example, Yarborough's example (included in section 3) of treating an unconscious, terminally ill patient for the benefit of family members who have yet to come to terms with the patient's condition.[15] The answer seems to be that if this is the only benefit generated by the treatment, it is still futile with respect to the patient's care even though it may be effective with respect to someone else's goals and values. This illustrates the relativity of futility judgments. "Futility, then, has to be socially as well as individually defined. A given course of action may be futile for the patient himself/herself, but it may have distinct value for the family, the community, or the medical team, and, therefore, not be futile in that sense."[16] However, one must be very cautious about treating patients in order to benefit others; as Yarborough points out, this is permissible only if the patient stands in an appropriate relationship to the beneficiary of the treatment and if the patient would have agreed to this treatment. So, in the narrow sense of futility that concerns itself only with the patient's well-being, this treatment would be futile.

## Futility Judgments as a Justification for Withholding or Withdrawing Treatment

The usual reason for classifying a medical intervention as futile is that such classification provides the basis of an argument for withdrawing or withholding a treatment. This has sparked considerable debate.

Treatments that are regarded as futile are not sharply different from many other treatments whose efficacy is low. Even so, futile-care policies would generate a sharp difference in how treatments that cross the threshold into futility are regarded.[17] This,

14. L. Schneiderman and N. Jecker, "Futility in Practice," *Archives of Internal Medicine* 153 (1993): 437–41.

15. M. Yarborough, "Continued Treatment of the Fatally Ill for the Benefit of Others," *Journal of the American Geriatrics Society* 36, no. 1 (1988): 63–67.

16. Loewy and Carlson, "Futility and Its Wider Implications," 430.

17. Lantos et al., "The Illusion of Futility in Clinical Practice."

too, illustrates a failure to handle treatment decisions in a coherent and evenhanded manner. Some, including Veatch and Spicer, have argued that many of the instances in which futility judgments are used to limit treatment involve ethical mistakes. They claim that withholding "futile" treatments when doing so leads to the death of the patient places too much emphasis on economics and not enough on respect for autonomy or personal dignity. Taking a similar position, Lantos and colleagues claim that "when the chance of success is low, but the alternative to treatment is death, and the patient desires therapy, the presumption should be in favor of treatment."[18] In some cases, they continue, providing a low-probability treatment will play a role in changing the patient's goals and evaluations of outcomes and burdens. But this position needs to be clarified. Are there some cases in which the chance of success is so low that the patient's desire is not enough to justify treatment? Should concerns about the scarcity or expense of the medical resources to be used in treatment always be overridden by our respect for a particular patient? Because the futility issue is often linked with questions of resource allocation, the balancing of individual against social interests, and so forth, we will ultimately have to *decide* on a definition of "futility" rather than simply discovering it, as Lawrence Schneiderman and Nancy Jecker argue in the first of the selections in this section.[19]

Tomlinson and Brody point out that if we refuse to use futility judgments to stop or withhold treatments (and accept the socially supported value judgments physicians must make in doing so), then unacceptable consequences follow. We would, for example, be required to continue resuscitation attempts as long as there was some possibility of recovery (for instance, until exhaustion makes CPR impossible). Also, we would have to provide CT scans and so forth to everyone that requested them. If it is ever appropriate for physicians to stop CPR or to deny people CT scans, they argue, then it must be acceptable for them to use the same value judgments involved to withdraw or withhold treatment in other cases as well.[20]

It should be remembered that many futile treatments are not benign or innocuous; instead, they may increase the patient's suffering. When patients or their families request such treatments, physicians should recognize that they are being asked, in effect, to cause suffering with no reasonable expectation of benefit.[21] Given the fact that most physicians are dedicated to alleviating suffering rather than augmenting it, one can certainly understand their unwillingness to provide these treatments.

Veatch and Spicer argue against this, however, pointing out that taking this attitude toward physicians' moral scruples would lead to an even worse outcome. They also argue that physicians are parties to a social contract that obliges them to put aside their own moral views in certain circumstances. (Unfortunately, they do not explain the full nature of this social contract, nor do they distinguish between hypothetical contracts a rational society might formulate and actual contracts that would be required to generate actual moral obligations.)

18. Ibid., 83.
19. Schneiderman and Jecker, "Futility in Practice."
20. T. Tomlinson and H. Brody, "Futility and the Ethics of Resuscitation," *Journal of the American Medical Association* 264 (1990): 1276–80.
21. Tomlinson and Brody, "Futility and the Ethics of Resuscitation."

## *Futility and Social Standards*

Lantos claims that the futility debate is usually framed in such a way as to conceal the real issues. The standard approach is to ask which treatments patients can insist upon receiving or to ask about the extent to which physicians may use their judgment to withhold a treatment or refrain from offering it. It is more helpful to recognize that patients are entitled to make informed choices about their treatments and then to ask which treatments should be offered in the first place. This shifts the focus from the power held by these actors in the futility drama to the background question of how people are permitted to spend social resources. This is a social and political question, not simply a medical one.[22]

Once the matter is put like this, it becomes reasonably clear that "given limited resources, it is ethically justifiable to limit access to treatments that are expensive and offer minimal benefit."[23] Although there will be discomfort about this approach in particular cases, it seems to accord well with the prevailing social view of resource use.

We seem to have chosen to leave decisions about treatment in questionable cases up to the individual (in large part, at least), but this is not the only possible approach. In many European countries, there are socially accepted standards of what medical care is "fitting," and these do not allow much of what we regard as futile treatment.[24] In much of Europe, for example, coronary artery bypass operations would never be performed on eighty-year-old patients, although such cases are not uncommon here. Not even the fact that many of these procedures yield medical and personal benefits would overcome the European sense that such operations are not "fitting." The North American approach places great emphasis on individual autonomy; "[i]t gives individuals or their surrogates enormous power to live and to die by their own values, however much they may fly in the face of medical judgment. It assumes, moreover, that we neither should, nor perhaps even could, reach some common social judgment about the moral validity of such choices."[25] This emphasis on autonomy is frequently in conflict with respect for physicians' professional integrity (which may lead them to object to providing useless or harmful treatments) and with economic pressures to limit our medical expenses.

Arriving at social standards may be very difficult in practice, however. Morreim argues that "questions about what sorts of life are valuable, and whether that basic value can ever be overshadowed by other values, are essentially matters of definition that lie at the cornerstone of further moral thinking. These are assumptions that cannot be fully defended because they are foundational."[26] In other words, this is a task that rational debate may be unable to settle.

---

22. J. Lantos, "Futility Assessments and the Doctor-Patient Relationship," *Journal of the American Geriatrics Society* 42, no. 8 (1994): 868–70.

23. Ibid., 869.

24. D. Callahan, "Necessity, Futility, and the Good Society," *Journal of the American Geriatrics Society* 42, no. 8 (1994): 866–67.

25. Ibid., 867.

26. Morreim, "Profoundly Diminished Life: The Casualties of Coercion," *Hastings Center Report* 24, no. 1 (1994): 33–42, at 34.

# Futility in Practice

LAWRENCE J. SCHNEIDERMAN
AND NANCY S. JECKER

ALTHOUGH THE TERM *FUTILITY* IS ACTIVELY used in medical discourse, critics object to the concept, calling it "elusive,"[1] "unsettling" (*Am Med News,* November 11, 1991: 28), "dangerous,"[2] and devoid of a "clear sense of public values."[3] If such objections prevail, they will effectively undermine assertions made by a wide variety of authorities that physicians are not obligated to provide futile treatment.[4-8] Must futility be construed only as an ambiguous concept, cited in the abstract, or can it be defined with sufficient specificity to be useful in clinical practice?

Much of the resistance to the notion of futility, we believe, derives from the fear that it will serve as a masquerade for less defensible motivations. For example, will its acceptance revive discarded abuses of medical paternalism? Will it reverse recent advances made in patient autonomy and shared decision making? Will the power to declare treatment futile provide a convenient excuse for physicians to neglect patients they deem unworthy? Will it entice nervous health care providers to avoid patients with life-threatening contagious illness? Will futility serve as a devious rationale for reducing medical costs?

We acknowledge these potential corruptions of the concept, yet we would argue that they are more likely to occur under the present state of ambiguity. In our view, only by seeking to develop a rigorous definition of futility will we encourage clarity of thinking with regard to the larger ethical problem of withholding and withdrawing medical treatment. It is particularly important, for example, to distinguish futility (implying no apparent therapeutic benefit) from rationing (acknowledging therapeutic benefit but raising questions about cost-worthiness).[9] In our experience, rationing is the notion most often confused with futility. Just as physicians find it painful to admit to a patient or family that they have run out of beneficial treatments, so too they find it difficult to upset egalitarian ideals by selectively apportioning such treatments.

Not long ago, a period of uncertainty preceded the establishment of a uniform definition of death based on the so-called whole-brain standard. After considerable debate and expert testimony within the medical, philosophical, and legal communities, the Uniform Brain Death Act has been adopted in most states.[10,11] Although it is unlikely that the definition of futility will ever be enshrined at the statutory level, nor should it be, since it is inherently dependent on a complex variety of clinical circumstances and treatments, we suggest that therapeutic futility be defined within the context of evolving "standards of care."

Just as empiric studies are always gathering data about treatments that provide significant clinical benefits, we believe that attention should be paid also to treatments that demonstratively do not provide such benefits.[12] Standards of care, therefore, can refer not only to the employment of useful treatments but also to the withholding of useless treatments. Since such standards of care will serve as guidelines to the court, physicians who decline to use futile treatments, even in the face of demands from patients and families, will be able to make these decisions with ethical and legal support.

From the *Archives of Internal Medicine* (1993) 153: 437–441.

We[13] have offered a definition of futility that takes into account the historical tradition of the goal of medical treatment, which is to achieve a benefit above a certain minimal quantitative or qualitative threshold. Specifically, we proposed "that when physicians conclude (either through personal experience, experiences shared with colleagues, or consideration of published empiric data) that in the last 100 cases a medical treatment has been useless, they should regard that treatment as futile. If a treatment merely preserves permanent unconsciousness or cannot end dependence on intensive medical care, the treatment should be considered futile."[13] Furthermore, physicians should distinguish between an *effect,* which is limited to some part of the patient's body, and a *benefit,* which the patient has the capacity to appreciate and which improves the patient as a whole. Treatment that fails to provide the latter, we have argued, whether or not it achieves the former, is "futile."[13]

It is important to note that we believe that, as in the case of the definition of death, the medical profession at best can *propose* a definition of futility, but ultimately society at large will *decide* the definition of futility.

In proposing the quantitative component, we have tried to overcome the problem of uncertainty in medicine by asking whether physicians would agree with the commonsense notion that if a treatment has not worked in the last 100 cases, it is almost certainly futile (upper limit of 95% confidence interval, 3%). Since it comports with what has become the traditionally conservative level of medical inference of statistical significance, expressed as $P < .01$, it is probably not surprising that other authors have independently arrived at a similar quantitative threshold when invoking futility on an empiric basis.[14-20]

With respect to the qualitative component, we have drawn attention to the distinction between a treatment effect, which merely alters some part of the patient's body, and a treatment benefit, which can be appreciated by the patient and enables the patient to escape total dependence on intensive medical care.

In our view, a treatment that cannot provide a minimum likelihood or quality of benefit should be regarded as futile, and such futile treatment is not owed to the patient as a matter of moral duty.

We acknowledge that there is no present consensus about the exact dimensions of futility. We have observed, however, that this lack of consensus has not kept the term from being invoked by health care providers to justify treatment or nontreatment decisions. In consultations and conferences, we occasionally hear futility cited when, in our view, it is not appropriate. On other occasions, we fail to hear the word when the concept is in everyone's mind. With the hope of encouraging debate and clarification, leading perhaps to a generally acceptable definition of medical futility, we herewith share a few representative experiences (which have been abbreviated without distorting the essential circumstances, and modified to protect the confidentiality of the participants).

## CASE I: FUTILITY CONFUSED WITH RATIONING

An 86-year-old man with chronic obstructive pulmonary disease was admitted to the hospital with severe pneumonia and renal failure. Gram-negative rods were found in his sputum and urine. Gram-negative sepsis was among the possible considerations, and the patient was treated with combined antibiotics. During a patient care conference, the ethics consultant, pointing out that the hospital had recently advised the staff on the availability of antiendotoxin monoclonal antibody, asked why this treatment was not being employed. (At that time a published report showed a 39% reduction in mortality with the agent's use,[21] although subsequent to the conference, further published commentary expressed doubts.[22,23]) The resident physician initially responded that this additional treatment was futile. After further questioning, however, the resident acknowledged that, in fact, this was just the situation in which antiendotoxin monoclonal antibody had been advocated. Several physicians then expressed concern about its cost and pointed out that other patients would be more likely to obtain a lasting benefit than an elderly man with chronic obstructive pulmonary disease and renal failure.

From this point on, the discussion clarified the distinction between futility (implying no therapeutic benefits) and rationing (implying possible therapeutic benefits but also implying concerns about cost and allocation of limited resources). Discussion then proceeded to the inappropriateness of making rationing decisions at the bedside of a single patient and on the importance of developing general institutional policies regarding the use of monoclonal antibody that are applied openly and fairly.[24]

## CASE 2: PHYSICIAN'S POSSIBLE FEAR OF CONTRACTING ACQUIRED IMMUNODEFICIENCY SYNDROME MASQUERADING AS FUTILITY

A 28-year-old man who was positive for the human immunodeficiency virus was referred to the orthopedic department for correction of a congenitally dysplastic hip. The surgeon refused to perform any operative procedure, however, insisting that it would be futile in view of the underlying incurable illness. The surgeon was not swayed by arguments that the treatment could not be regarded as futile, since the average latent period from infection to the full-blown acquired immunodeficiency syndrome is approximately 10 years, and therefore the patient could have many years of life ahead of him.[25] On further discussion, it became evident that the surgeon was accustomed to deciding whether or not to operate, with his reasons ranging from his estimate of the risk and the technical feasibility of the procedure to whether or not the patient had sufficient third-party coverage. The surgeon, there-

fore, saw nothing unethical about his refusal. Although refraining from raising the issue in a confrontational manner, the ethics consultant thought that the most likely explanation for the surgeon's claim for futility was his own fear of contracting the human immunodeficiency virus infection from the patient.

## CASE 3: FUTILITY SEPARATING TREATMENT FROM EXPERIMENT

The 66-year-old white man with long-standing chronic obstructive pulmonary disease was admitted for treatment of a stage IV small-cell carcinoma of the lung. During the patient's hospitalization, he developed an acute myocardial infarction, followed by periods of marked arrythmia. The patient had previously executed an advance directive advising his physicians that he wanted no cardiopulmonary resuscitation (CPR) if his lung cancer proved to be unresponsive to treatment. However, before therapy was started, the patient underwent a cardiac arrest. The resident physicians reasoned that the acute myocardial infarction had not been anticipated by the patient and therefore did not come within the purview of the patient's advance directive; they attempted CPR, which failed.

Because of the considerable debate among the physicians who cared for the patient about the appropriateness of carrying out CPR, an ethics conference was called. One side agreed that the patient's wishes had been inappropriately overridden. The other side claimed that these physicians were unduly discouraged by the diagnosis of cancer, which in this man's case was potentially curable. The only empiric data involving cases similar to those in this patient, however, were a meta-analysis reporting no successful survival to hospital discharge when CPR was attempted in as many as 127 patients with metastatic cancer.[19] The ethics consultant suggested that the issue was not one of patient autonomy, but rather of the ethical implications of demonstrated futility. Since the article indicated that CPR was unsuccessful in more than 100 patients with metastatic cancer, the consultant argued that the procedure should be regarded as quantitatively futile and therefore should be attempted only in the context of experimental therapy with appropriate human subject approval and patient informed consent. In other words, the patient would be consenting to therapy of no proven benefit with the hope of possibly benefiting, while serving to advance knowledge in a systematic way. Advocates of the procedure would be posing the hypothesis that this patient's particular circumstances (e.g., the type and stage of disease) represented an exception to the already demonstrated failure of CPR in a large group of more than 100 patients with various types of metastatic cancer.

## CASE 4: FAILURE TO DISTINGUISH BETWEEN EFFECT AND BENEFIT

A 92-year-old, severely and chronically demented woman was transferred to the hospital from the nursing home because of high fever and suspected pneumonia. Her physicians had no knowledge of any previously expressed treatment wishes, and there was no known family. During the previous year, the woman had undergone several surgical procedures on her large bowel to correct bleeding vascular malformations and had also been hospitalized for two episodes of aspiration pneumonia. On this hospital admission, pneumonia was again diagnosed and treatment started. The attending physician also elected to have a gastrostomy feeding tube inserted to facilitate nutrition.

An ethics consultation was called because of increasing conflicts among the physicians and nurses about the treatment plans for the woman. During the consultation, the attending physician, the residents, and all the nursing staff

agreed that the woman's baseline mental status was so impaired that even after resolution of the pneumonia, she had no interaction with her environment. Her only sounds and gestures seemed to be expressive of discomfort. The attending physician acknowledged her own personal distress at having ordered the gastrostomy tube, but she believed that she had been ethically and legally obligated to do so because the patient "would die without it and there was nothing more we can do." During the discussion, all the physicians and nurses concurred that, although the gastrostomy tube undoubtedly would prolong the patient's survival, it did not provide any benefits that the patient seemed capable of appreciating—a clear example of producing an effect without achieving a benefit. Thus, the idea of futility was acknowledged by all, but its ethical implications were not appreciated until they were raised by the ethics consultant.

At the conclusion of the consultation, all the health care providers agreed that from the patient's perspective the only treatments that could be considered beneficial were those emphasizing comfort care, including moistening the lips and medication for pain. The decision was made that the gastrostomy tube represented futile treatment and should be withdrawn.

## CASE 5: FUTILITY VS. A PATIENT'S 'RIGHT' TO UNPROVED TREATMENT

A 32-year-old man who was positive for the human immunodeficiency virus was admitted for his second episode of *Pneumocystis carinii* pneumonia. His condition failed to improve, and he remained for several weeks either in respiratory distress or in an obtunded state. While conscious, the patient never rescinded his wishes for full care; after the patient lost consciousness, his physician refused to agree to a "do not resuscitate" order.

The physician, a strong advocate for allowing patients access to unconventional as well as conventional medical treatment for the acquired immunodeficiency syndrome, demanded that the patient be administered all the medications the patient had obtained through underground channels. The physician claimed that the patient had a "right" to all treatments, even unproved and futile treatments, because from the patient's perspective, they represented his only hope.

The patient's condition continued to deteriorate, with failure developing in three major organ systems. The physicians in the intensive care unit argued that, in their judgment, based on empiric data, the patient had only a negligible (i.e., much less than one in 100) chance of ever leaving the intensive care unit alive and that, therefore, continued aggressive treatment was futile.[26,27] They further argued that the prior wishes of the patient did not impose on them a duty to apply futile care. After numerous discussions, the referring physician was finally persuaded that medical efforts should be redirected toward helping the patient die as comfortably and with as much dignity as possible.

## CASE 6: FUTILITY REJECTED IN HOPES OF A MIRACLE

As part of another case, the ethics consultant learned about a 14-month-old infant who had been in the intensive care unit since his premature birth more than a year ago. Never giving up hope for a miraculous recovery, the family insisted that aggressive lifesaving treatment be continued despite the patient's persistent vegetative state. Although the physicians acknowledged that recovery was out of the question and made every effort to persuade the family to agree to treatment withdrawal, they feared the legal—but even more the public relations—consequences of acting unilaterally against the adamant wishes of the family. In other words, the physicians were in complete agreement about

the futility of what they were doing—that the infant had far less than a one in 100 chance of ever regaining consciousness—but felt extremely vulnerable for the consequences of making a medical decision on their own.

The ethics consultant suggested that the hospital might consider developing a policy clearly stating that long-term life support of patients in a persistent vegetative state with such a prognosis does not conform with an acceptable standard of medical care. This would make it possible then for health care providers to feel more comfortable concentrating their efforts on assisting families to cope with their loss rather than feeling obligated to persist in efforts that offer no benefit.

## COMMENT

These examples represent some of the cases we have encountered in which the concept of medical futility was in some way misused. In our view, they illustrate the early and inevitable fumbling steps of defining this concept in the clinical setting. Furthermore, they illustrate that the abuses of the concept referred to at the beginning of this article are occurring now—namely, inappropriate paternalism, erosion of patient autonomy, unjustified avoidance of the duty to treat, and disguised and arbitrary rationing.

In cases 1, 2, and 3, there was conceptual confusion about the difference between futility and such related issues as rationing, patient autonomy, and physician autonomy. In case 4, the physician failed to recognize futility and failed to consider the ethical implication that futile treatment is nonobligatory. In cases 5 and 6, there were no disagreements about the futility of treatment, but confusions surfaced about the implementation of the concept in the clinical setting, in other words, its ethical implications.

We wish to underline these two distinct aspects of futility, namely its definition and its ethical implications. With respect to the latter, it seems clear that (despite the initial objection by the physician who treated the acquired immunodeficiency syndrome in case 5) overwhelming agreement has been reached in the medical community that physicians are not required to provide futile treatment.

Can the medical community achieve a consensus about the specific definition of futility? Callahan[3] doubts this possibility, arguing that there is "no political process to allow physicians and laypeople together to develop appropriate standards for futility." We agree with that assessment, although we are not thereby discouraged. Whatever "political process" Callahan has in mind, he cannot realistically expect physicians and society at large to unite spontaneously in a generally acceptable definition. Nor, in our opinion, is the well-known Oregonian process for establishing rationing priorities adaptable to defining futility. Nor will the courts await such a development; rather, they will continue to make ad hoc, emotionally propelled decisions (*Chicago Tribune,* January 10, 1991; *New York Times,* October 18, 1991: A8; *Am Med News,* January 28, 1992: 2; *New York Times,* January 10, 1991: A1) causing physicians and patients to become mired in ever more intractable confusion.

Therefore, in our view, it is up to the medical profession to take the initiative by offering specific standards and guidelines in the hope of first achieving consensus within the medical community and ultimately gaining acceptance in society at large. The steps we propose are as follows:

1. Acknowledge that the word *futility* is widely used in medical practice and agree to use it in a more consistent and explicit fashion than it is used today.

2. Seek a specific meaning for the concept through open debate and consensus seeking. Start with the general proposal that *futility* means treatment that fails to achieve the goals of medicine, in that it offers no benefit to the patient above a minimum quantitative or qualitative

threshold. Then see whether the medical profession can agree as to what counts as a minimum probability or minimum quality of benefit.

3. Introduce this definition of *futility* into practice by encouraging publication of studies reporting not only positive therapeutic outcomes (to be adopted) by negative therapeutic outcomes (to be avoided). These empiric studies will form the basis for defining standards of care for clinical situations.

4. Seek to enlighten and obtain the concurrence of society at large by declaring these standards of care openly, as institutional policies for the information of the public (including legislatures and governmental agencies) and as guidelines to the courts.

REFERENCES

1. Lantos JD, Singer PA, Walker RM, et al. The illusion of futility in clinical practice. *Am J Med.* 1989; 87: 81–84.

2. Capron AM. In re Helga Wanglie. *Hastings Cent Rep.* 1991; 21 (5): 26–28.

3. Callahan D. Medical futility, medical necessity: the-problem-without-a-name. *Hastings Cent Rep.* 1991; 21 (4): 30–35.

4. *Deciding to Forgo Life-Sustaining Treatment: Ethical, Medical and Legal Issues in Treatment Decisions.* Washington, DC: President's Commission for the Study of Ethical Problems in Medicine and Biomedical and Behavioral Research; 1983.

5. *Guidelines on the Termination of Life-Sustaining Treatment and the Care of the Dying.* Briarcliff Manor, NY: Hastings Center; 1987.

6. Council on Ethical and Judicial Affairs. *Current Opinions.* Chicago, Ill: Council on Ethical and Judicial Affairs, American Medical Association; 1989.

7. Task Force on Ethics of the Society of Critical Care Medicine. Consensus report on the ethics of forgoing life-sustaining treatments in the critically ill. *Crit Care Med.* 1989; 18: 1435–1439.

8. American Thoracic Society. Withholding and withdrawing life-sustaining therapy. *Ann Intern Med.* 1991; 115: 478–485.

9. Jecker NS, Schneiderman LJ. Futility and rationing. *Am J Med.* 1992; 92: 189–196.

10. *Defining Death*. Washington, DC: President's Commission for the Study of Ethical Problems in Medicine and Biomedical and Behavioral Research; 1981.

11. Guidelines for the determination of death. *JAMA*. 1981; 246: 2184–2186.

12. Rennie D, Flanagin A. Publication bias: the triumph of hope over experience. *JAMA*. 1992; 267: 411–412.

13. Schneiderman LJ, Jecker NS, Jonsen AR. Medical futility: its meaning and ethical implications. *Ann Intern Med*. 1990; 112: 949–954.

14. Kellerman AL, Staves DR, Hackman BB. In-hospital resuscitation following unsuccessful pre-hospital advanced cardiac life support: 'heroic efforts' or an exercise in futility? *Ann Emerg Med*. 1988; 17: 589–594.

15. Lantos JD, Miles SH, Silverstein MD, Stocking CB. Survival after cardiopulmonary resuscitation in babies of very low birth weight: is CPR futile? *N Engl J Med*. 1988; 318: 91–95.

16. Taffet GE, Teasdale TA, Luchi RJ. In-hospital cardiopulmonary resuscitation. *JAMA*. 1988; 260: 2069–2072.

17. Murphy DR, Murray AM, Robinson BE, Campion EW. Outcomes of cardiopulmonary resuscitation in the elderly. *Ann Intern Med*. 1989; 111: 199–205.

18. Bonnin MJ, Swor RA. Outcomes in unsuccessful field resuscitation attempts. *Ann Emerg Med*. 1989; 18: 507–512.

19. Faber-Langendoen K. Resuscitation of patient with metastatic cancer: is transient benefit still futile? *Arch Intern Med*. 1991; 151: 235–239.

20. Gray WA, Capone RJ, Most AS. Unsuccessful emergency medical resuscitation: are continued efforts in the emergency department justified? *N Engl J Med*. 1991; 329: 1393–1398.

21. Ziegler EJ, Fisher CJ Jr, Sprung CL, et al. Treatment of gram-negative bacteremia and septic shock with HA-1A human monoclonal antibody against endotoxin: a randomized, double-blind, placebo-controlled trial. *N Engl J Med*. 1991; 324: 429–436.

22. Warren HS, Danner RL, Munford RS. Anti-endotoxin monoclonal antibodies. *N Engl J Med*. 1992; 326: 1153–1157.

23. Wenzel RP. Anti-endotoxin monoclonal antibodies: a second look. *N Engl J Med*. 1992; 326: 1151–1153.

24. Schulman KA, Glick HA, Rubin H, Eisenberg JU. Cost-effectiveness of HA-1A monoclonal antibody for gram-negative sepsis. *JAMA*. 1991; 266: 3466–3471.

25. Biggar RJ. AIDS incubation in 1981 HIV seroconverters from different exposure groups. *AIDS*. 1990; 4: 1059–1065.

26. Knaus WA, Wagner DP, Lynn J. Short-term mortality predictions for critically ill hospitalized adults: science and ethics. *Science*. 1991; 254: 389–394.

27. Knaus WA, Wagner DP, Draper EA, et al. The APACHE III prognostic system: risk prediction of hospital mortality for critically ill hospitalized adults. *Chest*. 1991; 100: 1619–1636.

# Medical Futility and Care of Dying Patients

## NANCY S. JECKER

In this article, I address ethical concerns related to forgoing futile medical treatment in terminally ill and dying patients. Any discussion of medical futility should emphasize that health professionals and health care institutions have ethical responsibilities regarding medical futility. Among the topics I address are communicating with pa-

From the *Western Journal of Medicine* (1995) 163(3): 287–291.

tients and families, resolving possible conflicts, and developing professional standards. Finally, I explore why acknowledging the futility of life-prolonging medical interventions can be so difficult for patients, families, and health professionals.

WITH THE DEVELOPMENT OF NEW MEDICAL technologies during the latter half of this century, medicine has been able to keep terminally ill patients alive for longer periods of time without curing or ameliorating their underlying disease condition. The widespread use of artificial feeding and nutrition, ventilator support, cardiopulmonary resuscitation, and renal dialysis has meant that patients diagnosed with metastatic cancer, coronary artery disease, kidney failure, and other life-threatening conditions no longer regard their diagnoses as lethal. Yet, life-sustaining interventions have sometimes been a double-edged sword. Medical treatments that extend life may also result in patients spending their final days and weeks confused and debilitated, unable to breathe, eat, or urinate without the assistance of ventilators, feeding tubes, and catheters. Although patients live longer, they may find themselves confined to hospitals and intensive care units, where they are sedated and unable to interact meaningfully or to obtain comfort and support from the company of others.

Under what circumstances should providers cease life-prolonging efforts? When a patient reaches the final stages of a terminal condition such as AIDS [acquired immunodeficiency syndrome], should the patient be admitted to a hospital for pneumonia, receive intravenous infusions for fluid loss with diarrhea, or be prescribed antibiotics for a bladder infection? What about more invasive procedures, such as the insertion of endotracheal tubes, the use of defibrillators, or surgical repair of a bowel obstruction? When should providers attempt to prolong life, and when should their efforts instead focus on palliative measures?

In this article I address the general problem of forgoing the use of life-sustaining medical treatment in terminally ill and dying patients. I defend a patient-centered definition of medical futility, placing it in the context of end-of-life care. The ethical responsibilities of health professionals and health care institutions are discussed with regard to communication with patients and families, conflict resolution, and the development of professional standards about medical futility. In closing, I explore the reasons why acknowledging the futility of life-prolonging medical interventions can be so difficult for patients, families, and health professionals. Despite possible obstacles, refraining from medically futile interventions is often the best way to care humanely for patients at the end of life.

## WHAT DOES FUTILITY MEAN?

At first glance it might seem that, if a patient's death is imminent, then the patient's entire situation is futile regardless of what physicians do. On the other hand, if a life-sustaining treatment is working, that is, keeping the patient alive, we may wonder how the question of futility can even arise.

To clarify these questions, it is helpful to note that the term "futile" refers to a specific medical intervention applied to a specific patient at a particular time. It does not refer to a situation generally or to a medical treatment globally. Nor should "futile" be used to refer to a patient, or to care, as this may convey the impression that the patient is being abandoned or that comfort measures will no longer be undertaken.

Finally, futile treatments sometimes succeed in producing physiologic effects, yet provide no benefit to the patient. For example, cardiopulmonary resuscitation of a permanently unconscious patient may restore heart function, yet be regarded as futile because it does not confer any benefit that the patient can appreciate. Those who regard the goal of medicine to be helping the patient, not merely producing effects on organ systems or body parts, accept what is thus called a "patient-centered" definition of medical futility.[1]

A patient-centered understanding of medical futility involves attention to situations in which many effects can be produced on a person's body; only some will be appreciated as benefits, others will be perceived as harm, and still others will not be experienced by the patient at all. For instance, resuscitating a heart attack victim and returning her to full functioning is clearly a medical benefit. On the other hand, when an emergency medical crew is called to a nursing home to assist a patient who suddenly has dyspnea and ventricular arrhythmia, followed by cardiac arrest, and who is known to have widespread pancreatic cancer, the effect of attempted life prolongation may not be experienced as a benefit by the patient, but may instead be regarded as a detriment by adding to the patient's pain and discomfort at the end of life. In contrast to these situations, prolonging the life of someone in a persistent vegetative state through the use of a feeding tube is not experienced as either a burden or a benefit by the unconscious patient.

Futility may become apparent in the context of caring for dying patients in at least two distinct ways. First, a treatment may be quantitatively futile because the likelihood that it will benefit a patient falls below a threshold considered minimal.[2] For example, it is futile for emergency workers to rush terminally ill patients to a hospital after a failed resuscitation effort in the field because there is virtually no chance that patients will survive and benefit from such efforts.[3,4] Second, a treatment may be qualitatively futile when the quality of benefit associated with an intervention falls well below a threshold considered minimal.[2] For instance, hemodialysis of a hospitalized patient dying of multiple organ system failure with no hope of survival to discharge is qualitatively futile.[5]

Some have objected to a patient-centered definition of medical futility, claiming that treatment should be called futile only when it fails to produce any physical effect on the patient's body.[6,7] Supporters of a "physiologic" definition of futility argue that health professionals should avoid imposing their values on patients and families and that patient autonomy should be seen as inviolable.[8,9] Limiting health professionals' judgments about futility to the narrow, technical evaluation of whether a treatment can produce an effect may appear to rid futility judgments of any value dimension.

My response is that the goal of medicine is not merely to produce physical effects on patients' bodies, but to help patients.[10] Expressed differently, "the subject of medical care is the suffering patient, not a failing organ system."[1] (p. 2197) In contrast to a physiologic approach, which pictures the health professional's role to be narrow, technical, and even value free, a patient-centered view regards the provider's role as promoting patients' good by producing effects that patients can appreciate.

This stance is consistent with the historical and contemporary ethics of the profession. Since its earliest beginnings, medicine has focused on the ethical goal of helping suffering patients. The ancient Greek physician, Hippocrates, reportedly identified the purposes of medicine as twofold: first, "to do away with the sufferings of the sick" and "to lessen the violence of their disease"; and second, to recognize medicine's limits, "to refuse to treat those who are overmastered by their diseases, realizing that in such cases medicine is powerless."[11] (p. 6) Reflecting a continued commitment to these goals, the

American Medical Association (AMA)[12,13] and many other medical organizations have affirmed medicine's inevitable limits.[14–18] According to the AMA's Council on Ethical and Judicial Affairs, physicians' obligation is to offer patients "medically sound" options, including interventions that can "cure or prevent a medical disorder" or "relieve distressing symptoms."[12] (p. 2230)

In addition to ignoring the ethics and goals of medicine, a physiologic approach overstates the value of autonomy, casting it as an ethical absolute. Although respect for the wishes of autonomous patients is clearly an important value, this value must be placed in context. Autonomy does not entitle patients to receive any treatment they want, nor does it obligate health professionals to provide interventions that are "countertherapeutic" or that are contrary to "role-related professional standards and conscientiously held personal beliefs."[19] (p. 44) Upholding autonomy as an ethical absolute belittles the importance of beneficence in medicine, by making the goal of benefiting patients a secondary, or even irrelevant, consideration. If the only task of medicine were to carry out patients' wishes, clinicians would be reduced to functioning merely as patients' instruments. By contrast, upholding standards of medical practice aimed at benefiting patients assigns importance to beneficence while preserving a role for patient autonomy.

Finally, defining medical futility in purely physiologic terms fails to deliver on the promise of offering a "value-free" role for the provider. A commitment to use all interventions that can produce some effect on a patient's body, unless a patient or surrogate explicitly refuses them, is hardly a value-free stance. Instead, it implies a strong commitment to biological life; a commitment to medical technology for its own sake, rather than as a means of promoting patients' good; and a disavowal of providers' ethical responsibility to promote patients' good and to avoid harming them.

## WHAT ARE PROVIDERS' ETHICAL OBLIGATIONS?

Once disagreements about the meaning of medical futility are resolved, there remains the question, What are health professionals' ethical responsibilities? Should providers offer futile treatments to patients or surrogates? Should providers instead explain and discuss the situation more generally? Should providers attempt to exclude a discussion of futile interventions with patients or families altogether, with an eye to preventing possible conflicts from arising? If conflicts do arise over the use of a futile intervention, what constitutes a fair process of conflict resolution? May a physician unilaterally override a patient or family? Or should physicians instead cede to patients' or families' wishes?

Where feasible, providers should communicate in advance with patients (or surrogates) about decisions to withhold or withdraw futile treatments. Sensitive communication serves many functions, including making providers accountable for their decisions, educating patients and families, building trust between providers and patients (or families), and averting concerns that resources are being rationed or that patients will be abandoned. Providers should use the occasion of discussing the withholding or withdrawal of futile treatment to affirm that everything possible will be done to support the patient at the end of life, including the aggressive use of palliative and comfort measures.

Although the ordinary obligation of health professionals is to refrain from offering or using futile treatments, in certain situations compassionate exceptions should be made. For example, a patient with widespread cancer whose death is imminent within a matter of hours or days may ask to be made a "full code" because the patient would like to live long enough to see a grandchild for the first time who is arriving from a distant state. Or a patient who will never leave the intensive care unit may want to stay on a ventilator long enough to provide emotional support to a grieving spouse who is in the process of slowly coming to terms with the patient's death. Agreeing to a time-limited trial may provide a patient or family an opportunity to come to terms with their situation and to gain a sense of control over their fate. These examples make evident that the appropriate steps for implementing general ethical guidelines to refrain from futile interventions vary from case to case.

In the event that a patient or family persistently requests a treatment that the health care team regards as futile, a process of sensitively negotiating the conflict should occur. Ideally, an institution's policy on withholding and withdrawing treatment will specify steps for resolving conflict. These steps may include, for instance, consulting with the institution's ethics committee or individual ethics consultants[20]; drawing on resources such as a chaplain or social worker to provide support to the patient or family; obtaining a second medical opinion; and facilitating further communication with the patient, family, or both. In most cases, pursuing a process of conflict resolution enables the patient, family, and health care team to reach agreement and bring the case to a point of closure. Even when the parties continue to disagree about what should be done, they may be willing to accept a compromise position. For example, if there is not a clear consensus in the medical community about the futility of a particular intervention for the patient, the medical team may agree to refer the patient elsewhere. Or if a treatment is clearly futile, the patient or family may agree in advance to discontinue treatment after a certain amount of time if there is no improvement in the patient's situation.

The final decision about whether or not a particular treatment is futile does not rest with any single person. Rather, the definition of medical futility must be grounded in general standards of care that are first articulated by the health care professions and then accepted by the broader society.[21,22] Guidelines about medical futility should be based on reliable empirical data about the effects of interventions on different patient groups, as well as careful ethical analysis concerning patients' benefit. Whereas debate about the meaning of futility and ethical implications continues, physician surveys show that physicians are already incorporating some concept of medical futility into decision making at the bedside.[23-25] Establishing general guidelines and standards that address medical futility is preferable to delegating decisions about medical futility to individual physicians at the bedside. Bedside decisions are often not thought through, not applied consistently, not accountable to the public, not decided democratically, and not insulated from arbitrary or invidious prejudice based on factors such as a patient's race or ethnic group. To minimize possible abuses, institutions should develop clear standards for withholding and withdrawing futile interventions. Such standards serve to educate and guide not only patients and families, but also health professionals and courts about the limits of medicine.[26]

Many institutions have already begun to incorporate the concept of futility explicitly into guidelines for the withholding and withdrawing of medical treatment. For example, Johns Hopkins Hospital (Baltimore, Maryland) has defined "futility" as any course of treatment that "is highly unlikely to have a beneficial outcome" or "is highly likely merely to preserve permanent unconsciousness or persistent vegetative state or require permanent hospitalization in an intensive care unit."[27] Local consensus is also developing in places like Denver, Colorado, where area hospitals jointly developed criteria for deciding that a treatment is futile.[28] Such guidelines establish, for example, that aggressive treatments, such as cardiopulmonary resuscitation, are futile and should not be provided for patients with AIDS who have had two or more episodes of *Pneumocystis carinii* pneumonia, or patients with multiple organ system failure with no improvement after three days of intensive care.

## WHAT MAKES ACKNOWLEDGING FUTILITY SO HARD?

Despite the importance of emphasizing patient benefit in care of dying patients, health professionals often feel compelled to continue with nonbeneficial interventions. Interviews with physicians and nurses found that almost half (47%) of all respondents reported acting contrary to conscience in providing care to the terminally ill, with four times as many providing overly burdensome treatment than undertreatment.[29] Especially if a patient or family member requests that "everything possible" be done, the health care team may be reluctant to go against the patient's or surrogate's wishes. Unbalanced respect for patient autonomy, well-meaning compassion for grieving family members, fear of legal liability, and avoidance of death are among the factors that can contribute to the use of futile treatments at the end of life.

Setting aside legal concerns and economic self-interest, what leads health care providers to prolong patients' suffering by futile attempts to beat the odds? What impels patients and families to request that "everything possible" be done when a loved one's death is clearly imminent? Finally, why do we as a society continue to expect medical miracles, rather than viewing death as an inevitable, natural part of life?

There is no single answer to these questions. Yet, the broader philosophical and historical context in which they arise may shed some light on why futile treatments are used and why acknowledging futility has been so difficult. One factor leading to the use of futile treatment is undoubtedly our contemporary conception of disease and corresponding attitudes toward death. Western medicine tends to view disease as an enemy to be fought, with death marking the ultimate defeat in this battle against disease. Such a conception has historical roots in the mid-19th century, when American medicine first began to identify itself with a more aggressive scientific approach.[30] It was also during this time that the germ theory of disease became predominant, with its emphasis on isolating and destroying a foreign organism. In contrast to ancient Greek physicians who saw disease as an imbalance within the body, modern western physicians picture disease as a war waged against outside invaders.

Susan Sontag depicted modern medicine in these terms when she described the controlling metaphor in the description of fatal diseases, such as cancer, as drawn from the language of warfare[31] (p. 64):

> [C]ancer cells do not simply multiply; they are "invasive" . . . "colonize" from the original tumor to far sites in the body, first setting up tiny outposts ("micrometastases"). . . . Rarely are the body's "defenses" vigorous enough to obliterate a tumor that has established its own blood supply and consists of billions of destructive cells. . . . the prospects are that "tumor invasion" will continue, or that rogue cells will eventually regroup and mount a new assault on the organism.

Likewise, the language of cancer treatment is infused with military images: in radiotherapy, "patients are 'bombarded' with toxic rays . . . chemotherapy is chemical warfare, using poisons"; all treatment aims to "kill cancer cells."[31] (p. 65)

A second factor that may contribute to a physiologic approach to end-of-life decisions is that the scientific method medicine employs tends to emphasize the physical signs of disease, while discounting the importance of patients' subjective experience of illness. According to some analyses, scientific medicine encourages a way of knowing in which people are seen as mechanical and deanimated. Thus, Hunter maintained that medicine "focuses on the measurable abnormalities of body and behavior that, by appearing regularly in cases of illness, are the indices of identifiable disease or injury."[32] (p. 53) Likewise, Keller argued that rather than encouraging empathic understanding or a "feeling for the organism," scientific medicine emphasizes the empirical observation of physical facts.[33]

Downplaying the importance of patients' experiences and subjective quality of life can lead to the mistaken equating of survival with success.

Third, the use of futile treatments at the end of life may reflect our own fear of death. In modern secular society, such fear may center on fear of the unknown, as well as the loss of the comfort afforded by previous religious understandings. As Callahan notes . . . , in contrast to the Puritans for whom death was a religious and family event, to put in God's hands, modern Americans tend to find little solace or meaning in death.[34]

Fourth, to the extent that the culture of medicine encourages actions over omissions and judges attempts to beat the odds as "heroic," the tendency will be to continue to use futile interventions. To the extent that practicing medicine is equated with using treatments, rather than with implementing a plan of care (which may include both actions and omissions), the tendency will be to regard withholding or withdrawing treatment as "doing nothing" or, worse, "abandoning the patient."[35]

Fifth, treatments may continue to be used beyond the point of benefit to patients merely as a result of not deciding what to do. One physician poignantly described his most frequent response when faced with decisions about using futile treatments for dying patients as avoidance[36] (p. 719):

> . . . not to make a conscious decision at all. . . . the problem is simply too difficult for me as a single human being to face in a conscious way. . . . On the other hand, how can I inflict the pain of aggressive treatment, and the suffering of further living, and spend the scarce resources of time and money on this person who is so obviously "trying" to die? And so, all too often, I don't make a conscious decision at all. I simply act, do something, make a decision without really considering the meaning of what I do.

Finally, whereas admitting medical futility requires acknowledging that medicine is some-times powerless in the face of disease, continued efforts to beat the odds hold out the hope, however slim, of eventually mastering disease. As Nuland observed, fear of the loss and pain death portends can make it "more important to protect one another from the open admission of a painful truth [than to] achieve a final sharing that might have snatched an enduring comfort and even some dignity from the anguishing fact of death."[37] (p. 244) As a consequence, patients and families may keep up the charade of denial until the bitter end, clinging all the while to false hope, expecting to achieve a miraculous cure. Rather than exercising responsibility by educating patients and families about the hazards of excessive medical optimism, providers may instead prefer to put off such conversations indefinitely.

## CONCLUSION

> Those—dying then,
> Knew where they went—
> They went to God's Right Hand—
> That Hand is amputated now
> And God cannot be found—
> The abdication of Belief
> Makes the Behavior small—
> Better an ignis fatuus
> Than no illume at all
>
> —Emily Dickinson, 1845

Futile treatments can offer patients the illusion of continued life. They can offer families the false comfort of doing something. For health care providers, futile treatments may symbolize caring. Futile treatments thus perform vital functions; they are what Dickinson called an "ignis fatuus," something deluding or misleading that yet seems preferable to the absence of any understanding at all.

Despite their appeal, futile treatments should have no place in the humane care of dying patients. Although continuing to apply futile measures can offer a comfortable illusion, it is only by acknowledging, and moving beyond, futility that the dying process can become more dignified. Thus, when patients and families are no longer preoccupied with futile attempts to prolong life, they can turn their attention to preparing emotionally for death and to making practical decisions about the value of different settings for dying, such as the hospital, home, or hospice.[38] When health professionals are no longer preoccupied by futile technologies, they can focus instead on spending time with the patient and minimizing the patient's pain and discomfort. When those who surround the patient stop fighting for "everything" to be done, they can express love and concern in a more direct and meaningful way.[39] Only by redirecting our collective efforts in these ways will physicians help patients and make care of the dying a more honest and compassionate part of medical practice.

## ACKNOWLEDGMENT

Gil Omenn, MD, provided valuable assistance with an earlier draft of this article.

## REFERENCES

1. Jecker NS, Schneiderman LJ: An ethical analysis of the use of "futility" in the 1992 American Heart Association guidelines for cardiopulmonary resuscitation and emergency cardiac care. Arch Intern Med 1993; 153: 2195–2198.

2. Schneiderman LJ, Jecker NS, Jonsen AR: Medical futility: Its meaning and ethical implications. Ann Intern Med 1990; 112: 949–954.

3. Kellerman AL, Hackman BB, Somes G: Predicting the outcomes of unsuccessful pre-hospital advanced cardiac life support. JAMA 1993; 270: 1433–1436.

4. Gray WA, Capone RJ, Most AS: Unsuccessful emergency resuscitation—Are continued efforts in the emergency department justified? N Engl J Med 1991; 325: 1393–1398.

5. Faber-Langendoen K: Resuscitation of patients with metastatic cancer. Arch Intern Med 1991; 151: 235–239.

6. Truog RD, Brett AS, Frader J: The problem with futility. N Engl J Med 1992; 326: 1560–1564.

7. Waisel DB, Truog RD: The cardiopulmonary resuscitation–not-indicated order: Futility revisited. Ann Intern Med 1995; 122: 304–308.

8. Veatch RM, Spicer CM: Medically futile care: The role of the physician in setting limits. Am J Law Med 1992; 18: 15–36.

9. Wolf S: Conflict between doctor and patient. Law Med Health Care 1988; 16: 197–203.

10. Schneiderman LJ, Jecker NS: The Wrong Medicine. Baltimore, MD, Johns Hopkins University Press, in press.

11. Hippocrates: Art, *In* SJ Reiser, AJ Dyck, WJ Curran (Eds): Ethics in Medicine: Historical Perspectives. Cambridge, MA, MIT Press, 1977.

12. American Medical Association (AMA), Council on Ethical and Judicial Affairs: Decisions near the end of life. JAMA 1992; 267: 2229–2233.

13. AMA Council on Ethical and Judicial Affairs: Guidelines for the appropriate use of do-not-resuscitate orders. JAMA 1991; 265: 1868–1871.

14. American Heart Association, Emergency Cardiac Care Committee and Subcommittees: Guidelines for cardiopulmonary resuscitation and emergency cardiac care. JAMA 1992; 268: 2171–2183.

15. American Academy of Pediatrics, Committee on Bioethics: Guidelines on forgoing life-sustaining treatment. Pediatrics 1994; 93: 532–536.

16. American Thoracic Society, Bioethics Task Force: Withholding and withdrawing life-sustaining treatment. Ann Intern Med 1991; 115: 478–485.

17. Society of Critical Care Medicine, Task Force on Ethics: Consensus report on the ethics of forgoing life-sustaining treatment in the critically ill. Crit Care Med 1990; 18: 39.

18. Joint statement on resuscitative interventions. Can Med Assoc J 1994; 151: 1176a–1176c.

19. President's Commission for the Study of Ethical Problems in Medicine and Biomedical and Behavioral Research: Deciding to Forgo Life Sustaining Treatments, publication no. 83-600503. Washington, DC, Government Printing Office, 1983.

20. LaPuma J, Scheidermayer D, Siegler M: How ethics consultation can help resolve dilemmas in dying patients, *In* Caring for Patients at the End of Life (Special Issue). West J Med 1995; 163: 263–267.

21. Jecker NS, Pearlman RA: Medical futility: Who decides? Arch Intern Med 1992; 152: 1140–1144.

22. Schneiderman LJ, Jecker NS: Futility in practice. Arch Intern Med 1993; 153: 437–441.

23. Asch DA, Hansen-Flaschen J, Lanken PN: Decisions to limit or continue life-sustaining treatment by critical care physicians in the United States. Am J Respir Crit Care Med 1995; 151: 288–292.

24. Pijenborg L, van der Maas PJ, Kardaun JWPF, et al.: Withdrawal or withholding of treatment at the end of life. Arch Intern Med 1995; 155: 286–292.

25. Curtis JR, Park DR, Krone MR, Pearlman RA: Use of the medical futility rationale in do-not-attempt-resuscitation orders. JAMA 1995; 273: 124–128.

26. Stell L: Stopping treatment on grounds of futility: A role for institutional policy. St Louis Univ Public Law Rev 1992; 11: 481–497.

27. Johns Hopkins Hospital Policy on Withholding or Withdrawing Futile Life-Sustaining Medical Interventions. Baltimore, MD, Johns Hopkins Hospital, January 28, 1992.

28. Fianelli DM: One community looks for consensus on 'futile care.' Am Med News, September 20, 1993, pp. 1, 10.

29. Solomon MZ, O'Donnell L, Jennings B, et al.: Decisions near the end of life: Professional views on life-sustaining treatments. Am J Public Health 1993; 83: 14–23.

30. Jecker NS: Knowing when to stop. Hastings Cent Rep 1991; 21: 5–8.

31. Sontag S: Illness as Metaphor. New York, NY, Farrar, Straus & Giroux, 1978.

32. Hunter KM: Doctors' Stories. Princeton, NJ, Princeton University Press, 1991.

33. Keller EF: Reflections on Gender and Science. New Haven, CT, Yale University Press, 1985.

34. Callahan D: Frustrated mastery: Cultural context of death in America, In Caring for Patients at the End of Life (Special Issue), West J Med 1995; 163: 226–230.

35. Jecker NS, Emanuel L: Are acting and omitting morally equivalent? A reappraisal. J Am Geriatr Soc, in press.

36. Hilfiker D. Allowing the debilitated to die. N Engl J Med 1983; 308: 716–719.

37. Nuland SB: How We Die—Reflections on Life's Final Chapter. New Haven, CT, Yale University Press, 1994.

38. Wanzer SH, Federman DD, Adelstein SJ, et al.: The physician's responsibility toward hopelessly ill patients—A second look. N Engl J Med 1989; 320: 844–849.

39. Schneiderman LJ, Faber-Langendoen K, Jecker NS: Beyond futility to an ethic of care. Am J Med 1994; 96: 110–114.

# Futile Care: Physicians Should Not Be Allowed to Refuse to Treat

ROBERT M. VEATCH AND CAROL MASON SPICER

Eighteen years after the era of Karen Ann Quinlan, the debate over futile care has shifted. Now some patients are asking for treatment that care givers believe to be useless. In virtually all cases of so-called futile care, the real disagreement is over whether some agreed-on potential effect is of any value.

An obvious reason to resist providing care believed to be futile is that it appears to consume scarce resources and therefore burden others. However, for care that affects the dying trajectory but appears to most of us to offer no benefit, the proper course is for society—not clinicians—to cut patients off.

Under certain circumstances patients should have the right to receive life-prolonging care from their clinicians, provided it is equitably funded, even if the clinicians believe the care is futile and even if it violates their consciences to provide it. Society is

From Health Progress, December 1993, pp. 22–27.

not in a position to override a competent patient who prefers to live even if life prolongation is burdensome. For incompetent patients, if a clinician believes a treatment is actually hurting a patient significantly, he or she may appeal to a court to have it stopped.

A society that forces people to die against their will produces more offense than one that forces healthcare providers to provide services that violate their consciences. And medical professionals have a social contract with society to control the use of medical, life-prolonging technologies. Thus clinicians should be obligated to render the desired care if at least the following conditions are met: an ongoing patient-physician relationship, no colleague capable and willing to take the case, a clinician competent to provide the desired service, equitable funding, and the care being predictably life prolonging.

AMERICANS ARE IN THE MIDST OF A GREAT reversal in medical ethics. We have come a long way from the era of Karen Ann Quinlan, when patients and their families were desperately trying to get treatment stopped. At that time clinicians believed they had a moral duty to treat to the last gasp. The outcome of that debate was a patients' rights movement, which gave patients the right to refuse medical treatment, even if refusal would lead to death. It also gave families the right and the responsibility to function as surrogates for patients, trying to do what patients would have wanted, when patients' wishes are known, and trying to determine patients' best interests in cases where they are not.

Now, 18 years later, the debate has shifted. Some patients are asking for treatment that some care givers believe to be useless. Some patients insist on receiving what physicians believe to be "futile care"; others are arguing that physicians should have the right to refuse to provide care they deem futile.[1]

## MEDICALLY INAPPROPRIATE: A MISNOMER

On December 14, 1989, 86-year-old Helga Wanglie slipped on a rug and broke her hip.[2] She was treated at Hennepin County Medical Center in Minneapolis. She developed a series of respiratory tract infections and was placed on a respirator from which physicians were unable to wean her. She was transferred to a nursing home, where she suffered cardiac arrest and was left in a persistent vegetative state (PVS), on a ventilator and nasogastric tube. The healthcare team's unanimous conclusion was that the treatment was futile and "medically inappropriate."

But what can *medically* inappropriate mean here? It is morally reasonable to support the withdrawal of ventilators or even feeding tubes in such cases. But calling the inappropriateness "medical" tells us absolutely nothing and, in fact, perpetuates a serious philosophical mistake that has horrendous implications.

If continuing treatment is inappropriate, it is inappropriate religiously, philosophically, or morally, but medically the treatment has a definite effect. It clearly prolongs her life and is therefore efficacious.

## TWO BASIC DISTINCTIONS

To understand the debate over futile care, two basic distinctions must be made:

- A critical distinction between physiologically futile care and "normatively futile care"

- A distinction between denying so-called futile care on the basis of allocating scarce resources and denying it on the grounds that it violates care givers' integrity.

### Physiological Versus Normative Futility

Some interventions labeled futile are really without physical effect. This is what Stuart J. Youngner has called "physiologically futile treatment."[3] Such treatment will not produce the effect sought by the one insisting on it. This must be distinguished from care that has the anticipated effect but is believed by someone to be of no net benefit. We will call this second kind of futility "normative futility" because it involves a value judgment that the effect is of no benefit.

Physiological futility is more or less a question of medical science. We say "more or less" because every scientific question involves some value judgments (e.g., a choice of $p$ values and a choice of the concepts used to describe the effects). In rare instances, clinicians will disagree over the facts because of these hidden value disputes. Laypersons may also disagree with clinicians over such matters. To the extent that they do, it is not irrational for society to require care that physicians have deemed physiologically futile. That occurs only in unusual circumstances, however. In virtually all cases of so-called futile care, the real disagreement is not over whether a treatment will produce an effect; it is over whether some agreed-on potential effect is of any value.

To distinguish physiological from normative futility, ask the question, Is the disagreement over the science (the judgment about what the effect will be) or over the value of the agreed-on outcome? We can presume that clinicians are correct on the science, but also that they have no special claim to expertise on the value of the outcomes.

### Rationing Versus Clinician Integrity

A second distinction is also important. There are two separate reasons to be concerned about patient demands for care deemed futile: issues of rationing and of care givers' integrity.

First, an obvious reason to resist providing care believed to be futile (in either sense) is that it appears to consume scarce resources and therefore burden others. Our communal resources are inevitably scarce. Surely, if a treatment's benefits are so debatable that most of us consider them to be nonexistent, that is an obvious place to cut. But that does not mean it is a clinician's role to do the cutting.

We have acknowledged the legitimacy and necessity of rationing healthcare,[4] provided it is done equitably and with full public participation in decisions. But historically the clinician's job has been to help patients, not to act as society's cost-containment agent. This gatekeeping role must be someone else's task. Just like a defense attorney's role in the legal system is to advocate for a client, even an unworthy client, a clinician's job in the medical system is to advocate for his or her patient.

We agree that care without effect should not be funded on scientific grounds. A clinician should not be permitted to authorize treatments that he or she is convinced will not produce the effect a patient or surrogate seeks. In fact, insurers who receive requests for reimbursement for such care ought not to pay for it. However, for care that affects the dying trajectory but seems to most of us to offer no benefit, the proper course is for society—not clinicians—to cut patients off. Subscribers to insurance should have a strong interest in limiting care that offers little or no benefit and should agree to exclude such coverage from their plans.

For example, most Americans apparently believe that providing continued, long-term life support serves no purpose for a patient who is in a PVS. Insurers or health maintenance organizations (HMOs) should ask whether subscribers want to include long-term support for PVS patients in their coverage. Insurers should be able to explain what premiums would be if coverage for PVS treatment is and is not included. Insurers should not care whether subscribers vote PVS treatment in or out as long as they set an appropriately larger premium if such treatment is included.

We believe that most subscribers would vote PVS treatment out. The minority of subscribers who have an interest in such care can decide to buy supplemental insurance (a PVS rider) or to pay for the care out of pocket. If the insured group votes to include the coverage, or if individuals self-fund or buy supplemental coverage, then there is no unfairness to society as a whole. We can call this "equitable funding."

Helga Wanglie was an HMO member. HMO administrators should have asked her and her fellow subscribers whether they wanted to fund care for PVS patients. However, the HMO was explicit in its willingness to provide the funding for the care. There was thus no economic reason why the hospital or the individual physicians responsible for Helga Wanglie's care should have felt compelled to resist on grounds of allocation of resources. Also, at the time there were no non-economic demands—a scarcity of time or of beds—that would force a rationing decision. Had there been such scarcities, the institution would have had a moral obligation to make allocational choices.

Concern about scarcity of resources, however, is increasingly not the reason physicians want to limit care they deem futile. More commonly physicians want to protect the "integrity" of the physician who feels that it violates professional norms to deliver care that will do no good. We argue that under certain circumstances patients should have a right to receive life-prolonging care from their clinicians, provided it is equitably funded, even if the clinicians believe the care is futile and even if it violates their consciences to provide it.

This is a serious conflict, and we do not endorse such a position lightly. But clearly in some cases a physician must be obligated to violate his or her conscience. Consider, for example, someone raised as a racist who sincerely believes that it is wrong to provide medical treatment for racial minorities. The mere fact that the preju-

diced belief is held sincerely surely would not permit the physician to refuse to treat all members of minority groups.

It is similarly clear that patients cannot be allowed to receive any medical treatment that they happen to crave. Certain conditions will have to be met before the duty to provide care deemed futile will prevail. We will detail these conditions later in this article, but first we will explain the moral reasons why some patients may have a legitimate claim to care that physicians believe will do no good.

## MORAL COMPLEXITIES SURROUNDING A DUTY TO TREAT

Let us return to the case of Helga Wanglie. She and her husband were members of the right-to-life movement. Previously she had told family members that she would never want anything done to shorten her life. Her husband is quoted as saying, "I'm a pro-lifer; I take the position that human life is sacred."[5] He said that his wife of 53 years felt the same way. Their daughter agreed.

There was no dispute about the medical facts. The physicians and the Wanglie family agreed that she was permanently unconscious, that providing a ventilator and nasogastric tube would prolong her life, albeit in a vegetative state. The only question was the value of vegetative life.

### A Comparison with Quinlan

Compare this "futile care" case with the classic treatment refusal case of Karen Ann Quinlan, the young woman who in 1975 suffered a respiratory arrest that left her in a PVS.[6] Her physician, Robert Morse, was absolutely convinced that a ventilator believed necessary to preserve her life was providing benefit. He considered it "medically appropriate," claiming, probably incorrectly, that letting a permanently vegetative patient die violated the professional standard of the time.

The most critical issue in the court battle was whether a clinician's judgment about benefit for a patient could take precedence over a patient's or surrogate's assessment of benefit. Karen Quinlan's family and lawyer successfully argued that a professional consensus about whether an effective treatment was beneficial was irrelevant. Her father was, in effect, given the power to decide whether his daughter would consider this treatment beneficial.

The *Quinlan* and *Wanglie* cases, despite the seemingly opposite values of the decision makers, are similar in that both involved an assessment of the value of vegetative life. This assessment is fundamentally not a technical medical matter. Different people with different beliefs and values can come to different conclusions about whether ventilating a permanently vegetative patient is a benefit. When a patient is competent, he or she has the right to decide. When the patient is not competent, then the designated surrogate has the responsibility to try to determine what is best.

The two types of cases differ, however, in that the moral issue confronting physicians in futile care cases is whether patients or surrogates who make the decision that such care serves a worthwhile purpose have a right to insist that it be provided and, if so, on what basis.

## Autonomy Problem

Some defenders of the right to access make the mistake of claiming that the moral principle of autonomy confers that right. Autonomy gives a patient a right to refuse treatment. By extension, it even gives family members a limited right to decline treatment on a patient's behalf. But that does not imply that autonomy can give the patient a right of access. There is a lack of symmetry. Autonomy is a liberty right. A patient has a right to cancel the patient-physician relationship and at least metaphorically walk away. But in so

far as autonomy is relevant, it also should give a provider the right to sever the relationship. Autonomy cannot be the basis of the claim to a right to access.

## Burden of Futile Care

A second complexity in the argument concerns the possibility that acting on the demand for care deemed futile might impose excessive burdens on a patient. Clinicians evaluate some care not only as providing no benefit, but as actually harming a patient. But if harm refers to pain and suffering, a patient must at least be conscious for harm to occur. It is difficult to understand how Helga Wanglie or Karen Quinlan can be burdened by continued life support. There may well be moral offense if, for example, the life support is administered against a patient's wishes, but a patient must be conscious to be burdened in any real sense.

If a patient is mentally alert, he or she could perceive burden, but if the patient is mentally competent, it is the patient's judgment of burdens and benefits that must prevail. The patient is the one who will suffer the burden and die if treatment is forgone. Surely, society is not in a position to override a competent patient who prefers to live even if life prolongation is burdensome. Only a monstrous society would permit a physician to impose death on a patient who wants to live because the physician believes the patient would be better off dead.

The same rationale applies to persons who are mentally incompetent and who have expressed their wishes while competent, but what about those who have never expressed their wishes while competent? If a clinician believes treatment is actually hurting a patient significantly, he or she may appeal to a court to have it stopped.

Courts routinely override parents and guardians who refuse treatment when the refusal seems to harm a patient (e.g., Jehovah's Witness parents who refuse lifesaving blood for their children).[7] No court has yet ruled that parents or guardians can be guilty of abuse by insisting on futile care for a ward who is made to suffer by continuing treatment that is not only futile, but, on balance, gravely burdensome. Someday soon one may. But a judge, not a clinician, should determine the care to be unacceptable. Even if a clinician believes there is a burden on an incompetent patient, he or she should continue treatment until authorized to stop.[8]

Consider the case of Baby L.[9] She had fetal hydronephrosis and oligohydramnios, leaving her blind, deaf, and quadriplegic, with a gastrostomy and recurrent pneumonia. At two years of age she had the mental status of a three-month-old and had had four cardiac arrests. But she was conscious and could feel pain. Her mother insisted on life support, but the medical staff opposed mechanical ventilation and cardiovascular support, which they thought was "futile" and "inhumane."

The treatment was clearly preserving Baby L's life. She had lived for more than two years. The real issue was whether it was normatively futile. There are good reasons why this treatment should be considered disproportionately burdensome. Nevertheless, a clinician has no *medical* basis for deciding that the effective treatment does more harm than good. Only a public agency with due process has that authority. If a clinician believes that an incompetent patient is being harmed by futile care demanded by a surrogate, the clinician's duty is to try to get the surrogate overridden.

John J. Paris and colleagues treat the Baby L case as a paradigm futile-care case. However, this is a special case. The patient has never been competent to evaluate the burdens, and the burdens could well exceed the benefits. But even in these circumstances the clinicians cannot withdraw life support on their own. It is appropriate and reasonable to try to get a court order to stop, but this is different from simply deciding to overrule the mother's judgment about the burdens and benefits of the life support.

## FUTILE CARE FOR PATIENTS WHO ARE NOT BEING HARMED

Cases involving burden to incompetent patients are really not the essence of the futile care debate, however. The real issue is futile care for patients who are not being harmed. This is true futile care (i.e., care that neither benefits nor burdens a patient). For the moment let us simplify the analysis by limiting the discussion to interventions that will predictably prolong life.

Clinicians always have the right to withdraw from a case, just as a competent patient might, provided someone else is willing to take the case. It is in neither a patient's nor a physician's interest to insist that the original physician continue. But if no colleague is willing to step forward, the treatment is life prolonging, and the treatment will not be burdensome, then a licensed professional responsible for and capable of providing the care has a duty to provide it even if he or she is morally opposed. Otherwise that clinician would have to argue that the patient is better off dead even though the patient is not being injured and even though the patient or surrogate disagrees. Effective, nonburdensome, life-prolonging care is always morally required if a patient or surrogate desires it.

But why should physician autonomy be violated in this one case when generally patient autonomy should not be violated? Two arguments can be offered: the argument from offense and the argument from contract.

### Argument from Offense

If a patient or surrogate is demanding life-prolonging care that his or her clinician believes is futile and a violation of his or her integrity to provide, we have a head-on clash between a patient's or surrogate's choice for life and the provider's autonomy. A society that forces people to die against their will produces more offense than one that forces healthcare providers to provide services that violate their consciences. If society must offend, the lesser offense is preferred.

## Argument from Contract

The second argument rests on the notion of the social contract or covenant between medical professionals and society. Licensed professionals are the only members of society licensed to control the use of medical, life-prolonging technologies. When they accept licensure, they accept a public trust to use their monopoly on medical knowledge to preserve lives when the appropriate decision makers want them preserved.

Imagine that society is contemplating creating monopoly control over certain life-prolonging technologies. Further, imagine that there will be cases in which a minority desperately wants these technologies used while a majority does not see any value in their use. Finally, imagine that we cannot know whether we will be in the majority or the minority. We believe a rational society will extract, as a condition of licensure, a promise that the clinician will use these technologies for people who want them.

Of course, some conditions would be attached to such a promise. These might include:

1. An ongoing patient-physician relationship

2. No colleague capable and willing to take the case

3. A clinician competent to provide the desired service

4. Equitable funding

5. The care being predictably life prolonging

At least if all these conditions were met, we believe clinicians would be obligated to render the desired care. All these conditions were met in the *Wanglie* case. Once the court determined that Helga Wanglie's husband was the proper surrogate, physicians wisely acknowledged their duty to provide the care they believed was futile even though it violated their sense of professional integrity. Once one realizes that the decision to forgo effective, life-prolonging care is a moral choice rather than a technical one, it seems hard to deny the right of the minority to access. If we have created a monopoly in the use of that technology, we would be wise to insist that minority interests be protected by ensuring that holders of minority views can have their lives prolonged. The alternative is to permit physicians to decide that a patient would be better off dead even though the patient is not being burdened and even though the patient or surrogate believes the life should be preserved.

## NON−LIFE-PROLONGING FUNDAMENTAL CARE

What we have said thus far is limited to care that can be expected to prolong life effectively, at least for a length of time that a patient or surrogate considers worthwhile. The argument for the duty to provide care deemed futile clearly does not extend to all non−life-prolonging treatments that may be of interest to the patient. Some patients' demands are too offensive or too trivial to make them part of the contract between professionals and society. For example, a patient's demand that a surgeon amputate a healthy limb would not have to be honored.

On the other hand, some care that does not prolong life may still be considered so fundamental that physicians would have a duty to provide it. Consider, for example, medication to relieve severe chronic pain. Some physicians may sincerely believe that providing such medication is wrong, for instance, because it may shorten a patient's life. A physician may consider the use of such risky medication immoral, even though Catholic moral theology and much secular thought acknowledges the legitimacy of risking the indirect side effects in such cases. Even if a physician is sincerely opposed, however, he or she may well be expected by society to administer the pain relief, provided no other physician will take the case.

The key is that some interests of patients and surrogates may be recognized as fundamental. Even if a majority would not consider the treatment worth pursuing, that majority might recognize the importance of the minority's claim. Life-prolonging care is fundamental in this way; certain non–life-prolonging care may be as well. If the care is perceived as fundamental, then it should be part of the social covenant between society and the profession. In such cases, as in ones involving life-prolonging treatment, if (1) there is an ongoing patient-physician relationship, (2) no other physician will take the case, (3) the clinician is competent to provide the care, and (4) the funding is equitable, the licensed professional who is given a monopoly over the control of life should be expected to promise to use that technology when patients or surrogates ask for it.

REFERENCES

1. Nancy S. Jecker and Robert A. Pearlman, "Medical Futility: Who Decides?" *Archives of Internal Medicine,* June 1992, pp. 1140–1144; Lawrence J. Schneiderman, Nancy S. Jecker, and Albert R. Jonsen, "Medical Futility: Its Meaning and Ethical Implications," *Annals of Internal Medicine,* vol. 112, 1990, pp. 949–954; Donald J. Murphy, "Do-Not-Resuscitate Orders: Time for Reappraisal in Long-Term-Care Institutions," *JAMA,* vol. 250, 1988, pp. 2098, 2101; Tom Tomlinson and Howard Brody, "Futility and the Ethics of Resuscitation," *JAMA,* vol. 264, 1990, p. 1277; Steven H. Miles, "Informed Demand for 'Nonbeneficial' Medical Treatment," *New England Journal of Medicine,* August 15, 1991, pp. 512–515;

Michael Coogan, "Medical Futility in Resuscitation: Value Judgment and Clinical Judgment," *Cambridge Quarterly for Healthcare Ethics,* vol. 2, 1993, pp. 197–217; John J. Paris, "Pipes, Colanders, and Leaky Buckets: Reflections on the Futility Debate," *Cambridge Quarterly for Healthcare Ethics,* vol. 2, 1993, pp. 147–149.

2. Steven H. Miles, "Informed Demand for 'Nonbeneficial' Medical Treatment," *New England Journal of Medicine,* August 15, 1991, pp. 512–515.

3. Stuart J. Youngner, "Who Defines Futility?" *JAMA,* vol. 260, 1988, pp. 2094–2095.

4. Robert M. Veatch and Carol Mason Spicer, "Medically Futile Care: The Role of the Physician in Setting Limits," *American Journal of Law and Medicine,* vol. 18, nos. 1 and 2, 1992, pp. 15–36; Robert M. Veatch, "DRGs and the Ethical Reallocation of Resources," *Hastings Center Report,* June 1986, pp. 32–40.

5. B. D. Colen, "Fight Over Life," *Newsday,* January 29, 1991, p. S64.

6. *In re Quinlan,* 70 N.J. 10, 355 A.2d 647 (1976), *cert. denied sub nom.; Garger v. New Jersey,* 429 U.S. 922 (1976), overruled in part; *In re Conroy,* 98 N.J. 321, 486 A.2d 1209 (1985).

7. Maureen L. Moore, "Their Life is in the Blood: Jehovah's Witnesses, Blood Transfusions and the Courts," *Northern Kentucky Law Review,* vol. 10, no. 2, 1983, pp. 281–304.

8. Hastings Center, *Guidelines on the Termination of Life-Sustaining Treatment and the Care of the Dying,* Hastings-on-Hudson, NY, 1987, p. 32.

9. John J. Paris, Robert K. Crone, and Frank Reardon, "Physicians' Refusal of Requested Treatment," *New England Journal of Medicine,* vol. 322, 1990, pp. 1012–1115.

## Discussion Questions

1. The following futile-care policy has been in effect at Santa Monica Hospital since 1991; it is used when care that the physician regards as futile is requested by the patient, surrogate, or family. Evaluate this policy in light of the preceding discussions of futility. In particular, consider whether it would lead to inappropriately withholding treatment from patients, or whether it would inappropriately provide futile care. Also bear in mind the need to control costs and conserve medical resources. If the policy is adequate, defend it. If it is inadequate, explain how it should be altered.

   1. The attending physician should take the time to carefully explain the nature of an ailment, the options, and the prognosis to the aware patient and to the family. The doctor should explain that abandoning the treatment does not mean abandoning the patient in terms of comfort, dignity, and psychological support.

2. The attending physician should provide the names of appropriate consultants to provide an independent opinion.
3. The assistance of the nurses, chaplain, patient care representative, and social services should be offered to the patient's family. A joint conference with the doctor is desirable.
4. At the attending physician's request, the bioethics committee may be called in to consider the matter and offer advice and counsel to the physician or family.
5. Adequate time should be given so that the patient and family can consider this information.
6. If all of these steps are taken and the family remains unconvinced, neither the doctor nor the hospital is required to provide care that is not medically indicated, and the family may be offered a substitute physician (if one can be found) and another hospital (if one is available).
7. If it is determined that the patient can no longer benefit from an acute hospital stay and the patient insists on staying, or the family insists that the patient should remain, the mechanism for personal payment can be invoked.[1]

2. The case of Helga Wanglie has been widely discussed. It has become a focal point for much that has been said about futile medical treatments. Read the following summary of this case and then decide whether it was appropriate for Ms. Wanglie to have been maintained on the respirator. Defend your position carefully, making clear which moral principles are relevant and how the discussions of futility in this section are to be applied.[2]

In January of 1990, this eighty-five-year-old woman was transferred from a nursing home to the emergency department of the hospital for treatment of a chronic bronchial infection. During this treatment she was intubated and placed on a respirator, on which she became dependent. During an attempt to wean her from this respirator, her heart stopped; although she was resuscitated, she remained unconscious. Examination showed that her higher brain centers had been extensively damaged by lack of oxygen; that is, there was no hope that she would ever regain consciousness. The medical team, believing that it no longer benefited her, suggested to her family that treatment be withdrawn. Her family strenuously objected to this, saying that doctors should not play God and that a miracle could occur. Attempts to resolve the disagreement between the medical staff and the family were unsuccessful, and other hospitals refused (on the basis of the patient's poor health) to take over her care. A court appointed her husband as conservator, and aggressive medical care continued under his direction until Helga Wanglie died in July 1991 of multisystem organ failure.

3. The case of Baby K. has been another focal point for the discussion of futile medical care. Before Baby K.'s birth in 1992, doctors had determined that she was anencephalic; that is, she had only a brain stem and no cerebral cortex. It was explained to the mother that her child would never be conscious and would either be stillborn or would die shortly after birth. Although many parents who are presented with this tragic news choose to abort the pregnancy, Mrs. H. (the mother) insisted that everything be done to keep her baby alive, including ventilatory support (if necessary). Baby K. was alive at birth, but she would never have more than unconscious reflex actions, such as sucking, swallowing, and coughing. At birth, Baby K. had difficulty breathing and was given respirator support; the medical team

1. From T. Hudson, "Are Futile-Care Policies the Answer?" *Hospitals and Health Networks* (Feb. 20, 1994): 26–32; policy presented on 28.
2. Much has been written about the Wanglie case, but you should begin with S. Miles, "Informed Demand for 'Non-Beneficial' Medical Treatment," *New England Journal of Medicine* 325 (1991): 512–15.

was troubled by this, however, and continued to seek permission to withdraw care and let the child die. When the mother continued to insist that "everything be done," the hospital went to court seeking permission to withdraw life-sustaining care. The lower court refused to grant this permission, the court of appeals upheld that decision, and the United States Supreme Court refused to review the decision. Despite periodic problems with breathing that required hospitalization and ventilator support, Baby K. continued to live in a nursing home.

Was the treatment of Baby K. futile in any of the senses discussed in this section? Why or why not? What decisions should have been made regarding this infant's treatment, and why? Make very clear which moral principles you are applying.

## Suggestions for Further Reading

### DEFINING AND ANALYZING FUTILITY

Callahan, D. "Medical Futility, Medical Necessity: The-Problem-without-a-Name." *Hastings Center Report* 21, no. 4 (1991): 30–35.

> The various ways in which the issue of futility can arise are explored, showing that this is a meeting place for several concerns that initially seem to be unrelated.

Jecker, N. "Is Refusal of Futile Treatment Unjustified Paternalism?" *Journal of Clinical Ethics* 6, no. 2 (1995): 133–37.

> Responding to Zawacki's argument that withholding futile care is paternalistic and unjustified, Jecker explains why these cases of withholding are morally parallel to other clear cases in which physicians are permitted to go against patients' wishes.

Lantos, J., et al. "The Illusion of Futility in Clinical Practice." *American Journal of Medicine* 87 (1989): 81–84.

> It is argued that futile treatments are not significantly different from effective ones, and that futility judgments should only rarely be used as a basis for withholding care.

### APPLICATIONS OF FUTILITY

Alpers, Ann, and Bernard Lo. "Avoiding Family Feuds: Responding to Surrogate Demands for Life-Sustaining Interventions." *Journal of Law, Medicine and Ethics* 27, no. 1 (Spring 1999): 74 ff. *InfoTrac Power Search #A54700017.*

> Futility judgments can be used to respond to inappropriate demands made by family members.

Annas, G. "Asking the Courts to Set the Standard of Emergency Care: The Case of Baby K." *New England Journal of Medicine* 330, no. 21 (1994): 1542–45.

> Laws that apply to emergency medical care require that this treatment be provided and make no exceptions for situations in which this care might be futile, inhumane, or inappropriate.

Callahan, D. "Necessity, Futility, and the Good Society." *Journal of the American Geriatrics Society* 42, no. 8 (1994): 866–67.

> Our problems with limiting care arise in part from our society's lack of a "sense of what is fitting." Comparisons are made with European practices.

Golenski, J., and L. Nelson. "The Wanglie Case: A Demand for Treatment Clashes with Medical Integrity." *Clinical Ethics Report* 6, no. 1 (1992): 1–8.

> The famous Wanglie case is presented and analyzed.

Jecker, N., and L. Schneiderman. "An Ethical Analysis of the Use of 'Futility' in the 1992 American Heart Association *Guidelines* for Cardiopulmonary Resuscitation and Emergency Cardiac Care." *Archives of Internal Medicine* 153 (1993): 2195–98.

> Although there is a great deal of discussion of futility in medical journals and policies, they often involve misunderstandings of what futility involves and how it should be applied. This article discusses a prominent example.

Murphy, D. "Can We Set Futile Care Policies? Institutional and Systemic Challenges." *Journal of the American Geriatrics Society* 42, no. 8 (1994): 890–93.

> Attempts to set policies that require withholding quantitatively futile care may result in withholding futile treatments only from those who cannot afford them.

Nelson, J. "Families and Futility." *Journal of the American Geriatrics Society* 42, no. 8 (1994): 879–82.

> Futility judgments often have the effect of taking decision-making authority away from families. Nelson argues that this is often unwarranted and that futility policies give physicians too much power to make treatment decisions.

Peabody, J. "When a Parent Demands What Health Care Providers Deem Foolish." *Clinical Ethics Report* 7, no. 4 (1993): 1–12.

> The case of Baby K. is presented and ethically analyzed.

# Section 5

# *Resuscitating the Dying Patient*

## Introduction

For many patients who die in hospital, the last medical procedure employed before death is some attempt at resuscitation. Although this reflects standard medical procedures, serious moral questions surround the use of resuscitative techniques at the end of a patient's life. Are the potential benefits of resuscitation attempts outweighed by the potential for harm? Are patients adequately informed about the nature of these techniques and about their alternatives for care at the end of life? Are resuscitation attempts as they are now employed a wise use of our medical resources?

### *CPR as a Medical Procedure*

Cardiopulmonary resuscitation (CPR) is a set of medical procedures whose emergence in 1960[1] was sparked by the development of closed-chest cardiac massage (an improvement over earlier procedures that involved cutting open the patient's chest in order to massage the heart directly). This new form of cardiac massage was quickly coupled with artificial respiration and electrical cardiac stimulation.[2] By 1966 this procedure was well established in American hospitals, although its limitations were evident—of those patients receiving CPR in a hospital in the 1960s, only about 15 percent survived to hospital discharge, and many of those survivors suffered impairments

1. W. Kouwenhoven, J. Jude, and G. Knickerbocker, "Closed-Chest Cardiac Massage," *Journal of the American Medical Association* 173 (1960): 1064–67.
2. G. Snider, "The Do-Not-Resuscitate Order: Ethical and Legal Imperative or Medical Decision?" *American Review of Respiratory Disease* 143 (1991): 665–74.

of various sorts. Although CPR techniques have been honed considerably in subsequent decades and supplemented by other methods of resuscitating patients whose heart or lungs have stopped functioning, CPR is still not a magic wand. As Young reports in this section, these procedures involve considerable risk, and many who receive CPR never leave the hospital alive.

Although CPR is clearly a medical procedure, it is generally treated in law and policy as being quite distinct from others. It is generally agreed that it is morally unacceptable to impose an invasive and risky medical treatment upon a patient who has not consented to it (or whose surrogate has not consented on his or her behalf—see section 3 for more details). And yet CPR is regularly provided to those who may not clearly understand it and who have not explicitly consented to it. Two reasons are usually offered for this exception. First, someone who is in cardiac or pulmonary arrest is in no position to be making complicated decisions. Nor is there generally time to find and consult an appropriate surrogate. Therefore, the decision must be made by those who are present and able to attempt resuscitation. Second, it is generally assumed that anyone who is in need of CPR would want it. Refusing this medical treatment would almost certainly lead to death, and death is generally regarded as a serious harm. Thus, the principle of beneficence indicates that one ought to benefit a person in cardiac arrest by attempting resuscitation.

This reasoning would be more convincing if CPR caused the patient no harm and was very likely to be successful. Unfortunately, this is not the case. A great many patients who receive CPR do not survive to hospital discharge. Those who do survive often suffer a number of ill effects (both from the procedures themselves and from the cardiac arrest that precipitated them). In addition to fractured ribs, trauma to upper abdominal organs, neurological damage, and so forth, there is also risk of delayed effects such as depression, memory loss, and diminished awareness of one's environment.[3] It is interesting that those who have a clear understanding of CPR techniques and outcomes (such as doctors, nurses, and a number of patients who have had CPR in the past) are significantly less likely to want CPR for themselves. This should lead us to ask whether our current practice of providing CPR to everyone who goes into cardiopulmonary arrest (without a do-not-resuscitate order) is well founded. In particular, close attention should be paid to whether CPR is futile in any of the senses delineated in the previous section.

The discussion of these issues will include an extended discussion of the do-not-resuscitate (DNR) order. (This is sometimes known as the do-not-attempt-resuscitation or DNAR order.) This is a medical order, included in a patient's chart, indicating that no attempt at resuscitation should be made if the patient goes into cardiopulmonary arrest. There are other variants on the DNR order. The order might specify which resuscitation techniques may be used and which may not; for example, a patient may have a do-not-intubate (DNI) order, or an order that allows basic CPR techniques and perhaps the use of certain drugs but not electrical defibrillation. Decisions

3. D. Miranda, "Quality of Life after Cardiopulmonary Resuscitation," *Chest* 106, no. 2 (1994): 524–30.

about whether resuscitation should be attempted are a component in broader issues of whether life-sustaining care should be withheld or withdrawn (see section 2) and whether particular forms of care are futile (see section 4).

The most common justifications offered for writing a DNR order are as follows: (1) CPR would be quantitatively futile; that is, the likelihood that the patient would survive the procedure to hospital discharge is too small to be worth pursuing. (2) CPR would be qualitatively futile; that is, the quality of life the patient would be likely to experience following CPR would be so low as to be not worth pursuing (from the patient's point of view). (3) The patient's current quality of life is so low as to be unacceptable to him or her, so cardiopulmonary arrest would be welcomed as a way of dying and thus escaping further suffering. This can be seen as a variant of the qualitative futility argument presented in (2). (4) The resources that would be used in providing CPR would be better used in providing some other treatment (perhaps to another patient). The justification for this reallocation might be found in one or more of the first three arguments.

## CPR and Voluntary Informed Consent

One of the issues surrounding resuscitation is voluntary informed consent. Although the patient will be unable to make such decisions when actually in arrest, medical care, including resuscitation preferences, can be planned in advance. Living wills and other documents provide a means of doing this formally, and these generally include discussion of whether the patient would want to be resuscitated. Unfortunately, patients are often asked to express preferences on the basis of seriously incomplete information. The Medical Directive, a widely used living will form, describes CPR as the use, in a patient "on the point of dying[,] . . . of drugs and electric shock to start the heart beating, and artificial breathing," and asks whether the patient would want this, or want it withheld, in four types of medical situations.[4] It is the physician's responsibility to fill in the details of these procedures, including risks and outcomes, but in many cases this information is either not provided or is not understood by the patient. As a result, many decisions people make about resuscitation fail to meet the requirements for informed consent. Young's article in this section is a first step in remedying this problem, although, as he points out, only a detailed discussion with a physician about one's particular circumstances can really solve it.

Strangely enough, physicians are generally required to obtain the consent of the patient or an appropriate surrogate before writing a DNR order. What is odd about this is that a DNR order is not a medical procedure, yet we apply informed consent requirements to it as though it were. Note that this requirement does not distinguish between cases in which CPR would confer a benefit and those in which it would merely make the process of dying longer and more painful.

4. L. Emanuel and E. Emanuel, "The Medical Directive: A New Comprehensive Advance Care Document," *Journal of the American Medical Association* 261, no. 22 (1989): 3288–93, at 3290.

Surrogates and those who make these decisions on a patient's behalf face two difficulties: They generally do not have a clear picture of the patient's quality of life, and they do not know how unpleasant the patient's life would have to be before he or she would prefer to be dead. Studies show that physicians tend to underestimate patients' quality of life.[5] One finding is that there are few clear correlations between quality-of-life factors (such as forgetfulness, pain, mobility, depression, and family relationships) and a patient's resuscitation preferences. This suggests that there is no commonly shared judgment about how low one's quality of life must be before resuscitation efforts should be abandoned. So even if one knew exactly what the patient's quality of life was, it would tell one little about whether a DNR order should be written.

Families who insist that "everything be done" for a dying patient, including CPR, are often mistaken about the place of CPR in that patient's medical care. First, they may believe that the patient would benefit from this medical intervention, when in fact it would only prolong his or her suffering. Second, they may mistakenly believe that withholding such care would be tantamount to abandoning or betraying the patient. This has been used as the basis for allowing physicians to write DNR orders without the family's consent:

> No matter how clearly the medical case against CPR is made, some families will find the decision to forgo it emotionally or ethically difficult, and some will find it impossible. There is no point in making families agonize over the matter and worry whether they are breaking faith with their loved ones. To do so may create unnecessary suffering, strife, or guilt and may produce deadlock with an unsophisticated, death-denying, or guilt-ridden family.[6]

Discussions with a physician can often clear up these mistakes, but some families will not listen or fail to understand. Protecting such families and the patients they care for from the results of these mistakes involves a twofold paternalism: interference in the decisions of the family to protect both the family and the patient. The patient is protected because the DNR order would enable the patient to escape the suffering CPR would cause. As Hackler and Hiller put it: "at a certain point, . . . respect for the family must give way to concern for the patient. Hospital policy should not force physicians to inflict additional suffering on their patients when surrogates insist on burdensome treatment for unacceptable reasons."[7]

5. See, for instance, R. Uhlmann and R. Pearlman, "Perceived Quality of Life and Preferences for Life-Sustaining Treatment in Older Adults," *Archives of Internal Medicine* 151 (1991): 495–97; T. Starr, R. Pearlman, and R. Uhlmann, "Quality of Life and Resuscitation Decisions in Elderly Patients," *Journal of General Internal Medicine* 1 (1986): 373–79; and R. Pearlman and R. Uhlmann, "Patient and Physician Perceptions of Patient Quality of Life across Chronic Diseases," *Journal of Gerontology* 43 (1988): M25–30.

6. J. Hackler and F. Hiller, "Family Consent to Orders Not to Resuscitate: Reconsidering Hospital Policy," *Journal of the American Medical Association* 264, no. 10 (1990): 1281–83, at 1282.

7. Ibid., 1283.

## CPR and Futile Care

It has been suggested that in certain circumstances physicians should be authorized to override patients' or surrogates' refusal of a DNR order. The usual defense for this position is that CPR would be futile in these cases. It is uncontroversial that some treatments may be withheld by the physician when these are deemed futile. For instance, extra-corporeal membrane oxygenation (ECMO), a technique for providing the patient with a continuous flow of oxygenated blood, is provided only when it would provide a clear benefit to the patient, not whenever a patient or surrogate demands it. Why, then, must CPR be provided when the patient is extremely unlikely to benefit from it?

There are several classes of patients for whom CPR is highly unlikely to provide much benefit. For such patients, the probability of surviving CPR to hospital discharge is generally less than 3 percent. Although this is higher than the 1 percent futility threshold proposed by Schneiderman and Jecker (see section 4), one can still build a compelling case for the conclusion that such treatment is quantitatively futile for these patients. One can also add a qualitative component to this futility discussion: Of those who do survive to hospital discharge, many have a lower quality of life because of various medical problems or deficits. If a good case can be made for the conclusion that CPR is futile in these cases, would this justify hospital policies that allow physicians to write DNR orders for these patients without the patients' (or surrogates') consent? How much force should the principle of respect for autonomy receive in this situation?

In working out whether CPR would be futile, it is important to be clear about what outcome one is pursuing. If CPR is being used as a means of returning the patient to his or her pre-morbid condition, it may well be quantitatively futile. But remember that the patient may have other goals in mind:

> What about the terminally ill patient who requests CPR to allow one last visit from a distant loved one hastening to the bedside? Even though the physician is convinced that CPR would have almost no chance of keeping the patient alive more than a day or so in the ICU, clearly the physician will want to make a compassionate exception to accommodate this short-term goal of the patient.[8]

As the previous section made clear, no treatment is futile, period. Futility is always relative to a specific goal.

Related to this are questions about how we want to allocate our medical resources, a matter that will be taken up in more detail in section 9. With CPR, the question is this: if providing this medical treatment to identifiable groups of patients for whom it will provide little or no benefit is very costly, is this allocation of our limited medical resources morally warranted? The facile claim that CPR provides a patient with the hope of continued life and that no price can be put on a human life is not enough here.

8. L. Schneiderman, "The Futility Debate: Effective versus Beneficial Intervention," *Journal of the American Geriatrics Society* 42, no. 8 (1994): 883–86, at 885.

First, we must ask what sort of life the patient would experience after resuscitation. How much are we willing to spend to prolong life if the patient never regains consciousness, or awakes to great pain and spends the last two weeks of life suffering in the intensive care unit? Second, it is misleading to claim that the choice is between saving a life using CPR and doing nothing (and thus saving no lives at all). But this is not necessarily the case. By reallocating our medical resources, we may be able to save more lives—and lives that will involve more pleasure, at that—than by providing CPR to dying patients.

# Emergency Department Resuscitation Techniques

## BRYAN YOUNG

CONSENT IS A CORNERSTONE OF ETHICAL medical practice. The traditional setting for gaining consent is the doctor's office; there the patient and physician, without interruption or time pressure, discuss the potential benefits and risks of a proposed procedure. In the emergency department things are quite different: illness or injury may cloud consciousness, patients may be distracted by pain, the patient-physician relationship is undeveloped, and the urgency of the condition may not allow time for in-depth discussions. The public, worried that unwanted procedures will be carried out on them when they are incapacitated, has pushed for the acceptance of advanced directives, also known as "living wills." Living wills, however, are often developed in isolation, without consultation, and with limited information.

In this article I describe several lifesaving procedures commonly used in the emergency department. The reason for using the procedure is first given, followed by a description of the technique, and ending with a comment about possible discomfort and potential harm. Although

benefits and risks are explained, quantifying these is beyond the scope of this chapter, and the reader would be ill advised to attempt to make decisions based solely on this information. Many factors influence benefit-to-risk ratios, including extent of illness or injury, timeliness of intervention, age, and prior medical conditions. The information is presented to enable readers to discuss these items with their physicians and then to reach some conclusions for themselves. These choices will hopefully better reflect patients' desires and physician-guided expectations.

Resuscitation in the emergency department starts with ensuring adequate oxygen delivery to the lungs. Sometimes sufficient oxygen can be given through a small tube placed under the nose or using the standard oxygen mask. However, in critical circumstances, more advanced techniques are required. One of these is a device called continuous positive airway pressure (CPAP). In some patients with advanced lung disease or heart failure, the chest muscles fatigue and the small airways in the lung collapse, so that the oxygen level falls and the carbon dioxide

Prepared for this volume.

level rises. A tight mask with large straps is applied to the nose (or nose and mouth) in order to deliver pressurized oxygen through a large tube. The patient breathes with and against this pressure for twenty minutes to an hour at a time. If successful, this can avert the need for more aggressive therapy. The patient is unable to speak while receiving this treatment, and there is some facial discomfort. Potential harm is minimal, but the procedure may be unsuccessful.

The most common technique to ensure breathing in a critically ill or injured patient is orotracheal intubation. Patients can lose muscle tone in the tongue, which then falls backward into the throat, blocking airflow into the lungs. Similarly, bleeding or swelling from injury can cause obstruction. During normal swallowing, a piece of cartilage closes off the opening to the windpipe. Any material that passes beyond that barricade is further blocked by spasms of the vocal cords, and coughing expels it from the airways. In unconscious patients, all these protective reflexes can be lost, so that material in the mouth or vomited up from the stomach may enter the lungs. Intubation provides an open passage from the mouth to the lungs and helps reduce the risk of aspiration. Intubation is also required when mechanical ventilation is needed. With the patient lying on his back, the doctor places a metal device similar to a long, lighted tongue blade over the tongue and deep into the throat. Then the tongue and jaw are lifted forward and downward, revealing the vocal cords, a plastic tube about seven to eight millimeters in diameter is passed between the vocal cords into the windpipe, and a balloon on the end of the tube inside the windpipe is inflated. The tube is taped to the lips and cheek or tied around the head. Usually a hard plastic device is inserted into the mouth to keep the patient from biting the breathing tube. In the vast majority of cases, the patient is either already unconscious or is given intravenous medication to make him or her unaware during this procedure. Occasionally it is done with the patient awake by spraying the tongue and throat with anesthetic. The tube remains in place until the patient has recovered enough to breathe well and is conscious enough to keep his airway open. This may take a few hours or several days.

There are many negatives to having this tube in place: no speech is possible, as the tube is between the vocal cords; similarly, eating is not possible. The patient experiences gagging and choking sensations. (These feelings generally diminish within minutes or hours). There is throat and mouth discomfort. The tube limits mobility, and sometimes restraints are required to prevent stuporous patients from pulling it out. Potential harm from this procedure includes damage to the teeth, lips, throat, and vocal cords. More serious harm would include failing to place the tube properly, in which case no air goes into the lungs, and death ensues.

Rarely, in patients in whom intubation is not possible because of injury or abnormalities of the mouth and throat, a surgical airway is required. This procedure, called a cricothyroidotomy, involves making an incision just below the thyroid cartilage (Adam's apple) in the front of the neck through the skin and into the airway. A plastic tube is inserted through this incision into the windpipe. Occasionally the incision is made lower in the neck; this is called a tracheostomy. Patients needing this procedure would be unconscious. The negatives are similar to those for intubation, including not being able to speak when awake. However, if the tube is required for days, the patient may be able to eat and drink. Damage to the structures in the neck is also possible. Again, failing to insert the tube properly can result in death.

After securing an airway, the next procedure in resuscitation is to provide ventilation, pumping air in and out of the lungs. This is done when the chest muscles or nervous system is not working to provide adequate breathing. Usually a stiff plastic bag is attached to the endotracheal tube; it is squeezed by hand to push oxygen into the lungs. If necessary, a machine is later used to continue this process for hours or days. Attaching the bag or the machine causes little additional discomfort to the patient, as he or she is already intubated. Sometimes coordinating the machine to the patient's own breathing pattern may be difficult. Potential harm includes failure to provide enough air exchange, resulting in lack of oxygen or build-up of carbon dioxide, possibly leading to death. High pressures may damage the airways and lungs, causing a small tear through which air can escape into the chest cavity, a pneumothorax.

Another resuscitation procedure used to maintain breathing is the placement of a chest tube. It is used most often in trauma patients when a fractured rib has punctured a lung. Air escaping from the injured lung fills the chest space, and the lung collapses; if this is not corrected, the patient becomes unable to breathe. Sometimes internal bleeding in the chest results in the same problem. After a local anesthetic has been injected, an incision is made in the skin on the side of the chest. Then the tissue between the skin and the ribs is separated. Finally, a space is opened between two ribs, and a plastic tube is inserted through this opening to lie between the lung and the chest wall. Suction is applied via this tube, removing the air or blood from the chest cavity.

Patients often experience pain and pressure discomfort during the procedure, and there is discomfort from the tube in the chest; mobility is limited by the suction device. Potential harm to the patient includes bleeding, infection, and damage to the ribs, lungs, or (rarely) other organs. Improper placement or connections can further compromise lung function.

After providing an airway and ventilation, the next step in resuscitation is to ensure adequate blood pressure. All critically ill patients need intravenous access, usually through a vein in the arm. When large amounts of fluid or blood must be given, or when concentrated medications such as adrenaline are required, larger veins are accessed in the neck, below the collarbone in the

chest, or in the groin. Starting these lines can be moderately painful, but local anesthetics are used. Risks include damaging the nearby arteries and nerves. Attempts to start these lines in the neck and chest can puncture the lungs. Finally, these "central" intravenous lines are more prone to potentially serious infections.

Resuscitation of the heart is a commonly performed emergency procedure, both in the hospital and at the scene of the arrest. A typical scenario would be that a patient collapses in public. A witness to the collapse gets a helper to call 911 and begins cardiopulmonary resuscitation (CPR). The rescuer first assesses the patient's breathing. Finding none, he gives the patient mouth-to-mouth breaths. Next, he checks for a pulse. After finding no pulse, he feels for the lower part of the breastbone. Locking his hands one on top of the other, he compresses the chest by pushing the breastbone about two inches down into the chest about eighty times a minute. After every fifteen compressions, another two breaths are given. The process is designed to provide oxygen to the lungs by rescue breathing and to force blood to be circulated to the brain and other vital organs by the chest compressions. Unfortunately, the process is not highly effective and is valuable only as a temporary measure until further intervention is possible. Patients do not experience discomfort during CPR, since they are unconscious; however, they may have pain after they wake up. Complications include rib fractures, which may damage the lungs or other internal organs.

When trained personnel take over the resuscitation, their first step is to diagnose the electrical rhythm of the heart. The most common cause of a cardiac arrest in our society is an electrical problem called ventricular fibrillation. Instead of having an organized electric impulse flowing across the heart, followed by a smooth contraction, the electrical impulses are scattered, causing the heart to quiver rather than beat. Therefore, no blood is pumped. If this rhythm is found, electric pads are placed on the patient's chest and a direct current of 100 joules is delivered. The intent is to stop all electrical activity in the heart and allow it to start back up in an organized manner. If unsuccessful, a second and possibly a third shock are given, each with higher energy. After these, if there is no response, CPR is continued, the patient is intubated, an intravenous line is started, and medications are given. Further electric shocks are used after each medication has been circulated in the blood. If the heart does not start after these medications are administered, the resuscitation efforts are stopped. This is typically after thirty or forty minutes.

The chances of successfully restarting the heart are directly influenced by the time CPR is started and the time the electric shocks, which are the most critical lifesaving step, are applied. Around 35 to 40 percent of patients with ventricular fibrillation will survive if defibrillated within three minutes. Few patients defibrillated after ten minutes survive. Some survivors experience chest pain from the electrical shocks, and a few will have minor skin burns. The possibility of resuscitating the heart after there has been irreversible brain injury is the most serious risk. Other causes of cardiac arrest include abnormally fast heart rhythms, which are also treated with electric shocks.

Another cause of cardiac arrest may be a heart rhythm that is too slow or that is not being conducted consistently. This condition may require pacing. Electrical pads are adhered to the chest surface, and a small shock is passed between them to stimulate the heart to contract. Generally, the heart must be shocked about sixty or seventy times per minute. Most patients find these shocks painful and are given sedating medications. The shocks are continued until a temporary pacemaker can be inserted. After a large intravenous line is started in the neck, a wire is slid through it down the vein and into the heart, stopping when it touches the heart muscle. Then, minute electric currents are passed through the wire to stimulate the heart muscle to contract. These are

generally not felt by the patient. If this internal pacing is successful, the pads on the chest are turned off. The potential complications of this technique are the same as those of the central intravenous line. Occasionally the pacing wire damages the heart. Rarely, applying electrical stimuli to the heart will make the heart's rhythm worse. Sadly, many times the heart will not respond to pacing.

In the unfortunate circumstance that the heart has no electrical activity, CPR and intubation are used and medication is given, but the patient's chances of survival are grim.

Occasionally the heart is not able to pump effectively because the sack that encloses it fills up with blood; this is most often seen when there have been penetrating wounds to the chest. Without proper heart function, blood pressure falls and the patient loses consciousness. Left untreated, the condition leads to death. To temporarily correct the problem, a physician inserts a needle from just below the breastbone into the sac around the heart, and fluid is withdrawn, allowing the heart to fill properly. A drain is left in place until the patient is taken to the operating room. Pain is seldom felt, since most patients with this condition are unconscious. Lung collapse, coronary artery injury with heart attack, heart muscle perforation, and heart rhythm problems can all result from the insertion of this needle.

The most invasive procedure done in an attempt to resuscitate someone in the emergency department is a thoracotomy. It is reserved for trauma patients who have just lost all vital signs. The left chest is cut open by making a deep incision below the nipple around to the back, and the ribs are spread with a ratchet device to expose the heart and large vessels. Damage to the heart, its sac, or a large blood vessel can be temporarily fixed, or the major artery to the body can be clamped, confining what remains of the blood flow to the heart and brain. This done, the patient is rushed to the operating room to complete the surgery and resuscitation. Patients requiring this are unconscious and therefore do not experience pain. There are many potential complications and the procedure is usually unsuccessful, but for these patients, there is no other chance for survival.

Three other procedures are commonly performed when resuscitating trauma patients. Almost all severely injured patients have a tube inserted through the nose or mouth into the stomach to relieve pressure, reducing the likelihood of vomiting. Another tube is inserted into the bladder to empty it and check for blood in the urine. The other procedure is a peritoneal lavage. A surgeon performs this procedure to check quickly for bleeding inside the abdominal cavity that might otherwise go undetected. The skin just below the navel is injected with an anesthetic. A needle is pushed through the skin into the abdominal cavity. Using a guide wire that has been slid through the needle, a tube is threaded into the abdomen. If blood is found, the patient is taken for an operation to stop the internal bleeding. This procedure is seldom performed on conscious patients, and discomfort from it is minimal due to the anesthetic. The potential harms include damaging abdominal structures such as the bowel, bladder, and stomach, or, occasionally, a major blood vessel with the needle.

Although they are not resuscitation techniques and are part of the routine care of a critically ill or injured person, there are some other issues that are of concern to most people. Patients are frequently isolated from family and friends when they are most vulnerable. They often feel a loss of dignity, being completely exposed in a large, cold room in front of a group of strangers. Private matters, such as rectal tone and bladder function, are openly, sometimes loudly, discussed by the whole team. The patient is commonly discussed in the third person by one team member "giving report" to another. Patients also suffer from loss of control. Physical examination, history taking, and line and catheter insertion are carried out simultaneously. The patient cannot respond individually to each action or person. Finally, communication is difficult or impossible, so anxieties and fears may go unaddressed.

There are many other procedures used in the emergency department that are encountered only by patients with special conditions. It is not possible to comment on all of these. In discussing those presented, the reader is advised to broaden communication with his or her physician to include any issues of concern.

# Resuscitation of Patients with Metastatic Cancer: Is Transient Benefit Still Futile?

KATHY FABER-LANGENDOEN

THIRTY YEARS AGO KOUWENHOVEN ET AL.[1] presented their experience with closed-chest cardiopulmonary resuscitation (CPR), ushering in an era of new possibilities for postponing death. Initially, CPR was restricted to acute care facilities and was employed in specific situations (generally when an acute cardiac catastrophe occurred in a previously stable patient) at the dis-

From the *Archives of Internal Medicine* 1991; 151: 235–239.

cretion of the responsible physician. Over the decades, thousands of medical personnel and lay persons have been trained, and CPR is performed in extended care facilities, in homes, and on the street. In most acute care hospitals, CPR at the time of clinical death has become the standard of care. Patient consent for this procedure is presumed, although a patient may refuse ahead of time and a do not resuscitate (DNR) order will be written. In the absence of a DNR order, all patients receive CPR. As experience accumulates with resuscitation of a wide range of patients in various settings, it has become apparent that some subgroups are much less likely to survive CPR. In light of these data, there is increasing talk of the "futility" of resuscitation, and that perhaps some patients, such as those with cancer, should not even be offered resuscitation as an option. This article reviews the changing use of CPR since its introduction, presents the available data on the outcome of CPR in patients with cancer, and examines whether, in the light of these data, offering CPR to patients with cancer is consonant with the goals of medicine.

## THE CHANGING USE OF CPR AND DEVELOPMENT OF DNR ORDERS

A historic review of the published guidelines for CPR illustrates intriguing changes in how the medical community views the applicability of CPR. In 1974, the National Conference on Cardiopulmonary Resuscitation and Emergency Cardiac Care, convened by the National Academy of Sciences and the American Heart Association to set standards for basic and advanced cardiac life support, wrote their first guidelines, stating:

> The purpose of cardiopulmonary resuscitation is the prevention of sudden unexpected death. Cardiopulmonary resuscitation is not indicated in certain situations, such as in cases of terminal irreversible illness where death is not unexpected . . .[2]

They went on to suggest that when CPR was contraindicated, this should not be noted in the medical record; no mention was made of discussion with the patient or family regarding this judgment. By 1980, major changes had occurred in the patient-physician relationship, with a new emphasis on patient autonomy and participation in decision making. Thus, while the 1980 National Conference reiterated that CPR was not indicated in terminal illness with language virtually identical to that of 1974, they made note of the current legal rulings about DNR orders. No comment was made about patient wishes, but they suggested that "the patient's family should understand and agree with the decision, although the family's opinion need not be controlling."[3]

The most recent guidelines were published in 1986, and these recommendations reveal less confidence regarding whether CPR is categorically not indicated in some circumstances.

It is generally accepted that resuscitation is a form of medical therapy that, like most others, is indicated in some situations, but not in others. When doubt exists, however, resuscitation should be instituted. One of the situations in which CPR is usually not indicated is the case of the terminally ill patient for whom no further therapy for the underlying disease process remains available and for whom death appears imminent.[4]

The National Congress suggests that "imminent death" is death likely to occur within 2 weeks. Parallel with the increased acceptability of DNR orders in the courts, among the public, and within the medical community, the new guidelines state clearly that a DNR decision should be made by the patient and the physician; the family's wishes are compelling only when the patient is unable to make the decision. According to these most recent guidelines, no longer is it the physician's responsibility to unilaterally decide when CPR is not indicated. As in the 1980 guidelines, recommendations are made for clear documentation of the DNR order in the medical record. Perhaps out of concern over subsequent changes in the medical care of patients designated

DNR,[5] the 1986 guidelines state that DNR orders "do not and should not be interpreted to imply any other change in the level of medical or nursing care."[4]

Current resuscitation policies reflect the changes in these guidelines, and there is now a strong presumption for CPR in all instances of cardiac or respiratory arrest. The major constraint on the universal use of resuscitation has been the recognition that patients have a right to forego CPR. Decisions to not be resuscitated in the event of an arrest have gained such status that hospitals are required to have written policies on DNR orders to be accredited by the Joint Commission on Accreditation of Healthcare Organizations.[6] The decision to not attempt resuscitation is generally only made with the agreement of the patient (or, if incapacitated, the patient's representative), a practice recently reaffirmed in the updated American College of Physicians Ethics Manual.[7] The legality of DNR orders has been upheld by the courts,[8] reflecting a widespread consensus that a competent patient (or representative) has a strong right to refuse any medical treatment, including life-prolonging measures such as resuscitation and mechanical ventilation. The issue of unilateral DNR orders made by the physician without patient consent has not been directly addressed by the courts. Over the past decade, living legislation has provided patients with a means outside of the hospital setting to designate their wishes regarding resuscitation; however, most living wills are, by law, restricted to situations of terminal and incapacitating illness.

Apart from patient refusal, two other constraints on the universal use of CPR have been suggested: limitation based on the patient's pre-arrest diagnosis and limitation based on the outcome of CPR in a specified population. In a survey using hypothetical clinical vignettes, Lawrence and Clark[9] found that physicians were less likely to favor resuscitation of patients with cancer than resuscitation of patients with other chronic end-stage illnesses. A recent study of DNR orders at Stanford[10] found that patients with cancer or with acquired immunodeficiency syndrome were far more likely to receive DNR orders than were those with cirrhosis or severe ischemic congestive heart failure, even though all four diseases have similar mortality rates. Noting that overall prognosis of cancer is no worse than that of other chronic end-stage diseases studied, the authors of both articles suggest there may be undue physician pessimism about the prognosis of patients with cancer. Neither study, however, commented on the possibility that DNR decisions might be based not on the overall mortality of a given disease, but on the survival after resuscitation for patients with a given disease. And neither study suggested that actual patients would not even be offered resuscitation because of their underlying disease.

However, as data accumulate on the success of CPR, there has been increasing support in the medical literature for restricting resuscitation based on outcome for specific groups of patients. In light of the dismal rate of success in patients with cancer, sepsis, and acute renal failure, Blackhall[11] suggested that patients with these diagnoses not be offered resuscitation. There is a growing body of literature examining survival of the elderly after resuscitation, but the data are in disagreement as to whether age is an independent determinant of outcome.[12,13] Yet the 1986 CPR guidelines quoted above betray hesitation in making categorical distinctions, saying only that "CPR is not *usually* indicated in the case of the terminally ill patient for whom no therapy for the underlying disease process remains available" (emphasis added).

## DATA ON ATTEMPTED RESUSCITATION IN PATIENTS WITH CANCER

A closer look at the data on survival after resuscitation shows in what circumstances CPR is useful. Although little is known about survival after resuscitation in extended care facilities or on the street, a fair amount is known about survival after attempted CPR in the hospital. The literature of the last decade is replete with reviews (largely retrospective) of survival after CPR, both in community and university hospitals as well as outside the hospital. Some of these reviews compare outcomes for patients with various pre-arrest diagnoses, such as cancer, sepsis, and myocardial infarction. Comparing studies is difficult because of differences in patient populations with respect to age and underlying illness, extent of resuscitative effort (e.g., some studies include patients who refuse intubation), and proportion of monitored or witnessed arrests. The end points of resuscitation have been variously defined. Immediate recovery of a pulse and stable cardiac rhythm, survival long enough to be transferred to an intensive care unit, or survival 24 hours after resuscitation have all been used to define initial response to CPR. Survival to discharge is always reported as an end point, but few studies present data on neurologic function at time of discharge, percent of survivors requiring extended skilled care, or survival after leaving hospital.

Despite the variability in study populations and the kinds of data reported, clear trends have emerged regarding the outcome of patients in general, as well as those with a diagnosis of cancer. Initial response to attempts at resuscitation in the general hospitalized population ranges from 40% to 50%, with 10% to 20% of all patients who received CPR ultimately being discharged. Of all the studies published from 1980 to 1989 that deal with survival after CPR, nine specifically report data on patients with cancer (Table 5.1). Far fewer patients with cancer survive to discharge compared with patients with other diagnoses. Not all studies distinguished patients with metastatic cancer from those with localized disease, and initial response is reported in only three studies. Of the nine studies of outcome after CPR, only two found patients with cancer who survived to discharge (total of seven patients of 243 resuscitated), and all seven patients had localized disease. There were no survivors in any study among patients with metastatic disease.

Various criticisms can be raised regarding these studies. Was the CPR performed adequately? Were patients with metastatic cancer more likely to receive "slow codes" or partial efforts? At least in one study, accounting for 57 patients, review of the records did not reveal any differences in "quality of the effort" at resuscitation.[14] Are the reported data misleading? Might, in fact, the survival after attempted resuscitation of patients with metastatic cancer be as good as that of the general hospitalized population (or, at least, not as poor as the literature review seems to indicate)? Possible reasons for making such an erroneous conclusion could include small sample sizes, selection biases, and unrecognized variables that affect outcome. These factors are minimized by a comprehensive look at all the studies reported from many different institutions in the recent decade. While it is not theoretically impossible that a patient with metastatic cancer could survive to be discharged after CPR, there is simply no reported evidence to support this premise, and certainly, given the relatively large number of patients in these combined studies, it would seem unlikely.

Certainly the studies are not without flaw or unanswered questions, but after three decades of experience, recently with virtually unlimited access to CPR, it is apparent that patients with metastatic cancer fare worse than those with other diagnoses. In fact, survival beyond the hospital is not reported in the literature to date. If one considers CPR a treatment, then, for patients with metastatic cancer it is a treatment without reported benefit with respect to survival to discharge, and, at most, it provides a minimal prolongation of life in the hospital; it is a therapy with, at best, only transient effect.

## ETHICAL CONCERNS: FUTILITY AND THE GOALS OF MEDICINE

How shall we view hospital policies and ethics manuals that suggest that all patients, regardless of diagnosis or prognosis, should be offered

**Table 5.1    Survival of Cancer Patients after Inhospital Cardiopulmonary Resuscitation, 1980 to 1989\***

| | All Patients | | | Patients with Cancer | | | | | |
| | | | | All Cancer Patients | | | Metastatic Cancer Patients | | |
| Source, year | No. of Patients | Initial Response, No. (%) | Survival to Discharge, No. (%) | No. of Patients | Initial Response, No. (%) | Survival to Discharge, No. (%) | No. of Patients | Initial Response, No. (%) | Survival to Discharge, No. (%) |
|---|---|---|---|---|---|---|---|---|---|
| Arena et al.,[1] 1980 | 48 | 24 (50) | 7 (15) | 39 | 23 (59) | 5 (13) | 23 | 13 (57) | 0 (0) |
| Hershey & Fisher,[2] 1982 | 79 | 53 (67) | 11 (14) | 6 | 5 (83) | 0 (0) | 5 | 4 (80) | 0 (0) |
| Bedell et al.,[3] 1983 | 294 | 128 (44) | 41 (14) | 57 | NA | 2 (4) | NA[†] | NA | 0 (0) |
| Sowden et al.,[4] 1984 | 108 | 50 (46) | 23 (21) | 11 | NA | 0 (0) | NA[†] | NA | 0 (0) |
| Kelly et al.,[5] 1986 | 62 | 29 (47) | 11 (18) | 7 | NA | 0 (0) | NA[†] | NA | NA |
| Urberg & Ways,[6] 1987 | 212 | 46 (38) | 13 (11) | 8 | NA | 0 (0) | NA[†] | NA | NA |
| Rozenbaum & Shenkman,[7] 1988 | 71 | 29 (41) | 13 (18) | 5 | NA | 0 (0) | 5 | NA | 0 (0) |
| Taffet et al.,[8] 1988 | 329 | 161 (49) | 21 (6) | 89 | 33 (37) | 0 (0) | 63 | NA | 0 (0) |
| Keating,[9] 1989 | 156 | 68 (44) | 17 (11) | 21[‡] | NA | 0 (0) | 21[‡] | NA | 0 (0) |

\*NA indicates not available.
†Metastatic cancer not separated from local disease.
‡Described as "incurable malignancy."

1. Arena FP, Perlin M, Turnbull AD. Initial experience with a 'code-no code' resuscitation system in cancer patients. *Crit Care Med.* 1980; 8: 733–735.

2. Hershey CO, Fisher L. Why outcome of cardiopulmonary resuscitation in general wards is poor. *Lancet.* 1982; 1: 31–34.

3. Bedell SE, Delbanco TL, Cook EF, Epstein FH. Survival after cardiopulmonary resuscitation in the hospital. *N Engl J Med.* 1983; 309: 569–576.

4. Sowden GR, Robins DW, Baskett PJF. Factors associated with survival and eventual cerebral status following cardiac arrest. *Anaesthesia.* 1984; 39: 39–43.

5. Kelly CA, Watson DM, Hutchinson CM, Pole JM. Prognostic factors in cardiac arrest occurring in a district general hospital. *Br J Clin Pract.* 1986; 40: 251–253.

6. Urberg M, Ways C. Survival after cardiopulmonary resuscitation for an in-hospital cardiac arrest. *J Fam Pract.* 1987; 25: 41–44.

7. Rozenbaum EA, Shenkman L. Predicting outcome of inhospital cardiopulmonary resuscitation. *Crit Care Med.* 1988; 16: 583–586.

8. Taffet GE, Teasdale TA, Luchi RJ. In-hospital cardiopulmonary resuscitation. *JAMA.* 1988; 260: 2069–2072.

9. Keating RM. Exclusion from resuscitation. *J R Soc Med.* 1989; 82: 402–405.

CPR? Setting aside the legal concerns and economic arguments, why do we offer resuscitation to patients dying of metastatic cancer? Twenty years ago one could plead uncertainty about outcome; given that physicians did not know who would benefit from attempts at resuscitation, CPR was given in all circumstances. Now, however, the data are reasonably clear and consistent from study to study; we can no longer invoke uncertainty in the case of patients with metastatic cancer. Blackhall,[11] citing Bedell and co-workers' study[14] of outcome of resuscitation at Beth Israel Hospital, urges: "In cases in which CPR has been shown to be of no benefit, as in patients with metastatic cancer, it should not be considered an alternative, and should not be presented as such."[11] Others have made similar suggestions regarding CPR of the elderly in nursing homes,[12] or very-low-birth-weight babies,[15] and after unsuccessful prehospital advanced cardiac life support,[16] deeming attempts at resuscitation in these circumstances to be "futile."

Is Blackhall[11] correct in arguing that resuscitation is of "no benefit" in patients with metastatic cancer? After all, review of the last decade's literature shows that not all patients with metastatic cancer die during attempts at resuscitation; a certain portion survive initially, making their way to an intensive care unit, often intubated, sedated, restrained, and monitored. There they will live for a few hours, days, or perhaps weeks, but all will die before leaving the hospital. Is this futile treatment?

Youngner[17] answers this question with another: futile with respect to what? Focusing on the diverse goals of therapy, Youngner suggests several meanings of futility, ranging from physiologic futility (inability of CPR to restore a heartbeat) to a slim chance of achieving a goal (curing lung cancer with chemotherapy) to "an absolute inability to postpone death." In as much as a treatment is unable to prolong life whatsoever, it may be judged futile; but if it can add even a few hours to a patient's life, it is not entirely without benefit and thus, Youngner argues, falls to the patient's autonomous choice. A physician's role, he continues, is "to frame the choice by describing prognosis and quality of life, as well as the odds for achieving them." A one in a hundred chance is not zero; an extra hour of life is not nothing. It is uniquely the patient's choice as to what burdens he or she will risk in gambling for improbable or transient success; this is a value-laden decision, and thus out of the scientific realm of the physician and into the realm of the autonomous patient.

Similarly, Lantos et al.[18] argue that futility must be defined carefully in terms of the goals of therapy, and that the goals of patients may differ significantly from those of physicians. Specifically, a few extra days of life in an intensive care unit after an arrest may "be of supreme value to a dying patient." Not only that, but Lantos et al. carry the argument a step further, saying that medical interventions may carry symbolic importance or emotional benefits (either for the patient or family) that should not be dismissed hastily. Although the authors acknowledge the importance of medical judgments regarding the chance of success, the bottom line remains whether the intervention may achieve the patient's goals.

This way of thinking is reflected in hospital policies that permit DNR orders only after the patient agrees with the foregoing CPR, requiring the physician to present resuscitation as an option as well as commenting on whether it is indicated in a specific situation. Do-not-resuscitate policies such as these allow no categorical contraindications to resuscitation; unlike the initial guidelines for resuscitation in the 1970s, CPR must be offered to the irreversibly dying patient. Taking Youngner's and Lantos and coworkers' comments into account, what might be the justification for offering a treatment that, on scientific evidence, only transiently delays an expected death?

First, perhaps patient autonomy and informed consent include the right to demand any technology, regardless of efficacy. In the evolution of the informed consent doctrine over the last century, firm ethical and legal obligations have been established for full disclosure of the risks and benefits of, and medically indicated alternatives to, a given proposed therapy. Then it becomes the patient's decision. What do patients decide? Patients choose which of the options they are willing to accept given the information provided (or refuse any therapy at all). However, it is not within the moral rights of patients to demand treatments judged by the medical community to be without benefit; the President's Commission states:

> The well-being principle circumscribes the range of alternatives offered to patients: informed consent does not mean that patients can insist upon anything they might want. Rather, it is a choice among medically accepted and available options, all of which are believed to have some possibility of promoting the patient's welfare . . .[19]

Unfortunately, this does not answer the question as to who determines the patient's welfare or what options might promote that welfare. If, as some have suggested, only the patient can decide what his or her health goals are, and if only the patient can define "well-being," then it seems that the range of alternatives is not circumscribed at all.

Second, perhaps a patient with widespread cancer may judge life to be of such absolute worth that no cost is too high and no suffering too great to gain a few more days of life. Putting aside the obvious objection that few of us would hold on to life under such extreme burdens, particularly in the context of an inevitable death, might it be that only the patient can assess the worth of a few more hours of life? Although the metastatic cancer is incurable, although resuscitation will do nothing to relieve pain or suffering, and although continued life past the hospital is unprecedented, Youngner insists that it is only "the absolute inability to postpone death" that defines futile treatments apart from the patient's assessment.

The other possibility, of course, is that resuscitation is more than just a treatment; perhaps it has become symbolic of fighting the good fight, of doing "everything." Thus, similar to the argument that nutrition should be provided apart from consideration of efficacy because it symbolizes our care for one another,[20] might we not argue along with Lantos and colleagues that CPR be given even when long-term survival is unprecedented, so patients can feel they have resisted death to the end? In Dylan Thomas' world, one raged against the dying of the light with his or her own physical and spiritual reserves; there was no technology to aid in the fight. Today resisting death to the end is a different battle. Modern medicine provides us with an armamentarium of defibrillators and ventilators, pressors and pacers, and the end has been redefined as unsuccessful resuscitation.

At every point, then, this argument is reduced to the patient's assessment of benefits. If patients dying from metastatic cancer believe a full resuscitative effort will contribute to their well-being, or that a few days of life are worth whatever cost, or that they have not resisted to the end if resuscitation is not attempted—any of these may be deemed "beneficial" by the patient, and thus resuscitative attempts become the patient's right. It is an argument of autonomy: a person is in charge of his/her own body, the patient determines his or her life plan, decides what risks to take and defines what is beneficial. Is autonomy the final word in how medicine is practiced?

Perhaps autonomy has become the final word because physicians have forgotten what the goals of medicine are; perhaps the medical community itself is at fault for caving in to a view of autonomy that renders patient self-determination the final arbiter of the goals and limits of medical care. Physicians should reexamine the goals of medicine and recognize that medicine is fundamentally unable to delay death forever. Although the ultimate goal of medicine is the healing of disease, medicine has long recognized that even this is often beyond its grasp. The Hippocratic writings urged physicians not to continue treating those overmastered by their disease;[21] the threefold dictum of the 15th century defines medicine's goal as "to cure sometimes, to relieve often, to comfort always." Time and again the primary goals of medicine have been described as the cure of disease and the relief of suffering,[22] and in 1989, the American College of Physicians reiterated that the goals of medicine are to prevent disease, restore health, and provide palliation and comfort for diseases that cannot be cured.[23]

Under none of these formulations is it the goal of medicine to eke out the last few possible days of life. Under no definition could a few additional days in an intensive care unit for an irreversibly dying patient be construed as health. Nowhere is it suggested that physicians have an obligation to press on until they reach that "absolute inability to postpone death." In our insistence that we present patients with the chance to transiently delay an inescapable death, we become slaves to our technology. Kass[24] makes an eloquent argument against redefining the primary goal of medicine as a relentless prolongation of life.

> If medicine takes aim at death prevention, rather than at health and relief of suffering, if it regards every death as premature, as a failure of today's medicine—but avoidable by tomorrow's—then it is tacitly asserting that its true goal is immortality. . . . Physicians should try to keep their eyes on the main business, restoring and correcting what can be corrected and restored, always acknowledging that death will and must come, that health is a mortal good, and that as embodied beings we are fragile beings that must stop sooner or later, medicine or no medicine.[24]

Clearly, temporary resuscitation of the patient with metastatic cancer falls well outside of these goals.

Even a look at current medical practice reveals that, at many other points, medicine does not allow the patient to demand interventions solely on the basis that the patient would consider it beneficial. Surgeons commonly decline to operate in the face of overwhelming risks of operative morbidity and mortality, oncologists will not offer bone marrow transplantation to breast cancer patients with refractory disease, and critical care physicians will not suggest extracorporeal membrane oxygenation to a patient with diffuse extensive pulmonary metastases from colon cancer.

Any of these interventions might prolong a dying patient's life slightly, but neither hospital policies nor the goals of medicine mandate that any of these be offered. Such decisions do not require the standard of absolute certainty that no patient will ever benefit. Physicians ought to reject the practice of offering an intervention "not for the good that it will do, but that nothing may be left undone on the margin of the impossible," to borrow T. S. Eliot's words.[25] Survival to discharge after CPR in patients with metastatic cancer falls squarely on that margin.

## CONCLUSIONS

Resuscitation of the patient dying from metastatic cancer is of only transient benefit at best, and should not generally be offered to patients without hope of survival to discharge. At this time, however, it may be part of the public expectation that resuscitation will be attempted in all situations if the patient has not consented to a DNR order. Thus, out of respect for patients as persons, physicians ought to discuss the goals and limits of medical care with patients with metastatic cancer, assuring patients that they will receive appropriate care, but that attempts at resuscitation are not indicated.

Physicians have an obligation to offer treatments consonant with the goals of medicine. A treatment that transiently prolongs life in the hospital, particularly the life of a patient dying of an irreversible disease, is without benefit with respect to regaining health, controlling the effects of disease, or relieving suffering: such a treatment is futile. Recommending that physicians not be required to offer resuscitation to the dying patient with metastatic cancer is not a return to the silent paternalism of medical practice before the 1960s. It is not fueled by concerns over the rising costs of health care (legitimate concern though that is) or a nihilistic attitude that the patient with metastatic cancer would be better off dead. If we broaden the goals of medicine to include prolonging life as long as possible regardless of the patient's health, medicine incurs great costs. We violate the principle of truth-telling if we present resuscitation as a way to regain health. We leave families with the perception that to consent to a DNR order is to stop short of doing everything, and patients with the sense that fighting to the end is defined by attempts at resuscitation. We require our house staff to attend to dying cancer patients with defibrillators and endotracheal tubes. While communication and patient autonomy remain of fundamental importance, physicians must not propose treatments that do not work, and CPR does not work in patients with metastatic cancer. To suggest otherwise to patients damages the integrity of medicine and does great harm to patients and to their physicians alike.

## ACKNOWLEDGMENTS

I am indebted to Arthur Caplan, PhD, B. J. Kennedy, MD, Bruce Peterson, MD, and Ann Russell, JD, for their critical review and constructive suggestions.

### REFERENCES

1. Kouwenhoven WB, Jude JR, Knickerbocker GG. Closed-chest cardiac massage. *JAMA*. 1960; 173: 1064–1067.

2. National Conference on Cardiopulmonary Resuscitation and Emergency Cardiac Care. Standards and guidelines for cardiopulmonary resuscitation and emergency cardiac care: medicolegal considerations and recommendations. *JAMA*. 1974; 227: 864.

3. National Conference on Cardiopulmonary Resuscitation and Emergency Cardiac Care. Standards and guidelines for cardiopulmonary resuscitation and emergency cardiac care: medicolegal considerations and recommendations. *JAMA*. 1980; 244: 507.

4. National Conference on Cardiopulmonary Resuscitation and Emergency Cardiac Care. Standards and guidelines for cardiopulmonary resuscitation and emergency cardiac care: medicolegal considerations and recommendations. *JAMA*. 1986; 255: 2981.

5. Youngner SJ, Lewandowski W, McClish D, Jukmalis BW, Coulton C, Bartlett ET. 'Do-not-resuscitate' orders: incidence and implications in a medical intensive care unit. *JAMA*. 1985; 253: 54–57.

6. Joint Commission on Accreditation of Healthcare Organizations. *Accreditation Manual for Hospitals*. Chicago, Ill: Joint Commission on Accreditation of Healthcare Organizations; 1987: 90.

7. American College of Physicians Ethics Committee. American College of Physicians ethics manual, II. *Ann Intern Med*. 1989; 111: 333.

8. In re *Dinnerstein*, 6 Mass App 466, 380 NE2d 134, 138–139 (1978).

9. Lawrence FA, Clark GM. Cancer and resuscitation: does the diagnosis affect the decision? *Arch Intern Med*. 1987; 147: 1637–1640.

10. Wachter RM, Luce JM, Hearst N, Lo B. Decisions about resuscitation: inequities among patients with different diseases but similar prognoses. *Ann Intern Med*. 1989; 111: 525–532.

11. Blackhall LJ. Must we always use CPR? *N Engl J Med*. 1987; 317: 1281–1285.

12. Murphy DJ, Murray AM, Robinson BE, Campion EW. Outcomes of cardiopulmonary resuscitation in the elderly. *Ann Intern Med*. 1989; 111: 199–205.

13. Taffet GE, Teasdale TA, Luchi RJ. In-hospital cardiopulmonary resuscitation. *JAMA*. 1988; 260: 2069–2072.

14. Bedell SE, Delbanco TL, Cook FE, Epstein FH. Survival after cardiopulmonary resuscitation. *N Engl J Med*. 1984; 310: 463–464.

15. Lantos JD, Miles SH, Silverstein MD, Stocking CB. Survival after cardiopulmonary resuscitation in babies of very low birth weight: is CPR futile therapy? *N Engl J Med*. 1988; 318: 91–95.

16. Kellerman AL, Staves DR, Hackman BB. In-hospital resuscitation following unsuccessful prehospital advanced cardiac life support: 'heroic efforts' or an exercise in futility? *Ann Emerg Med*. 1988; 17: 589–594.

17. Youngner SJ. Who defines futility? *JAMA*. 1988; 260: 2094–2095.

18. Lantos JD, Singer PA, Walker RM, et al. The illusion of futility in clinical practice. *Am J Med*. 1989; 87: 81–84.

19. President's Commission for the Study of Ethical Problems in Medicine and Biomedical and Behavioral Research. *Making Health Care Decisions: the Ethical and Legal Implications of Informed Consent in the Patient-Practitioner Relationship*. Washington, DC: Government Printing Office; 1982: 42–44.

20. Callahan D. On feeding the dying. *Hastings Cent Rep.* 1983; 13:22.

21. Chadwick J, Mann WN, eds. *The Medical Works of Hippocrates.* Boston, Mass: Blackwell Scientific Publications Inc; 1950: 85.

22. Cassel EJ. The nature of suffering and the goals of medicine. *N Engl J Med.* 1982; 306: 639–645.

23. American College of Physicians Ethics Committee. American College of Physicians ethics manual: I. *Ann Intern Med.* 1989; 111: 247.

24. Kass LR. Ethical dilemmas in the care of the ill, II: what is the patient's good? *JAMA.* 1980; 244: 1947.

25. Eliot TS. The family reunion. In: *The Complete Poems and Plays: 1909–1950.* New York, NY: Harcourt, Brace, & World Inc; 1971: 237–238.

# Must Consent Always Be Obtained for a Do-Not-Resuscitate Order?

## RITA T. LAYSON AND TERRANCE MCCONNELL

Using cardiopulmonary resuscitation for cardiac or respiratory arrest unless there is an explicit do-not-resuscitate order is a policy adopted by all hospitals. Such a policy usually requires the patient's (or surrogate's) consent for a do-not-resuscitate order to be instituted. This article, however, presents the argument that consent need not always be obtained. In the case discussed, the well-being of the patient, other patients, and the health care providers all support a unilateral decision by the physician not to attempt resuscitation at the time of death. The medical community and society need to acknowledge that such cases exist and to develop policies that respect not only the interests of patients but also those of health care providers and society.

CARDIOPULMONARY RESUSCITATION (CPR), first described in 1960,[1] was initially used for otherwise healthy persons who experienced cardiac arrest during a medical procedure or as a result of a near drowning.[2] With time, health care providers recognized that CPR might be administered to any individual who experiences cessation of cardiac or respiratory function, and CPR became routinely available in acute care hospitals and fire and rescue services by the late 1960s. Today CPR is a procedure that will be administered to all patients who experience cardiopulmonary arrest unless otherwise specified. Such specification in a hospital setting is normally conveyed in the form of a do-not-resuscitate (DNR) order.

Significant ethical changes have occurred during the last 35 years as well. Medical decisions, once regarded as solely in the hands of physicians, are now seen as a joint enterprise involving both patients and health care providers. Increasing emphasis on individual autonomy has led to the conclusion that, in the end, competent patients have a moral and legal right to consent to or refuse any recommended medical intervention.[3] This is thought to apply to the issuance of DNR orders as well. Different rationales have been identified for issuing DNR orders, 2 of which are that the patient does not want CPR performed and that physicians judge that CPR will offer no medical benefit.[2] These considerations can exist together or separately. Tomlinson and Brody[4] cite the second rationale and argue that when physicians judge that resuscitation will offer no medical benefit, they are warranted in writing a DNR order.

Others, making a similar point, claim that physicians are not required to administer CPR in cases where they believe that the procedure is futile.[5] The general principle at work here is that a patient's preference for an intervention should be honored only if there is at least a modicum of potential medical benefit.[6] However, when the appropriateness of a DNR order is based on the judgment that CPR will offer no medical benefit, it is important to ask what role the patient (or, in the case of an incompetent patient, the surrogate) should play in the decision-making process.

Some say that the patient should be informed of the medical realities and persuaded of the reasonableness of the DNR order.[4] Others contend that patients should be informed of the DNR order, but not offered the choice of CPR.[5,7] Common to each suggestion is the important point that the right to autonomy does not given patients the right to demand treatment beyond that which physicians judge to be appropriate.[5] Clearly, this gives rise to another question. What should be done if the patient cannot be persuaded of the reasonableness of the DNR order? What if the patient continues to demand CPR?

A consensus has emerged about how to answer these questions. In the face of such an intractable disagreement between the patient and the physician, arrangements should be made for an orderly transfer of care to another physician.[5,8] What if such a transfer cannot be arranged? This

is not merely a logical possibility, for at least 2 scenarios are plausible: there may be no time to arrange for a transfer, or there may be no other physician willing to accept the responsibility of care. Indeed, the latter possibility is likely when there is agreement among physicians that CPR would offer the patient no medical benefits. Guidance is needed here. Does patient autonomy demand that CPR be provided? Must physicians in such cases act contrary to their consciences? A particular case will provide the occasion for focusing on these issues.

## REPORT OF A CASE

A 34-year-old man was admitted to the hospital for terminal care. He had acquired immunodeficiency syndrome with severe wasting. A thorough workup for treatable causes of his rapid weight loss and increasing weakness was fruitless. Consequently, he was referred to a hospice for palliative care. He had been under the care of the local hospice for several months. On the day of admission, he weighed 27 kg, was bedridden, was unable to feed himself, and could talk only for short periods. It was clear to physicians and staff that he had only a few days to live.

The patient was admitted to an inpatient hospice unit. The hospital's policy mandates that patients admitted to the hospice unit have a DNR order within 48 hours of admission because the unit is not equipped for resuscitation. Soon after admission, an intern approached the patient about writing a DNR order. The patient adamantly insisted that he wanted "everything done."

The following day the attending physician, having been informed of these details, initiated a discussion with the patient and his brother. The physician was aware that doing everything means different things to different people; for some, it is merely a plea not to be abandoned and to be provided with pain relief. But discussion with this patient made it clear that he was afraid of dying and was denying the inevitable imminence of his death; he really meant do everything. Indeed, he said, "I don't want to talk about this again." His brother confirmed the physician's assessment, saying, "He will deny that he is dying until he takes his last breath." Because of his fear and denial, he was unwilling even to discuss the possibility that some therapies, such as CPR, would not promote his goal of living as long as possible.

Without a DNR order, the physician would have been forced to transfer the patient to a general medicine unit. The physician judged that attempted resuscitation would not achieve the patient's goals and that his needs would be better served on the hospice unit because of the expertise of its staff. The physician also believed that CPR was not a medically indicated treatment and should not be offered as an option. While CPR in this case might not qualify as futile in the narrow sense of providing brain perfusion,[9] it was the physician's judgment that it would not restore cardiac rhythm sufficient to add a meaningful measure of time to his remaining life. Arranging for transfer of this patient to another physician's service was impractical because of time constraints and the unlikely willingness of another physician to accept responsibility for the patient. The brother probably would have agreed to a DNR order, but soliciting his permission would add little moral validity to the decision since the patient was still capable of making his own decisions.

Consequently, a DNR order was written without informing the patient. The patient remained on the hospice unit and died 2 days later. Did the physician violate the patient's autonomy? Was the case handled properly?

## COMMENT

It is tempting to say that the physician in this case did not try hard enough to find another physician who would take this patient on his own

terms. If such a transfer had occurred, the main moral problem would disappear for the original physician. Such an avoidance strategy, when available, is regarded by many as desirable. To assume that transferring a patient to another physician is *always* a possibility is simply to assume that the moral problem mentioned above can never arise, and that is false. How should a case be handled when what the patient wants conflicts with what the physician believes are defensible principles of medical ethics, and transferring the patient to another physician is not feasible?

Given the preeminence that society assigns to the principle of autonomy, one might think that it should prevail here and that the patient's wishes should be honored. The status quo has assured a preeminence of autonomy in decision making by requiring seeking explicit consent for DNR orders. This is problematic for 2 reasons. First, it is not obvious that autonomy should *always* trump other moral considerations. Second, even if autonomy does take precedence, it may not entail that the patient's wishes must be honored. Autonomy is most naturally understood as imposing negative moral requirements, requirements that others not interfere with one's freedom and choices. Autonomy is seldom understood as preempting the freedom and choices of others.[10] At best, invoking autonomy produces a stalemate, because physicians too can appeal to this principle. Physicians can argue that autonomy precludes others from forcing them to act against conscience.

It would be a mistake to focus only on autonomy in analyzing this case; other values are relevant too. One cannot discuss a case like this without considering the allocation of scarce medical resources. Some will contend that any investment other than comfort care in a clearly terminal patient is inappropriate. However, here we put aside the issue of the utilization of society's scarce resources, since arguably policymakers, not physicians at the bedside, should make these decisions.

How the time of nurses and physicians is used is also important. All agree that patients like the one in this case should not be abandoned; beneficence directs that comfort care be provided. That is why the hospice unit, with staff experienced and trained to deal with such cases, is the ideal place for this patient. Having nurses and physicians provide interventions that can result in no medical benefits is unjustified; directly or indirectly, this is apt to have adverse effects on others. For example, staff involved in the resuscitation of one patient will be unavailable to provide care to other patients.

Perhaps the most significant value at stake in this case is nonmaleficence, the principle that directs agents not to cause harm. If suffering results from using CPR, that is an important moral consideration. Would anyone suffer from calling a code in this case? Whether patients are aware of any suffering as a result of a code probably varies from case to case. In situations where they are aware, they probably suffer a great deal. Patients' families probably suffer as the result of CPR. While they are not in the room to witness the indignities of the procedures and in most cases are probably ignorant of what is going on, they do miss the chance to share those last moments with their loved one. One study[11] has documented increased anxiety in family members who are deprived of this opportunity.

There are other important players in this drama. Health care providers themselves may suffer significantly when they participate in futile codes. Nurses who have nurtured and cared for a patient must now mark the patient's death by performing CPR and feeling ribs crack under their hands. As one nurse said, "While doing CPR on a patient riddled with bone cancer, I could feel the crunch of broken bone on each compression. What was I doing?"[12] Residents and other physicians must order violent acts in an unsuccessful attempt to prolong life. When the goal of saving a life is no longer achievable, the sense is that CPR is being performed on a *dead* body. Health care providers have normal human reactions to death, and performing procedures on dead bodies violates their sense of humanity. They appropriately feel a deep sense of having done something inhumane after participating in the macabre ritual of violence associated with futile CPR. Individuals who are forced repeatedly to participate in such codes may incur permanent psychological and spiritual wounds.[13] This is surely undesirable if we want health care providers to be caring, sensitive people.

All the previous arguments in this case have been independent of the specific diagnosis of end-stage human immunodeficiency virus infection; they are relevant to any patient in a similar situation with a clearly terminal disease. However, one cannot ignore the increased risk of transmission of an infectious agent such as human immunodeficiency virus during the "controlled chaos" of an attempted resuscitation. One nurse, describing a code performed on a patient with infectious hepatitis and acquired immunodeficiency syndrome, said,

> When his pulse stopped, a code was called. It was terrible. With every compression, blood flowed from his mouth, so giving him oxygen was nearly impossible. There was blood all over the bed, and some splattered on the equipment and floor. Wasn't our futile attempt to save his life unfair to him and to us?[12]

While most health care workers willingly risk potential exposure to deadly infectious agents in the process of caring for sick patients, exposing them to this risk is senseless if there is no meaningful benefit to the patient.

These considerations make it clear why nurses are often more insistent than physicians that a patient's code status be defined early in the terminal course. Many physicians who have the authority for writing DNR orders do not conduct the codes themselves and so are spared the adverse consequences just noted. Moreover, the option of transferring such a patient to another physician's care, when that option is available, may provide moral cover for the first physician, but it fails to protect the nurses and other staff from the suffering caused by a futile code. So using the widely recommended avoidance strategy—what Annas [14] has called ethical dumping—is morally suspect. The physician who effects the transfer still has a prominent though more distant place in the causal chain that results in harm to caregivers.

It is tempting to characterize this patient's desire for CPR as irrational. But since rational decision making is usually understood in terms of the patient's own aims and values,[15] it is difficult to say whether such a characterization is accurate. Although CPR will not advance the patient's aims and values, neither will it thwart them. What is odd is that the patient's goal is unachievable; the desire for CPR is, then, at best nonrational. If a pejorative label must be attached to the patient's preferences in this case, it may be more apt to say that he or she is selfish since what the patient wants will provide him or her no benefit and will affect others adversely. Of course, the same denial that prompts the patient's preference for this intervention will make him or her unable to see that the request is selfish; because of this, we conclude that this is selfishness for which the individual is not culpable.

Some will object that the physician in this case lacks the courage to confront the patient with the truth. Just as physicians in the past routinely withheld bad news from patients to protect themselves rather than the patient, in this case our physician may also be engaged in self-protection. While there may be an element of truth in this accusation, it was not the principal motivation in this case. The physician believed, based on conversations with the patient and his brother, that the patient was engaged in denial as a means of coping with the fear of death and that it would be cruel to take this away from him. Confronting this patient with the fact that a DNR order had been written would only pierce his coping mechanism and at best force him to acknowledge the reality that death was imminent. Normally physicians should inform patients that they will not provide requested treatments because this allows patients to exercise various options, such as finding a new physician or seeking alternative care. In this case, transfer to another physician's service was not feasible and the patient was so close to death that these other choices were not readily available. Because comfort care was the only thing that could provide benefits to this patient, the physician also believed that the hospice unit was uniquely equipped to meet his needs and that he would be poorly served by being transferred to another unit. As Schneiderman and Jecker [16] have said,

> Saying no to futile treatment does not mean saying no to caring for the patient, but rather means transferring aggressive efforts away from life prolongation and toward life enhancement in the waning hours and days of existence.

Overall, there was an element of paternalism in the physician's actions, but paternalism is not always wrong, nor is it the primary justification for this physician's actions.

Contrary to the position defended herein, Wear and Logue [17] have argued that even if CPR may be unilaterally withheld when using it would be futile, such a result is trivial because it does not include the option to withdraw or withhold other life-sustaining measures, and when CPR is futile, health care providers "will know this within a few minutes, and the problem will be 'solved' with cold finality." [17] These claims are inadequate, however, because they disregard or underestimate the immediate harm done to health care professionals who are forced to participate in futile codes. Moreover, they fail to take into account the adverse *cumulative* effects that such participation can have on the psyches of these same individuals. We agree with the contention of Wear and Logue that the most important thing is to develop "an overall management plan for any patient for whom any limitation of treatment is considered." However, this will not eliminate difficult cases of the sort considered here.

One final worry should be addressed. If physicians are allowed to write DNR orders unilaterally, there is the potential for abuse of power. It is not unreasonable to think that society's most vulnerable, such as minorities, the elderly, and persons infected with human immunodeficiency virus, would most likely be the victims of such abuse. To deal with this "slippery slope" concern, many think that there should be an absolute prohibition against unilateral DNR orders. When complying with the absolute prohibition seems unreasonable, such as in the case discussed herein, physicians often implement "slow codes." This practice has the worse features of each of the alternatives: like our proposal, selected patients are not informed of their status, and like the policy of doing a full code, a slow code puts nurses and house staff through the sort of suffering documented earlier. Moreover, slow codes may subject nurses and house staff to legal liability. The ideal response to the possibility of abuse would be to develop rules that state in detail the circumstances in which unilateral DNR orders may be implemented. We doubt, however, that such rules can be constructed. What is right is context dependent, and these situations must be handled on a case by case basis. When confronted with a case of the type discussed herein, we recommend that physicians seek the advice of their institution's ethics committee and that hospitals develop policies that support this practice. Such consultation can usually be arranged promptly. Physicians contemplating writing unilateral DNR orders are apt to experience doubts and should welcome the input that ethics consultations provide.

Using CPR for cardiac or respiratory arrest unless there is an explicit DNR order is an appropriate policy. What is at issue is whether such a policy requires the patient's (or surrogate's) consent for a DNR order to be instituted. There

is no doubt that consent should be obtained in most cases. Our argument in this article is that consent need not always be obtained. In the case discussed, a disagreement between the patient and the physician over the appropriateness of attempted resuscitation at the time of death was resolved by the physician writing a unilateral DNR order. The well-being of other patients, of the staff, and of the patient himself all supported this action. Currently, the approved way of dealing with such a conflict is either to attempt resuscitation or to transfer the care of the patient to a different physician. In this case, both of these alternatives were morally suspect because of harm to others, especially caregivers. The medical community and society need to acknowledge that such cases exist and to develop policies that respect the interests of patients, health care providers, and society.

## REFERENCES

1. Kouwenhoven WB, Jude JR, Knickerbocker GG. Closed-chest cardiac massage. *JAMA.* 1960; 173: 94–97.
2. Guidelines for the appropriate use of do-not-resuscitate orders. *JAMA.* 1991; 265: 1868–1871.
3. Faden R, Beauchamp T. *A History and Theory of Informed Consent.* New York, NY: Oxford University Press Inc.; 1986.
4. Tomlinson T, Brody H. Ethics and communication in do-not-resuscitate orders. *N Engl J Med.* 1988; 318: 43–46.
5. Emergency Cardiac Care Committee and Subcommittees, American Heart Association. Ethical consideration in resuscitation. *JAMA.* 1992; 268: 2282–2288.
6. Brett AS, McCullough LB. When patients request specific interventions. *N Engl J Med.* 1986; 315: 1347–1351.
7. Lo B. Unanswered questions about DNR orders. *JAMA.* 1991; 265: 1874–1875.
8. Task Force on Ethics of the Society of Critical Care Medicine. Consensus report on the ethics of forgoing life-sustaining treatments in the critically ill. *Crit Care Med.* 1990; 18: 1435–1439.
9. Waisel DB, Truog RD. The cardiopulmonary resuscitation-not-indicated order: futility revisited. *Ann Intern Med.* 1995; 122: 304–308.

10. Blackhall LJ. Must we always use CPR? *N Engl J Med.* 1987; 317: 1281–1285.

11. Doyle CJ, Post H, Burney RE, Maino J, Keefe M, Rhee KJ. Family participation during resuscitation: an option. *Ann Emerg Med.* 1987; 16: 673–675.

12. Dolan MB. Coding abuses hurt nurses, too. *Nursing.* 1988; 18: 46–47.

13. Bell MH. Teachings of the heart. *JAMA.* 1984; 252: 2684.

14. Annas G. Transferring the ethical hot potato. *Hastings Cent Rep.* 1987; 17: 20–21.

15. Brock DW, Wartman SA. When competent patients make irrational choices. *N Engl J Med.* 1990; 322: 1595–1599.

16. Schneiderman LJ, Jecker NS. *Wrong Medicine.* Baltimore, MD: Johns Hopkins University Press; 1995.

17. Wear S, Logue G. The problem of medically futile treatment falling back on a preventive ethics approach. *J Clin Ethics.* 1995; 6: 138–148.

## Discussion Questions

1. Is there ever any moral justification for slow codes, the illegal practice of starting and carrying out a resuscitation attempt so slowly that it is extremely unlikely that the patient will survive? This practice is sometimes used when the medical team believes strongly that resuscitation would only harm a dying patient but the family insists that "everything be done." Make clear how paternalism, resource allocation decisions, and the principle of nonmaleficence are involved in your conclusion.

2. A five-year-old child is brought into the emergency department of the hospital. He has been found unconscious and face down in the family's swimming pool after an apparent head injury, probably following an accident involving the diving board. No one is sure how long he had been like that, but no sounds had been heard from the pool area for about forty-five minutes prior to the discovery of the child. The parents had tried basic CPR in the car while on the way to the hospital but were not sure they had remembered the procedure correctly. The physician realizes that although the child may be resuscitated, there is a good chance that he has suffered very serious brain damage from lack of oxygen and may never regain consciousness. The parents are blaming themselves for not watching the boy more closely and are screaming at the physician to "do something." What should the physician do, and why?

3. Mr. R., a sixty-eight-year-old man, is in the last stages of a terminal illness and is only vaguely conscious of his surroundings. He has earlier indicated that his physician should not employ any "heroic measures" in prolonging his life, and his daughter, Janet, understands and supports this decision; a DNR order has been written. But now Ken, his son, has arrived from a distant city and wants his father to receive full and aggressive treatment. Ken and his father have never been on friendly terms, and communication between the two has been limited to a few telephone calls each year. Ken accuses his sister of abandoning their father and of wanting to get her hands on the life insurance money. He hints that if the DNR order is not reversed, he will take legal action against the medical team. What should the attending physician do, and why? How are the principles of beneficence and respect for autonomy to be balanced against other considerations?

## Suggestions for Further Reading

### ETHICAL ANALYSIS OF RESUSCITATION AND DNR ISSUES

Bruce-Jones, P. "Resuscitation Decisions in the Elderly: A Discussion of Current Thinking." *Journal of Medical Ethics* 22 (1996): 286–91.
   Common arguments are reviewed, and flaws in them are pointed out.

Hackler, J. C., and F. C. Hiller. "Family Consent to Orders Not to Resuscitate: Reconsidering Hospital Policy." *Journal of the American Medical Association* 264, no. 10 (1990):
1281–83.
> Physicians should be authorized to override family refusals of DNR orders.

Heilicser, B., C. Stocking, and M. Siegler. "Ethical Dilemmas in Emergency Medical Services:
The Perspective of the Emergency Medical Technician." *Annals of Emergency Medicine* 27,
no. 2 (1996): 239–43.
> The special circumstances and considerations involved in the work of emergency medi-
cal technicians (EMTs) lead to different concerns and different moral conclusions. This
article reviews the results of a survey of 340 EMTs.

Tomlinson, T., and H. Brody. "Futility and the Ethics of Resuscitation." *Journal of the American Medical Association* 264, no. 10 (1990): 1276–80.
> Rejecting the usual arguments for the conclusion that CPR must be provided to every
patient who is in arrest and does not have a DNR order, the authors argue that CPR
should be unilaterally withheld by physicians when it is futile.

### OUTCOMES OF CPR AND DNR

Bonin, M., et al. "Distinct Criteria for Termination of Resuscitation in the Out-of-Hospital
Setting." *Journal of the American Medical Association* 270, no. 12 (1993): 1457–62.
> This study of 139 patients shows that most who do not respond to resuscitation efforts
in the field within twenty-five minutes will not survive.

Gray, W., R. Capone, and A. Most. "Unsuccessful Emergency Medical Resuscitation: Are
Continued Efforts in the Emergency Department Justified?" *New England Journal of
Medicine* 325, no. 20 (1991): 1393–98.
> This study of 185 patients shows that not only are these continued efforts usually un-
successful, but they also cost a lot of money.

Miranda, D. "Quality of Life after Cardiopulmonary Resuscitation." *Chest* 106, no. 2 (1994):
524–30.
> This study shows the many difficulties faced by those who recover after CPR, including
several delayed cognitive problems.

Wenger, N., et al. "Outcomes of Patients with Do-Not-Resuscitate Orders: Toward an
Understanding of What Do-Not-Resuscitate Orders Mean and How They Affect Patients."
*Archives of Internal Medicine* 155 (1995): 2063–68.
> Patients who have DNR orders may be sicker than those who have the same diagnosis
but no DNR order. DNR orders written very late in the course of a patient's illness may
be an indication of poor medical care.

### PRACTICAL ISSUES

Cammer Paris, B., et al. "Roadblocks to Do-Not-Resuscitate Orders: A Study in Policy Implementation." *Archives of Internal Medicine* 153 (1993): 1689–95.
> This study compares the problems experienced by attending physicians and interns in
getting surrogates to agree to DNR orders. Communication problems and unclear policies are highlighted.

Miller, D., et al. "Factors Influencing Physicians in Recommending In-Hospital Cardiopulmonary Resuscitation." *Archives of Internal Medicine* 153 (1993): 1999–2003.
> Although most physician recommendations are appropriate, there is still a tendency to
overestimate the effectiveness of CPR.

Wachter, R., et al. "Decisions about Resuscitation: Inequities among Patients with Different Diseases but Similar Prognoses." *Annals of Internal Medicine* 111, no. 6 (1989): 525–32.
> The likelihood that a patient has a DNR order seems to have more to do with diagnosis than with prognosis. This may indicate a misuse of DNR orders.

Wenger, N., et al. "Epidemiology of Do-Not-Resuscitate Orders: Disparity by Age, Diagnosis, Gender, Race, and Functional Impairment." *Archives of Internal Medicine* 155 (1995): 2056–61.
> Reveals how patients view the usefulness of CPR and indicates that DNR orders may be underused among the sickest patients.

## CASES

"Nurse Fails to Follow DNR Order: 'Wrongful Living' Suit." *Regan Report on Nursing Law* 37, no. 7 (Dec. 1996): 1 ff. *InfoTrac Power Search #A19590393.*

Tammelleo, David. "'No Heroic Efforts' Directive by Parents Ignored by RN." *Regan Report on Nursing Law* 39, no. 9 (Feb. 1999): 4 ff. *InfoTrac Power Search #A54117373.*

# Section 6

## *Assisted Suicide*

## Introduction

Many people who believe that their futures hold unacceptable suffering wish to avoid rather than endure it. Suicide is seriously considered by many who find themselves in this position. But this raises troubling questions. Is death really better than the suffering that lies ahead of me? Is killing myself morally acceptable? Do I know how to kill myself? If I try to take my own life, will I succeed, or will I just make my situation worse? As a result, some seek the assistance of others in ending their own lives, mostly to ensure success, but also in part to find in another's assistance some reassurance that this course of action is acceptable. Although this issue is often put in terms of *physician*-assisted suicide, such assistance might be asked of family members or close friends. Nonetheless, this section will deal primarily with cases in which a physician is helping someone to commit suicide; this raises several of the most interesting moral questions, and much that is said here can be applied (with appropriate changes) to assistance provided by others.

Assisted suicide differs in important ways from euthanasia and raises a somewhat different set of moral issues. Although many of the questions and considerations raised in the next section are relevant to assisted suicide (such as the questions to ask about slippery-slope arguments and whether death is always a harm), new issues are raised as well. One difference between assisted suicide and euthanasia is that in euthanasia the patient is killed (or allowed to die), but in assisted suicide someone provides the patient with the means to take his or her own life. In the case of physician-assisted suicide, this usually involves providing the patient with a lethal dose of some drug. This is an important distinction, because committing suicide even with a physician's assistance is not possible for those who are so incapacitated that they cannot take medications (or perform related actions) by themselves. Thus, there are many patients who might be candidates for euthanasia who could never be candidates for assisted suicide (such as those who are in a persistent vegetative state and those who are profoundly demented). Notice that simply having the physical capability to take one's own life is not enough for one to be a candidate for assisted suicide. Suicide necessarily involves a decision and intention to end one's own life, and many people are mentally incapable of this regardless of their physical capabilities.

Assisted suicide has received more support than euthanasia, largely because the final, lethal act is left in the hands of the patient rather than those of a physician or other medical professional. This makes assisted suicide somewhat less vulnerable to abuse than euthanasia.[1] A patient could be inappropriately euthanized by physicians who take this action with little or no consultation with the patient, but so long as the patient must take the final step of committing suicide, it will be less easy to push a reluctant person into this course of action. (In his article in section 9, Daniel Sulmasy presents a scenario in which a patient is bullied into committing suicide; physician-assisted suicide may make abuse more difficult, but certainly not impossible.)

Those who are too poor to be able to afford good medical care at the end of life might be particularly vulnerable to the abuse of assisted suicide. Because good end-of-life care is often not available to this segment of the population, their only options might be either enduring their suffering or committing suicide. In other words, we might see the development of two standards of medical care: for those with good medical insurance, more therapeutic options and access to hospice programs would be available; but for those with poor or no insurance, physicians would "help them exercise their autonomy" by assisting in their suicides.

Arguments against assisted suicide that focus on the potential abuses of such a practice usually take the form of slippery-slope arguments. These claim that if we allow a few cases of assisted suicide, even if assisted suicide seems morally appropriate in these few cases, then we will inevitably find ourselves with many unacceptable cases as well. When presented with such an argument, one should ask three questions: (1) What evidence is there that these abuses would actually take place? Does the argument simply assert that such abuses will follow? If evidence is offered, how convincing is it? (2) Would these abuses result in harms that outweigh the benefits of allowing assisted suicide? Simply pointing out that there would be abuses of a law or policy permitting assisted suicide is not enough. It might be that we are willing to tolerate these abuses in order to gain the benefits the law provides. (3) What risks of abuse are we, as a society, willing to take? Simply showing that allowing assisted suicide exposes us to the risk of abuse is not enough. We must find out whether this risk is worth running. The answers to these questions might prevent us from being convinced by slippery-slope objections to assisted suicide.

---

1. T. Quill, C. Cassell, and D. Meier, "Care of the Hopelessly Ill: Proposed Clinical Criteria for Physician-Assisted Suicide," *New England Journal of Medicine* 327, no. 19 (1992): 1380–84.

In this connection, it is interesting to note what has happened in Oregon, where physician-assisted suicide has been legal since November 1997. In 1998, twenty-three people received prescriptions for lethal doses of medication under this legislation.[2] Of these, fifteen died from taking the medications, six died from their illnesses, and two were still alive at year's end. Interestingly, there was no indication that those who chose assistance in committing suicide tended to be poor, uneducated, underinsured, or members of a minority or oppressed group. In fact, all of the fifteen who committed suicide were white, eight were male, four had college degrees (eight more had high school diplomas), and eight had private insurance. None of these people expressed any concern about the financial burden of their care upon their families. Instead, their primary concerns seemed to be loss of autonomy or of bodily functioning. (Only one person expressed concern about inadequate pain control.) There seems to be no indication that there is any rush for people to take advantage of this new law or that people are flocking to Oregon from other states to receive assistance in committing suicide.

Apart from questions of abuse, there are, of course, those who argue that the role physicians are to play in caring for patients is inconsistent with helping them to commit suicide. The American Medical Association (AMA), for instance, is opposed to physician-assisted suicide, saying that it "threatens the very core of the medical profession's ethical integrity."[3] But others claim that the medical professional's responsibility does not stop with prolonging life and that helping patients commit suicide may have an appropriate role in the profession.

When patients face incurable illness, medicine's job is to help control symptoms, help patients adjust to growing disabilities or changing circumstances, and so forth. But its goal is not simply to extend life as much as possible; there are those who argue that medicine should provide patients with a good death when the time comes. Howard Brody, for instance, says that

> medicine produces a good death when it uses life-prolonging interventions as long as they produce a reasonable quality of life and a reasonable level of function (defined in terms of the patient's own life goals) and when it then employs the highest quality of hospice-style terminal care.[4]

But not all patients get good deaths; medical interventions may not be able to handle the ravages of disease, or these interventions may prolong life without dignity or functioning. Comfort care may be provided carefully and competently and still fail to manage suffering. (Remember the discussion of suffering at the beginning of section 4: there is much more involved here than just pain.) These are medical failures. In such cases,

2. A. E. Chin et al., "Legalized Physician-Assisted Suicide in Oregon: The First Year's Experience," *New England Journal of Medicine* 340, no. 7 (1999): 577–83.

3. American Medical Association, Council of Ethical and Judicial Affairs, "Physician Assisted Suicide," *Issues in Law and Medicine* 10, no. 1 (1994): 91–97, at 91.

4. H. Brody, "Assisted Death: A Compassionate Response to a Medical Failure," *New England Journal of Medicine* 327, no. 19 (1992): 1384–88, at 1385.

walking away, denying that medicine can do anything to help in the patient's plight, is an immoral abrogation of medical power, especially in cases in which the prior exercise of the medical craft has extended the patient's life and resulted in the complications that have brought the patient to the present state of suffering.[5]

Therefore, Brody concludes, the moral duties that arise with the practice of medicine require that physicians be allowed to offer patients an easier exit. It is interesting to note that this line of argument, which would support both euthanasia and physician-assisted suicide, invokes not only the moral principles of beneficence and nonmaleficence, but also a moral principle that obliges one to make reparation for harm that one has caused. (This is sometimes presented as a form of the principle of justice.)

5. Ibid.

# Death and Dignity: A Case of Individualized Decision Making

TIMOTHY E. QUILL

DIANE WAS FEELING TIRED AND HAD A rash. A common scenario, though there was something subliminally worrisome that prompted me to check her blood count. Her hematocrit was 22, and the white-cell count was 4.3 with some metamyelocytes and unusual white cells. I wanted it to be viral, trying to deny what was staring me in the face. Perhaps in a repeated count it would disappear. I called Diane and told her it might be more serious than I had initially thought—that the test needed to be repeated and that if she felt worse, we might have to move quickly. When she pressed for the possibilities, I reluctantly opened the door to leukemia. Hearing the word seemed to make it exist. "Oh, shit!" she said. "Don't tell me that." Oh, shit! I thought, I wish I didn't have to.

Diane was no ordinary person (although no one I have ever come to know has been really ordinary). She was raised in an alcoholic family and had felt alone for much of her life. She had vaginal cancer as a young woman. Through much of her adult life, she had struggled with depression and her own alcoholism. I had come to know, respect, and admire her over the previous eight years as she confronted these problems and gradually overcame them. She was an incredibly clear, at times brutally honest, thinker and communicator. As she took control of her life, she developed a strong sense of independence and confidence. In the previous 3½ years, her hard work had paid off. She was completely abstinent from alcohol, she had established much deeper connections with her husband, college-age son, and

From the *New England Journal of Medicine,* 1991; 324(10): 691–694.

several friends, and her business and her artistic work were blossoming. She felt she was really living fully for the first time.

Not surprisingly, the repeated blood count was abnormal, and detailed examination of the peripheral-blood smear showed myelocytes. I advised her to come into the hospital, explaining that we needed to do a bone marrow biopsy and make some decisions relatively rapidly. She came to the hospital knowing what we would find. She was terrified, angry, and sad. Although we knew the odds, we both clung to the thread of possibility that it might be something else.

The bone marrow confirmed the worst: acute myelomonocytic leukemia. In the face of this tragedy, we looked for signs of hope. This is an area of medicine in which technological intervention has been successful, with cures 25 percent of the time—long-term cures. As I probed the costs of these cures, I heard about induction chemotherapy (three weeks in the hospital, prolonged neutropenia, probable infectious complications, and hair loss; 75 percent of patients respond, 25 percent do not). For the survivors, this is followed by consolidation chemotherapy (with similar side effects; another 25 percent die, for a net survival of 50 percent). Those still alive, to have a reasonable chance of long-term survival, then need bone marrow transplantation (hospitalization for two months and whole-body irradiation, with complete killing of the bone marrow, infectious complications, and the possibility for graft-versus-host disease—with a survival of approximately 50 percent, or 25 percent of the original group). Though hematologists may argue over the exact percentages, they don't argue about the outcome of no treatment—certain death in days, weeks, or at most a few months.

Believing that delay was dangerous, our oncologist broke the news to Diane and began making plans to insert a Hickman catheter and begin induction chemotherapy that afternoon. When I saw her shortly thereafter, she was enraged at his presumption that she would want

treatment, and devastated by the finality of the diagnosis. All she wanted to do was go home and be with her family. She had no further questions about treatment and in fact had decided that she wanted none. Together we lamented her tragedy and the unfairness of life. Before she left, I felt the need to be sure that she and her husband understood that there was some risk in delay, that the problem was not going to go away, and that we needed to keep considering the options over the next several days. We agreed to meet in two days.

She returned in two days with her husband and son. They had talked extensively about the problem and the options. She remained clear about her wish not to undergo chemotherapy and to live whatever time she had left outside the hospital. As we explored her thinking further, it became clear that she was convinced she would die during the period of treatment and would suffer unspeakably in the process (from hospitalization, from lack of control over her body, from the side effects of chemotherapy, and from pain and anguish). Although I could offer support and my best effort to minimize her suffering if she chose treatment, there was no way I could say any of this would not occur. In fact, the last four patients with acute leukemia at our hospital had died very painful deaths in the hospital during various stages of treatment (a fact I did not share with her). Her family wished she would choose treatment but sadly accepted her decision. She articulated very clearly that it was she who would be experiencing all the side effects of treatment and that the odds of 25 percent were not good enough for her to undergo so toxic a course of therapy, given her expectations of chemotherapy and hospitalization and the absence of a closely matched bone marrow donor. I had her repeat her understanding of the treatment, the odds, and what to expect if there were no treatment. I clarified a few misunderstandings, but she had a remarkable grasp of the options and implications.

I have been a longtime advocate of active, informed patient choice of treatment or nontreatment, and of a patient's right to die with as much control and dignity as possible. Yet there was something about her giving up a 25 percent chance for long-term survival in favor of almost certain death that disturbed me. I had seen Diane fight and use her considerable inner resources to overcome alcoholism and depression, and I half expected her to change her mind over the next week. Since the window of time in which effective treatment can be initiated is rather narrow, we met several times that week. We obtained a second hematology consultation and talked at length about the meaning and implications of treatment and nontreatment. She talked to a psychologist she had seen in the past. I gradually understood the decision from her perspective and became convinced that it was the right decision for her. We arranged for home hospice care (although at that time Diane felt reasonably well, was active and looked healthy), left the door open for her to change her mind, and tried to anticipate how to keep her comfortable in the time she had left.

Just as I was adjusting to her decision, she opened up another area that would stretch me profoundly. It was extraordinarily important to Diane to maintain control of herself and her own dignity during the time remaining to her. When this was no longer possible, she clearly wanted to die. As a former director of a hospice program, I know how to use pain medicines to keep patients comfortable and lessen suffering. I explained the philosophy of comfort care, which I strongly believe in. Although Diane understood and appreciated this, she had known of people lingering in what was called relative comfort, and she wanted no part of it. When the time came, she wanted to take her life in the least painful way possible. Knowing of her desire for independence and her decision to stay in control, I thought this request made perfect sense. I acknowledged and explored this wish but also thought that it was out of the realm of currently accepted medical practice and that it was more than I could offer or promise. In our discussion, it became clear that preoccupation with her fear of a lingering death would interfere with Diane's getting the most out of the time she had left until she found a safe way to ensure her death. I feared the effects of a violent death on her family, the consequences of an ineffective suicide that would leave her lingering in precisely the state she dreaded so much, and the possibility that a family member would be forced to assist her, with all the legal and personal repercussions that would follow. She discussed this at length with her family. They believed that they should respect her choice. With this in mind, I told Diane that information was available from the Hemlock Society that might be helpful to her.

A week later she phoned me with a request for barbiturates for sleep. Since I knew that this was an essential ingredient in a Hemlock Society suicide, I asked her to come to the office to talk things over. She was more than willing to protect me by participating in a superficial conversation about her insomnia, but it was important for me to know how she planned to use the drugs and to be sure that she was not in despair or overwhelmed in a way that might color her judgment. In our discussion, it was apparent that she was having trouble sleeping, but it was also evident that the security of having enough barbiturates available to commit suicide when and if the time came would leave her secure enough to live fully and concentrate on the present. It was clear that she was not despondent and that in fact she was making deep, personal connections with her family and close friends. I made sure that she knew how to use the barbiturates for sleep, and also that she knew the amount needed to commit suicide. We agreed to meet regularly, and she promised to meet with me before taking her life, to ensure that all other avenues had been exhausted. I wrote the prescription with an uneasy feeling about the boundaries I was exploring—

spiritual, legal, professional, and personal. Yet I also felt strongly that I was setting her free to get the most out of the time she had left, and to maintain dignity and control on her own terms until her death.

The next several months were very intense and important for Diane. Her son stayed home from college, and they were able to be with one another and say much that had not been said earlier. Her husband did his work at home so that he and Diane could spend more time together. She spent time with her closest friends. I had her come into the hospital for a conference with our residents, at which she illustrated in a most profound and personal way the importance of informed decision making, the right to refuse treatment, and the extraordinarily personal effects of illness and interaction with the medical system. There were emotional and physical hardships as well. She had periods of intense sadness and anger. Several times she became very weak, but she received transfusions as an outpatient and responded with marked improvement of symptoms. She had two serious infections that responded surprisingly well to empirical courses of oral antibiotics. After three tumultuous months, there were two weeks of relative calm and well-being, and fantasies of a miracle began to surface.

Unfortunately, we had no miracle. Bone pain, weakness, fatigue, and fevers began to dominate her life. Although the hospice workers, family members, and I tried our best to minimize the suffering and promote comfort, it was clear that the end was approaching. Diane's immediate future held what she feared the most—increasing discomfort, dependence, and hard choices between pain and sedation. She called up her closest friends and asked them to come over to say goodbye, telling them that she would be leaving soon. As we had agreed, she let me know as well. When we met, it was clear that she knew what she was doing, that she was sad and frightened to be leaving, but that she would be even more terrified to stay and suffer. In our tearful goodbye, she promised a reunion in the future at her favorite spot on the edge of Lake Geneva, with dragons swimming in the sunset.

Two days later her husband called to say that Diane had died. She had said her final goodbyes to her husband and son that morning, and asked them to leave her alone for an hour. After an hour, which must have seemed an eternity, they found her on the couch, lying very still and covered with her favorite shawl. There was no sign of a struggle. She seemed to be at peace. They called me for advice about how to proceed. When I arrived at their house, Diane indeed seemed peaceful. Her husband and son were quiet. We talked about what a remarkable person she had been. They seemed to have no doubts about the course she had chosen or about their cooperation, although the unfairness of her illness and the finality of her death were overwhelming to us all.

I called the medical examiner to inform him that a hospice patient had died. When asked about the cause of death, I said, "acute leukemia." He said that was fine and that we should call a funeral director. Although acute leukemia was the truth, it was not the whole story. Yet any mention of suicide would have given rise to a police investigation and probably brought the arrival of an ambulance crew for resuscitation. Diane would have become a "coroner's case," and the decision to perform an autopsy would have been made at the discretion of the medical examiner. The family or I could have been subject to criminal prosecution, and I to professional review, for our roles in support of Diane's choices. Although I truly believe that the family and I gave her the best care possible, allowing her to define her limits and directions as much as possible, I am not sure the law, society, or the medical profession would agree. So I said "acute leukemia" to protect all of us, to protect Diane from an invasion into her past and her body, and to continue to shield society from the knowledge of the degree of suffering that people often undergo in the process of dying. Suffering can be lessened to some extent, but in no way eliminated or made benign, by the careful intervention of a competent, caring physician, given current social constraints.

Diane taught me about the range of help I can provide if I know people well and if I allow them to say what they really want. She taught me about life, death, and honesty and about taking charge and facing tragedy squarely when it strikes. She taught me that I can take small risks for people that I really know and care about. Although I did not assist in her suicide directly, I helped indirectly to make it possible, successful, and relatively painless. Although I know we have measures to help control pain and lessen suffering, to think that people do not suffer in the process of dying is an illusion. Prolonged dying can occasionally be peaceful, but more often the role of the physician and family is limited to lessening but not eliminating severe suffering.

I wonder how many families and physicians secretly help patients over the edge into death in the face of such severe suffering. I wonder how many severely ill or dying patients secretly take their lives, dying alone in despair. I wonder whether the image of Diane's final aloneness will persist in the minds of her family, or if they will remember more the intense, meaningful months they had together before she died. I wonder whether Diane struggled in that last hour, and whether the Hemlock Society's way of death by suicide is the most benign. I wonder why Diane, who gave so much to so many of us, had to be alone for the last hour of her life. I wonder whether I will see Diane again, on the shore of Lake Geneva at sunset, with dragons swimming on the horizon.

# Giving Death a Hand: When the Dying and the Doctor Stand in a Special Relationship

NANCY S. JECKER

WHAT SHOULD A PHYSICIAN DO WHEN A patient suffering from a terminal illness asks for aid in dying? With a few exceptions,[1-4] both medical ethics literature[5-12] and the policies of professional medical organizations[13-15] agree that physicians should not actively assist patients in dying. Arguments against physician involvement in active euthanasia are more widely known and frequently cited than arguments for it. Most call attention to the potential deleterious effects of a policy assigning physicians a role in voluntary active euthanasia. It is argued that such a policy may undermine trust in the medical profession or may place elderly or incompetent patients at risk of being euthanized without their fully informed consent. The case against the legislation of physician-assisted voluntary active euthanasia is presented in detail in this issue of the journal.[16] To furnish a broader perspective, this paper considers the possibility that, under special circumstances, physicians who stand in a close personal relationship with a patient are ethically permitted to assist their patient in dying.

From the *Journal of the American Geriatrics Society,* August 1991; 39(8): 831–835.

## UNETHICAL CASES

There clearly are many, many cases in which voluntary active euthanasia is ethically *indefensible*. Many agree, for example, that the Michigan pathologist who connected a 54-year-old woman who was newly diagnosed as having Alzheimer's disease to a homemade suicide device participated in an unethical death.[17] Although the latter states of this disease destroy every trace of higher brain function, medical experts call attention to the fact that it is difficult to make an accurate diagnosis of Alzheimer's, and even after an accurate diagnosis is made a patient's condition worsens only gradually.[18] The patient, Ms. Adkins, enjoyed excellent physical health and functional status at the time of her death, and no safeguards were introduced to ensure the accuracy of her diagnosis or to evaluate her capacity to make a decision to end her life.

There are numerous other cases in which, although hastening death may be ethically defensible, it is not morally acceptable for a particular physician to participate. For example, even if we assume that it is morally acceptable to provide some aid in dying to the 20-year-old woman, known only as "Debbie," reported dying of ovarian cancer in a recent issue of the *Journal of the American Medical Association*,[19] it was clearly unethical for a sleepy resident-in-training who had never met Debbie to administer a lethal injection of morphine in the middle of the night. Even assuming that Debbie had competently requested aid in dying, a stranger who stumbled into her room, physician or not, had no ethical justification for ending Debbie's life. Referring to abstract points, such as the "gallows scene" at her bedside and the "cruel mockery of her youth and unfulfilled potential," hardly provides ethical warrant for killing a particular suffering person.

Yet suppose, for the purpose of argument, that active euthanasia is ethically allowable under certain circumstances. For example, a competent patient who is terminally ill and imminently dying requests aid in dying. This request is based on the patient's current situation; the situation involves intolerable suffering with no prospect of relief; the decision is reviewed by an ethics or other institutional committee; and procedural safeguards, such as evaluation of patient competency, are in place. If active euthanasia is ethically acceptable under these (or other) circumstances, is it ever ethically suitable for physicians to participate actively? Assuming physicians themselves accept the desirability of euthanasia, can they ever ethically give death a hand? What are the scope and limits of whatever ethical role they may have?

## DIANE'S CASE

To begin to address these questions I refer to a recent case described in the *New England Journal of Medicine*[20] in which a physician, Timothy Quill, describes how he prescribed barbiturates that a 45-year-old female patient, identified only as "Diane," needed to kill herself. Diane was diagnosed as having acute myelomonocytic leukemia and refused treatment offering a 25% chance of long-term survival. Withholding treatment for this severe form of cancer produces certain death in days, weeks, or at most a few months. Undergoing treatment (induction chemotherapy, consolidation chemotherapy, and bone marrow transplantation) brings certain suffering from hospitalization, from lack of control over one's body, from side-effects of chemotherapy, and from pain and anguish.

Quill's role in the case was to respond to Diane's request for aid in dying by informing her that information was available from the Hemlock Society; prescribe barbiturates, an essential ingredient in a Hemlock Society suicide; make sure that Diane knew the amount of barbiturates needed to commit suicide; meet regularly in order to make certain that Diane was not overwhelmed in a way that might color her judgment; confirm that all other avenues were exhausted before she actually took the barbiturates; withhold information about the cause of death from the medical examiner so as to prevent criminal prosecution of himself or Diane's family; and make known Diane's case so that the public is not shielded from knowledge of the degree of suffering that people undergo in the process of dying.

In support of his decision to aid Diane, Quill makes the following points. Diane's suffering could be lessened to some extent, but in no way eliminated. Her preoccupation with or fear of a lingering death might interfere with getting the most out of the time remaining. The consequences of an ineffective suicide or violent death on Diane's family could be disastrous. And all other avenues had been exhausted. But what figures most prominently in Quill's rendition of his moral choices is his specific perception of who Diane was and of his special relationship with her. According to Quill, Diane was an "incredibly clear, at times brutally honest, thinker and communicator" whom he had come to "know, respect, and admire" over the course of 8 years as she confronted and overcame other serious medical problems.

Throughout his discussion, Quill's personal investment in Diane's welfare is evident. He reports as much, or more, on Diane's and his own subjective feelings as he does on the objective medical facts of her case. We learn, for example, that "she was terrified, angry, sad"; "we both clung to the thread of possibility that it might be something else"; "I felt the need to be sure that she and her husband understood"; "something disturbed me"; "I feared"; "I . . . felt strongly that I was setting her free"; "she had periods of intense sadness"; "our tearful goodbye"; "she seemed to be at peace." The lesson Quill draws from Diane's case is that "I can take small risks for people that I really know and care about." The question that continues to trouble him, however, is that present laws and policies prohibiting physician involvement shroud such acts

in secrecy and thereby limit the ethical support and care he can give. "I wonder whether Diane struggled in that last hour and whether the Hemlock Society's way of death by suicide is the most benign. I wonder why Diane . . . had to be alone for the last hour of her life."

## PERSONAL RELATIONSHIPS

Quill's narrative casts in vivid relief values that ethical analysis often couches in more formal, abstract terms. Rather than citing bare principles of beneficence and autonomy untethered to individual life and social reality, Quill enlivens these values by weaving them into the texture and fabric of Diane's life. In so doing, Quill makes evident the value of examining issues in context, appreciating the particular persons involved in an analysis, and looking at the nature of the relationships at stake. These lessons offer insight into how moral debates about euthanasia should be conducted and how deeply our method of debate infects the problems and options we perceive. The particular moral quandary Quill faced was whether or not to help a patient he had come to know and care about over a period of many years. Geriatricians and other physicians who treat chronically ill patients over a period of time may face similar dilemmas. So might health care providers who serve rural populations and small towns, where opportunities to know patients better and over a longer period of time are greater.

How are moral exigencies altered when physicians' relationships with patients are personal as well as professional? One additional responsibility physicians incur is to avoid depersonalizing either the patient or the relationship with the patient. It is helpful to distinguish three qualities or kinds of relationships.[21] First, in a personal relationship, one holds the other person's ends and good as one's own. A physician who stands in such a relationship focuses on a particular and unique individual, the patient. By contrast, in a second kind of relationship, a quasi-personal relationship, having a certain *kind* of relationship is one's end, but the particular person with whom one stands in a relationship is not essential to the structure of one's desire. For example, as a patient it may matter to me to have the kind of physician who is a good communicator or a sensitive human being. In these cases, a relationship is defined in terms of roles, and rules for roles, yet the particular person who instantiates the role is incidental. The other party is replaceable rather than carrying some unique significance. Finally, what keeps a quasi-personal relationship from becoming completely impersonal is that in an impersonal relationship one wants *something*, rather than wanting something *from* a certain sort of person. My desire is, for instance, for a good reputation; excellent patient care is how I aim to realize this desire.

Were Quill to view his moral situation in terms of what a physician, i.e., *any* physician, should do, this would focus the ethical lens on the quasi-personal features of the relationship at hand. Yet sustaining precisely this focus would be required for Quill to justify standing by and doing nothing were he persuaded that active euthanasia was the right course for Diane. In reasoning about Diane's plight, Quill would need to detach from Diane's specific needs and invoke global rules governing his role as a doctor. Quill might reason, for example, that patients' trust in the medical profession would be undercut by a policy sanctioning physician involvement while ignoring the actual basis of Diane's trust in him. Or he might refer to the Hippocratic maxim, "Do no harm," while discounting what harm means to Diane. Although a quasi-personal focus may be adequate if a physician's relationship with a patient is *merely* quasi-personal, it is a facile method when physician and patient are close associates who know each other well. Keeping an abstract and distant gaze then becomes a way of

retreating and pulling back. It renders moral reasoning instrumental to the purpose of denying the moral claims personal relationships make.

In addition to preserving the quality of one's relationship with the patient, a physician should make an effort not to succumb to temptations, pressures, and impulsive or selfish desires that might betray the patient's trust. The temptations to which many physicians may be especially vulnerable include a single-minded devotion to conquering the patient's disease;[22] a tendency to hold fast to the promise of a successful outcome under futile circumstances;[23] and an inclination to place emphasis on the cure and treatment, rather than the care, of patients.[24] The temptations to which medical ethical thinking falls prey include seeking refuge in ironclad rules and principles while discounting the importance of the circumstance, relationships and the patients' lived world.[25] In Diane's case, Quill resists both sets of temptations. Describing his as "a case of individualized decision making," he recounts that "as a former director of a hospice program, I know how to use pain medicines to keep patients comfortable and lessen suffering." After explaining the philosophy of comfort care to Diane, however, he accepted that she wanted no part of a lingering death and "controlled" pain. Quill recognized that her request made perfect sense, although it was beyond the realm of currently accepted medical practice.

## THE PERSONAL AND THE PROFESSIONAL

Although the relationship between Quill and Diane is a personal relationship, it also displays qualities associated with a quasi-personal relationship. It is a certain *kind* of relationship. How should the fact that Quill is a physician inform proper conduct toward Diane? As others note, ethical arguments rest, in part, on cultural and social conceptions of the roles persons fill and the responsibilities and expectations attached to those roles in particular times and places.[26] It might appear that killing is not consistent with the exercise of Quill's particular skills and virtues as a physician. Unlike the foregoing of futile treatment, which depends, at least in part, on competent medical judgment that treatment is highly unlikely to attain medical goals, the decision to end a life need not incorporate the application of medical skill and judgment.

In response it can be noted that new tasks are added to the physician's role when the physician's relationship with a particular patient becomes personal, not just quasi-personal. Although being a doctor does not itself entitle someone to offer aid in dying, being a doctor in a personal relationship with a patient may. Such a relationship enables one to appreciate what the patient's experience is like, become aware of the patient's feelings, understand the patient's personal history, and gain access to the patient's deep, as well as surface, desires. Personal relationships sometimes heighten our responsibility to others and may temper the stringency of rules designed to protect our rights and liberties against strangers.

To see that this is so, consider an analogous case of aid in dying provided by close family members. Suppose an elderly and devoted couple, married for over 40 years, agree that should either be afflicted with a serious terminal illness such that their last days would involve torturous and degrading suffering, the other will support a request for aid in dying. If we permit such a pact to be carried out, it is not because of the mere fact that someone is a family member. Rather, moral justification for our permission lies in the fact that these two knew and cared for each other. This enables them to do exceptional acts to further the other's good, and it also may provide grounds for excepting each from moral rules and principles to which the rest of us are subject.

Of course, the license that personal relationships give is not unlimited. While we may create patterns of giving or agree to perform future acts in the context of a personal relationship, the patterns we set and services we promise are subject to external moral constraints. First, I cannot rightly serve others to the point of servility. The servile person displays an absence of self-respect by acting as if his or her own rights are nonexistent or insignificant.[27] Physicians who feel compelled to provide aid to the dying when they themselves oppose euthanasia belittle the importance of their own moral agency and values. Second, personal relationships cannot be exempted from impersonal moral criticism.[28] Figuring out what one ought, morally, to do is not simply a matter of getting clear about what specific relationships call for. Relationships have moral pre-conditions: certain agreements cannot legitimately be made. They also have moral side-constraints: under certain conditions, even legitimate agreements cannot be kept. An example of the former is if a patient lobbies me to poach and hoard scarce medical resources to another's detriment. An example of the latter is where a patient entreats me to keep a prior promise to care for him over the course of a long and protracted illness in a situation where my other personal and professional demands are morally overriding.

In summary, personal relationships can ground moral authority and license health professionals or family members to participate in acts that persons who stand in only impersonal or quasi-personal relationships cannot, in good conscience, do. In relationships that are impersonal or quasi-personal only, a lack of intimacy can impede one's ability to grasp another's plight in its uniqueness and particularity. Personal distance can make one prone to calculate the moral course in terms that stray dangerously far from the lives of those actually involved.

Just as intimate others can have a role in medical decision-making that others cannot fill,[29] so, too, close associates may have a moral function in the dying process that only they can ethically meet. A competent colleague could not step into Quill's position and take his place. Quill was not *merely* Diane's doctor, and his moral role was not *merely* to discharge doctorly duties. Quill grew dedicated to the particular person who was Diane. Diane learned to trust the particular individual who was her doctor. Quill's importance to Diane was not simply that he accorded her respect or respected her goals and values. Rather, Quill demonstrated to Diane that the fulfillment of *her* goals had become synonymous with the fulfillment of *Quill's own* goals.

## CONCLUSION

The approach I am suggesting is that the physician's ethical role in euthanasia is contingent on the physician's relationship with the patient. Needless to say, a multitude of questions remain. First, if my reasoning is sound, it remains to be seen what the scope of application of this reasoning is. Clearly, many professional relationships are more impersonal or quasi-personal than personal. Often, "professionalism" is thought to require distancing oneself from those that one serves, separating off the personal dimensions of life from the professional arena in which one works, and holding back feelings and emotions in the course of interacting with others. In addition, individuals may change physicians relatively frequently or may see different medical specialists for different complaints. These factors make it less likely that close relationships will be formed and sustained between physician and patient. Second, even when close relationships emerge, not all personal relationships are benevolent. One can feel personal animosity and ill will, as well as personal devotion, to others. Third, it is far from clear what criteria we as a society might apply in order to judge whether particular physi-

cians and patients stand in benevolent and personal relationships.[30] Finally, uninsured patients and patients who rely on Medicaid are less likely than other patients to have a continuing relationship with a doctor and more likely to receive basic care in a hospital emergency room or clinic.[31] This places these groups at a disadvantage if moral authority to participate in active euthanasia is granted only to physicians who stand in special relationships with their patients.

While these questions and concerns remain, the emotionally wrenching dilemmas physicians encounter do not abate. The public at large appears sharply divided on what the proper role of the physician should be. While 53% of Americans questioned in a recent New York Times/CBS News Poll said that they want doctors to be allowed to assist a seriously ill person to take his or her own life, a substantial minority (42%) took the opposite view.[32] At the same time, many express reservations about being treated by doctors who admit to helping patients commit suicide.[32] Our thoughts and feelings on voluntary active euthanasia are muddled by the denial of death and dying which runs rampant in our society. That the specter of death is not faced squarely is evidenced by the fact that only one-third of Americans have a will when they die,[33] still fewer (15%) have executed a directive to physicians (living will),[34] and only 56% have spoken with family members about their wishes at the end of life.

Many medical ethicists flatly oppose any physician involvement in hastening death because of the potential negative impact of such a policy. I have emphasized instead the costs born by patients, families, and health providers when terminally ill patients are left to languish and suffer. Viewed from this perspective, the love and care one harbors for a particular person may impel one to intervene and hasten death. Care for another may make it morally impossible to simply step aside and watch a protracted illness run a painful course.

REFERENCES

1. Vaux KL. Debbie's dying: mercy killing and the good death. JAMA 1988; 259: 2140–2144.

2. Cassel CK, Meier DE. Morals and moralism in the debate over euthanasia. N Engl J Med 1990; 323: 750–752.

3. Wanzer SH, Federman DO, Adelstein SJ et al. The physician's responsibility toward hopelessly ill patients. N Engl J Med 1989; 320: 844–849.

4. Williams G. Euthanasia legislation: a rejoinder to the nonreligious objections. In: Beauchamp TL, Perlin S, eds. Ethical Issues in Death and Dying. Englewood Cliffs, New Jersey: Prentice-Hall, 1978, 232–240.

5. Sprung CL. Changing attitudes and practices in foregoing life-sustaining treatments. JAMA 1990; 263: 2211–2215.

6. Callahan D. Can we return to death from disease? Hastings Cent Rep 1989; 19 supplement: 4–6.

7. Wolf S. Holding the line on euthanasia. Hastings Cent Rep 1989; 19 supplement: 13–15.

8. Singer PA, Siegler M. Euthanasia: a critique. N Engl J Med 1990; 322: 1881–1883.

9. Feingsen R. A case against Dutch euthanasia. Hastings Cent Rep 1989; 19 supplement: 22–30.

10. Gaylin W. Doctors must not kill. JAMA 1988; 259: 2139–2140.

11. Foot P. Euthanasia. Philosophy and Public Affairs 1977; 6: 85–112.

12. Kamisar Y. Euthanasia legislation: some nonreligious objections. In: Beauchamp TL, Perlin S, eds. Ethical Issues in Death and Dying. Englewood Cliffs, New Jersey: Prentice-Hall, 1978: 220–232.

13. Judicial Council of the American Medical Association. Opinions of the Judicial Council, 1982. Reprinted in President's Commission for the Study of Ethical Problems in Medicine and Biomedical and Behavioral Research. Deciding to Forgo Life-Sustaining Treatment. Washington, DC: US Government Printing Office, 1983, pp. 299–300.

14. President's Commission for the Study of Ethical Problems in Medicine and Biomedical and Behavioral Research. Deciding to Forgo Life-Sustaining Treatment. Washington, DC: US Government Printing Office, 1983, p. 72.

15. American Geriatric Society. Voluntary active euthanasia. J Am Geriatr Soc 1991; 39: 826.

16. Teno J, Lynn J. Voluntary active euthanasia: the individual case and public policy. J Am Geriatr Soc 1991; 39: 827–830.

17. Belkin L. Doctor tells of first death using his suicide device. New York Times, 7 June 1990, A1 and B6.

18. Angier N. Diagnosis of Alzheimer's is no matter of certainty. New York Times, 7 June 1990, D22.

19. It's over, Debbie. JAMA 1988; 259: 272.

20. Quill TE. Death and dignity: a case of individualized decision making. N Engl J Med 1991; 324: 691–694.

21. Hardwig J. In search of an ethics of personal relationships. In: Graham G, LaFollette H, eds. Person to Person. Philadelphia: Temple University Press, 1989: 63–81.

22. Jecker NS. Learning restraint in medically futile cases: Hippocratic medicine and Baconian science. Hastings Cent Rep 1991; 21: 1–4.

23. Schneiderman LJ, Jecker NS, Jonsen AR. Medical futility: its meaning and ethical implications. Ann Intern Med 1990; 112: 949–954.

24. Jecker NS. Separating cure and care: historical and contemporary images of nurses and physicians. J Med Philos 1991; 16.

25. Jonsen AR, Toulmin S. The Abuse of Casuistry: A History of Moral Reasoning. Berkeley: University of California Press, 1988.

26. Jonsen AR. Beyond the physician's reference: the ethics of active euthanasia. Western J Med 1988; 149: 195–198.

27. Hill TJ. Servility and self-respect. In: Feinberg J, West H, eds. Moral Philosophy: Classic Texts and Contemporary Problems. Belmont, California: Dickenson Publishing Co Inc, 1977: 484–493.

28. Jecker NS. Impartiality and special relationships. In: Meyers DT, Kipnis K, Murphy C, eds. Kindred Matters: Rethinking the Philosophy of the Family. Ithaca, NY, Cornell University Press, 1991.

29. Jecker NS. The role of intimate others in medical decision making. Gerontol 1990; 30: 65–71.

30. Altman LK. More physicians broach forbidden subject of euthanasia. New York Times, 12 March 1991: B6.

31. US Physician Payment Review Commission. Report to Congress. In: Pear R. Low Medicaid fees seen as depriving the poor of care. New York Times, 2 April 1990: A1, A12.

32. New York Times/CBS News Poll: Should a doctor help someone die? New York Times, 1 September 1990: A6.

33. Malcom AH. Giving death a hand: rending issue. New York Times, 6 June 1990: A6.

34. American Medical Association. Medical World News 40 (4): 24; July 1989, 26–27.

# The Reasons So Many People Support Physician-Assisted Suicide—And Why These Reasons Are Not Convincing

YALE KAMISAR[1]

IT WOULD BE HARD TO DENY THAT THERE is a great deal of support in this country—and ever-growing support—for legalizing physician-assisted suicide (PAS). Why is this so? I believe there are a considerable number of reasons. In this article, I shall discuss five common reasons and explain why I do not find any of them convincing.

## THE COMPELLING FORCE OF HEARTRENDING INDIVIDUAL CASES

Many people, understandably, are greatly affected by the heart-wrenching facts of individual cases, e.g., a person enduring the last stages of ALS (Lou Gehrig's disease), who gasps: "I want . . . I want . . . to die." In this regard the media, quite possibly inadvertently, advances the cause of PAS.

A reporter often thinks that the way to provide in-depth coverage of *the subject* of assisted suicide and euthanasia is to provide a detailed account of a particular person suffering from a particular disease and asking: "How can we deny this person the active intervention of another to bring about death?" Or "What would you want done if you were in this person's shoes?" But we should not let a compelling individual case blot out more general considerations. The issue is not simply what seems best for the individual who is the focal point of a news story, but what seems best for society as a whole.

Everyone interested in the subject of PAS and active voluntary euthanasia (AVE) has heard emotional stories about people suffering great pain and begging for someone to kill them or help them bring about their death. But people like Kathleen Foley, the Memorial Sloan-Kettering Cancer Center's renowned pain control expert, and Herbert Hendin, the American Suicide Foundation's executive director, can tell very moving stories, too—stories *militating against* the legalization of PAS and AVE. They can tell us how suicidal ideation and suicide requests commonly dissolve with adequate control of pain and other symptoms or how, for example, after much conversation with a caring physician, a suicidal patient—one who had become convinced that suicide or assisted suicide was his best option—changed his mind, how his desperation subsided, and how he used the remaining months of his life to become closer to his wife and parents.[2]

I can hear the cries of protest now. "Let terminally ill people (and perhaps others as well) obtain assistance in committing suicide if that is what they want. They're not bothering anybody else. Letting them determine the time and manner of their death won't affect anybody else."

But I am afraid it *will*. "We are not merely a collection of self-determining individuals";

From *Issues in Law and Medicine* 1996; 12(2): 113–131.

"[w]e are connected to others in many different ways."[3] Therefore, PAS and AVE are social issues and matters of public policy.[4]

Suppose a healthy septuagenarian, who has struggled to overcome the hardships of poverty all his life, wants to assure that his two grandchildren have a better life than he did. So he decides he will sell his heart for $500,000 and arrange to have a trust fund established for his grandchildren. This does not strike me as an irrational or senseless act. But would "society" allow this transaction to take place? I think not. But why not? How can a prohibition against selling one's body parts be reconciled with the view that we have full autonomy over our lives and our bodies?

This article is being written at a time when the firmly established right to refuse or to terminate lifesaving medical treatment is being used as a launching pad for a right to PAS.[5] However the issue of assisted suicide is ultimately resolved, it will reflect society's views about life and death, as did resolution of the debate over disconnecting the respirator and pulling the feeding tube.

Many want to believe—and loose talk about the "right to die" encourages them to do so—that the termination of life support for dying or seriously ill patients, a considerable number of whom are no longer competent, is merely an exercise of individual autonomy. But "[m]edical technology has forced the law to resolve questions concerning termination of medical treatment . . . by making largely social decisions involving our attitudes toward life, and the ways in which society allocates resources best to preserve it and its quality."[6] That many of us prefer to believe that we have simply been deferring to personal autonomy is hardly surprising. On the one hand, confronting questions about the quality of life "worth" preserving is discomfiting, even frightening; on the other hand, individual autonomy is highly prized in our society.[7] But "this model of mere deference to individual wishes does not ring true in many 'right to die' cases."[8]

Although I sometimes disagree strongly with Professor Charles Baron, a leading proponent of physician-assisted suicide,[9] I share his view that in many, probably most, persistent vegetative state cases "[w]hat actually drives death decisions . . . is an objective test based on the convergence of 'best interests' and economic criteria. [But] the extreme discomfort of making death decisions for other people and our fear of the slippery slope . . . lead us to pretend that we are merely complying (however reluctantly) with the wishes of the patient. The result in most states is mere lip service to substituted judgment."[10]

More generally, as Professor Donald Beschle has pointed out:

One way or another, . . . society will label certain types of decisions about death as 'right' and others as 'wrong,' some as courageous and noble, others as at least disappointing, possibly cowardly, or even disgraceful. These social labels cannot fail to influence subsequent individual choices. In addition, such attitudes can cause decision makers to interpret the statements and actions of the individual patient in ways that are at least problematic.[11]

The "right to die" is a catchy rallying cry, but here as elsewhere we should "turn up [our] collars against windy sloganeering, no matter from which direction it is blown."[12] The right to die focuses on what is only one aspect of a multidimensional problem. I think Seth Kreimer put it well when he summarized the "fearsome dilemma" presented by the assisted suicide issue as follows:

Forbidding [assisted suicide] leaves some citizens with the prospect of being trapped in agony or indignity from which they could be delivered by a death they desire. But permitting such assistance risks the unwilling or manipulated death of the most vulnerable members of society, and the erosion of the normative structure that encourages them, their families, and their doctors to choose life.[13]

It is noteworthy, I believe, that although some members of the New York Task Force on Life and the Law regarded assisted suicide, and even voluntary active euthanasia, as "ethically acceptable" in exceptional cases,[14] all twenty-four members of the task force concluded that heartbreaking individual cases could not justify significant changes in current law and moral rules.[15] The realities of existing medical practice, observed the task force, "render legislation to legalize assisted suicide and euthanasia vulnerable to error and abuse for all members of society, not only for those who are disadvantaged."[16] "Constructing an idea or 'good' case is not sufficient for public policy," added the task force, "if it bears little relation to prevalent medical practice."[17]

John Arras, a philosopher and bioethicist who served on the task force that issued the aforementioned report on death and dying, recently disclosed that during work on that project he was one of several members who recognized that in certain rare instances PAS or AVE "might constitute both a positive good and an important exercise in personal autonomy for the individual"—but who nevertheless balked at legalizing these practices "due to fears bearing on the social consequences of liberalization."[18] Professor Arras emphasized that whether we maintain the total prohibition against PAS and AVE *or whether we lift the ban* for certain groups, "there are bound to be victims."[19] He continued:

> The victims of the current policy are easy to identify; they are on the news, the talk shows, the documentaries, and often on Dr. Kevorkian's roster of so-called 'patients.' The victims of legalization, by contrast, will be largely hidden from view: they will include the clinically depressed 80-year-old man who could have lived for another year of good quality if only he had been treated; the 50-year-old woman who asks for death because doctors in her financially stretched HMO cannot/will not effectively treat her unrelenting but mysterious pelvic pain; and perhaps eventually, if we slide far

enough down the slope, the uncommunicative stroke victim whose distant children deem an earlier death a better death. Unlike Dr. Kevorkian's 'patients,' these victims will not get their pictures in the paper, but they all will have faces and they will all be cheated of good months or perhaps even years.[20]

Although Professor Arras and other members of the task force were deeply moved by the sufferings of some patients, they were ultimately convinced that these patients could not be given publicly sanctioned assistance in committing suicide without endangering a much larger number of vulnerable patients. Thus Arras and others who shared his views joined a report that focused not on the alleged immorality of assisted suicide and voluntary euthanasia, but on consequentialist arguments against these practices, such as the well-founded fear—considering "the pervasive failure of our health care system to treat pain and diagnose and treat depression"—that legalizing PAS and physician-administered voluntary euthanasia "would be profoundly dangerous for many individuals who are ill and vulnerable" (especially "those who are elderly, poor, socially disadvantaged, or without access to good medical care").[21]

## THE NOTION THAT THE ONLY SUBSTANTIAL OBJECTIONS TO LEGALIZING ASSISTED SUICIDE OR ACTIVE VOLUNTARY EUTHANASIA ARE BASED ON RELIGIOUS GROUNDS

Another reason I think the assisted suicide–active voluntary euthanasia movement has made so much headway is that its proponents have managed to convince many that the only substantial objections to their proposals are based on religious doctrine.

In November of 1994, Measure 16, the Oregon ballot initiative, was narrowly approved by the voters, and Oregon became the first state to legalize PAS. According to press reports, Oregon Right to Die and other proponents of PAS either hammered away at the Roman Catholic Church explicitly, or, somewhat vaguely, attacked those who "think they have the divine right to control other people's lives." [22]

There is nothing new about these tactics. Forty years ago, the British legal scholar Glanville Williams, probably the leading Anglo-American proponent of AVE at the time, maintained that "euthanasia can be condemned only according to a religious opinion." [23] And the eminent philosopher Bertrand Russell, a great admirer of Williams's writings on the subject, called euthanasia "one of the subjects of sharpest conflict between theology and humane feeling." [24]

I agree that *if* assisted suicide or euthanasia can be condemned only on religious grounds their prohibition should not be imposed on those who do not share these beliefs, but I strongly disagree that the prohibition can only be defended on religious grounds. Indeed, this is the principal reason I first wrote about the subject way back in 1958. (In resisting Professor Williams's arguments, I took pains to call my article *Some Non-Religious Views Against Proposed "Mercy-Killing" Legislation*,[25] and, so far as I know, I have never made a religious objection to either PAS or AVE.)

I think many people share Professor Williams's view and that proponents of PAS and AVE have done their best to exploit this feeling.[26] But I believe the New York Task Force Report amply demonstrates that any jurisdiction prohibiting assisted suicide and euthanasia can advance substantial justifications for the ban that go well beyond the law's conformity to religious doctrine or "morality." *Non*religious concerns were what led the task force members to reach the unanimous conclusion that the total ban against assisted suicide and voluntary euthanasia should be kept intact.

## PHYSICIANS ARE DOING IT ANYWAY, SO WE MIGHT AS WELL LEGALIZE IT—AND REGULATE IT

Another argument for PAS that appeals to a goodly number of people goes something like this: A significant number of physicians have been performing assisted suicide anyway, so why not legalize it? Wouldn't it be better to bring the practice out in the open and to formulate clear standards than to keep the practice underground and unregulated?

It is not at all clear how prevalent the underground practice is. As Daniel Callahan, president of the Hastings Center, and Margot White, a lawyer specializing in bioethics, have pointed out in a recent article, however, if it is truly the case that current laws against euthanasia (and assisted suicide) are widely ignored by doctors, "why should we expect new statutes to be taken with greater moral and legal seriousness?" [27] Evidently no physician has ever been convicted of a crime for helping a suffering patient die at her request. But, as Callahan and White ask, why should we expect that there will be any more convictions for violating the new laws than there have been for violating the laws presently in effect? [28]

What Dr. Herbert Hendin warned a congressional subcommittee earlier this year in his testimony about the impact of legalizing euthanasia applies to the legalization of PAS as well: Absent "an intrusion into the relationship between patient and doctor that most patients would not want and most doctors would not accept," no law or set of guidelines covering euthanasia (or assisted suicide) *can* protect patients.[29] Adds Dr. Hendin:

> After euthanasia [or assisted suicide] has been performed, since only the patient and the doctor may know the actual facts of the case, and since only the doctor is alive to relate them, any medical, legal, or interdisciplinary review committee will, as in the Netherlands, only know what the doctor chooses to tell them. Legal

sanction creates a permissive atmosphere that seems to foster not taking the guidelines too seriously. The notion that those American doctors—who are admittedly breaking some serious laws in now assisting in a suicide—would follow guidelines if assisted suicide were legalized is not borne out by the Dutch experience; nor is it likely given the failure of American practitioners of assisted suicide to follow elementary safeguards in cases they have published.[30]

# THERE IS NO SIGNIFICANT DIFFERENCE, THE ARGUMENT RUNS, BETWEEN THE TERMINATION OF LIFE SUPPORT AND ACTIVE INTERVENTION TO PROMOTE OR TO BRING ABOUT DEATH; IN BOTH INSTANCES THE RESULT IS THE SAME

This March, in the course of ruling that mentally competent, terminally ill patients, at least, have a constitutionally protected right to assisted suicide,[31] an 8-3 majority of the U.S. Court of Appeals for the Ninth Circuit (covering California, Washington, Oregon, and other western states) wrote that it could see "no ethical or constitutionally cognizable difference between a doctor's pulling the plug on a respirator and his prescribing drugs which will permit a terminally ill patient to end his own life."[32] According to the Ninth Circuit, the important thing is that "the death of the patient is the intended result as surely in one case as in the other."[33] Thus, the Ninth Circuit found "the state's interests in preventing suicide do not make its interests substantially stronger here than in cases involving other forms of death-hastening medical intervention."[34]

The Ninth Circuit found the right to assisted suicide grounded in the due process clause. A month later, a three-judge panel of the U.S. Court of Appeals for the Second Circuit (covering New York, Connecticut, and Vermont) struck down New York's law against assisted suicide on equal protection grounds.[35]

Although it ultimately arrived at the same result the Ninth Circuit had via a different route, the Second Circuit did so only after "repudiat[ing] the reasoning of Judge Reinhardt's opinion [for the Ninth Circuit], which [it] found open-ended and unconvincing."[36] Nevertheless, the Second Circuit was no more impressed with the alleged distinction between "letting die" and actively intervening to promote or to bring about death than the Ninth Circuit had been.

It "seem[ed] clear" to the Second Circuit that "New York does not treat similarly circumstanced persons alike: those in the final stages of terminal illnesses who are on life-support systems are allowed to hasten their deaths by directing the removal of such systems; but those who are similarly situated, except for being attached to life-sustaining equipment, are not allowed to [do so] by self-administering prescribed drugs."[37]

The Ninth Circuit's due process analysis would seem to apply to active voluntary euthanasia as well as to PAS.[38] So would the Second Circuit's equal protection analysis. If persons *off* life support systems are similarly situated to those on such systems, why aren't terminally ill people who are *unable* to perform their last, death-causing act themselves, and thus need a physician to administer a lethal injection, similarly situated to terminally ill people who *are* able to perform the last, death-causing act themselves?

If a mentally competent, terminally ill person is determined to end her life with the active assistance of another, but needs someone else to administer the lethal medicine, how can she be denied this right simply because she cannot perform the last, death-causing act herself? Applying the reasoning of the Second Circuit, wouldn't denial of the latter person's right or liberty constitute—and at this point I am quoting the very language the Second Circuit used—a failure to "treat equally all competent persons who are in the final stages of fatal illness and wish to hasten their deaths"?[39]

I think both the Ninth and Second Circuits went awry by lumping together *different kinds* of rights to die. Few slogans are more stirring than the right to die. But few phrases are more fuzzy, more misleading, or more misunderstood.

The phrase has been used at various times to refer to (a) the right to refuse or to terminate unwanted medical treatment, including lifesaving treatment; (b) the right to commit suicide, at least "rational suicide"; (c) the right to assisted suicide; and (d) the right to active voluntary euthanasia, i.e., the right to authorize another to kill you intentionally and directly.[40]

Until March of this year the *only* kind of right to die any American appellate court, state or federal, had ever established—and the only right or liberty that the New Jersey Supreme Court had recognized in the *Karen Ann Quinlan* case[41] and the Supreme Court had assumed existed in the *Nancy Beth Cruzan* case[42]—was the right to reject life-sustaining medical treatment or, as many have called it, the right to die a natural death.[43] Indeed, the landmark *Quinlan* case had explicitly distinguished between "letting die" on the one hand and both direct killing and assisted suicide on the other.[44]

When all is said and done, both the Second and Ninth Circuit rulings turn largely on the courts' failure to keep two kinds of rights to die separate and distinct—the right to terminate life support and the right to assisted suicide. And their failure to do so indicates that, when faced with the specific issue, they are unlikely to keep a third kind of right to die separate and distinct—active voluntary euthanasia.

I believe the Ninth Circuit was quite wrong when it claimed an inability to find any "constitutionally cognizable difference" between a doctor's "pulling the plug" on a terminally ill patient and his providing a patient with lethal medicine so that she could commit suicide.[45] I think the Second Circuit was equally wrong when it concluded that terminally ill patients on life support systems and those not on such systems are "similarly situated" or "similarly circumstanced."

"As [various] courts have recognized, the fact that the refusal of treatment and suicide may both lead to death does not mean that they implicate identical constitutional concerns."[46] The right to terminate life support grows out of the doctrine of informed consent, a doctrine "firmly entrenched in American tort law."[47] "The logical corollary" of that doctrine, of course, is "the right not to consent, that is to refuse treatment."[48] The other tradition, which has "long existed alongside" the first one, is the anti-suicide tradition.[49] This is evidenced by society's discouragement of suicide (indeed, by the state's power to prevent suicide, by force if necessary) and by the many laws criminalizing assisted suicide.

In the 1990 *Cruzan* case, the only right to die case ever decided by the U.S. Supreme Court up to now, a majority of the Court, perhaps as many as eight justices, evidently decided that the termination of artificial nutrition and hydration was more consistent with the rationale of the cases upholding the right to reject treatment. Of course, we cannot know for sure what the other eight members of the Court thought, but only Justice Scalia, who wrote a lone concurring opinion, expressed the view that the case implicated the anti-suicide tradition.

In *Quill v. Vacco* the Second Circuit judges looked with favor at Justice Scalia's concurring opinion in *Cruzan*. Judge Miner, who wrote the majority opinion in *Quill,* pointed out that "Justice Scalia, for one, has remarked upon 'the irrelevance of the action-inaction distinction,' noting that 'the cause of death in both cases is the suicide's conscious decision to "pu[t] an end to his own existence."'"[50] Judge Calabresi, who wrote a concurring opinion in *Quill,* referred to "the powerful arguments" Justice Scalia had made against the alleged distinction between "'active' assisted suicide" and the "passive" removal of life supports or feeding tubes.[51]

There is no evidence, however, that any of his eight colleagues on the U.S. Supreme Court thought any of the arguments Justice Scalia